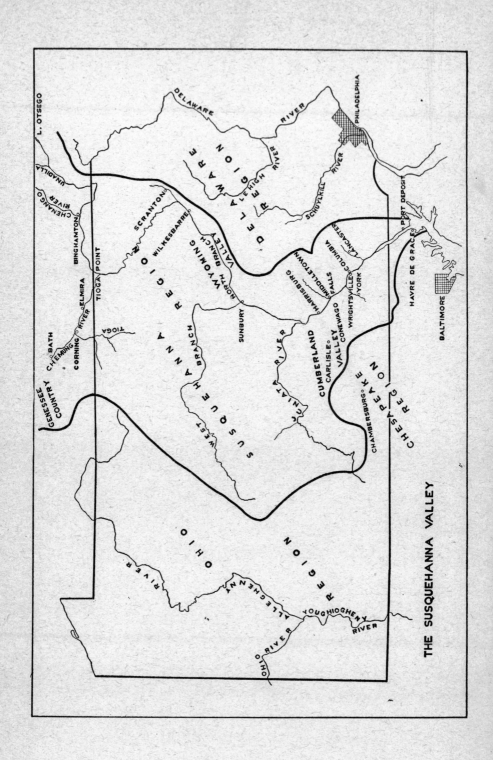

THE SUSQUEHANNA VALLEY

The Philadelphia-Baltimore Trade Rivalry

1780-1860

by

JAMES WESTON LIVINGOOD

COMMONWEALTH OF PENNSYLVANIA

THE PENNSYLVANIA HISTORICAL AND MUSEUM COMMISSION

HARRISBURG, 1947

 3

THE PENNSYLVANIA HISTORICAL AND MUSEUM COMMISSION

PREFACE

The rivalry between Philadelphia and Baltimore for the trade of the Susquehanna Valley is an episode of American history which recurred many times in all parts of the country. The first settlers along the seacoast were dependent upon ocean transportation to Europe. Later waves of advancing settlements were in like manner dependent on rivers, roads, canals, and railroads to get their raw materials and semi-finished goods to market and to obtain other goods produced in distant regions. This was especially true during the early stages of development when local products and commodities were likely to be bulky in character, of low value in relation to their bulk, and in some cases perishable. The economic life of the new settlement was dependent on transportation since surpluses could not be marketed at home where all neighbors tended to have a satisfactory quantity of local products.

Just as the producers were dependent on transportation media, so too were the merchants of the seaport cities who had ready orders for grain, flour, whiskey, iron, lumber, coal, etc. The cities needed hinterlands that would furnish these commodities and also buy return goods, which meant double profits for the city tradesmen. Since the interior had limited funds as well as inexperience in business methods, it was only natural that the initiative for improved transportation and the funds invested in it, came from the seacoast metropolitan centers. The desire for better trading arrangements naturally became keenest when rival cities found that their hinterlands overlapped. Philadelphia and Baltimore both hoped to increase their trade; both looked to the Susquehanna farmers and artisans as potential producers and consumers. Since trade and transportation are but two sides of a single question, the rivalry for trade between the two cities soon expressed itself in an ambition to extend internal improvements into the valley.

The history of the struggle between the two rival cities is thus one of trade and transportation. As such it was of interest to every man of the region involved in that day. It is the story of hopes and ambitions; of blueprints, politics, finance, construction; and of trade carried over the different transportation avenues constructed. In dealing with this story it has been deemed advisable to treat the subject topically rather than chronologically in spite of the limitations of the former method.

It is impossible to arrive at definite conclusions as to which city was victorious during the part of the tournament reviewed. Statistics of the amount of goods which flowed from the Susquehanna Valley to each are not available and as the different channels of trade become more complex it is very difficult to follow even a single shipment from its origin to its final market. Moreover, by the latter years of this study the influence of the growing western trade overshadowed that of the Susquehanna Valley and caused prime attention to be turned away from this arena.

This volume is nothing more in its ambitions than a preliminary survey and as such its shortcomings are obvious. There are many in the Susquehanna Valley today who could add points of local interest, and many documents, day-books, letters, and musty newspaper files with untold stories to tell have not been touched. It is hoped that those who read this book will not censure it for what it has not done but that they will themselves constructively add to the history of this region by bringing their own findings before the student and scholar.

Since no attempt was made to consider the much larger field of rivalry between Philadelphia and Baltimore in the lands west of the mountains, little mention is made of the mongrel State Works of Pennsylvania which wound through the heart of the Susquehanna Valley. The complete history of the struggle of the two cities is an attractive field for future study.

In the preparation of this study I am especially indebted to the aid, suggestions, and friendly criticism of Professor Robert G. Albion, Professor of History at Princeton University, where the original manuscript was presented as a doctoral dissertation, and to Professor Robert Fortenbaugh, Chairman of the History Department at Gettysburg College, who first introduced me to the lure of Pennsylvania history. To many others who have assisted generously in many ways I wish to tender thanks. I also wish to express my appreciation for the courtesies extended and the professional assistance given by the library staffs of Princeton University, the Historical Society of Pennsylvaina, the York County Historical Society, the Lancaster County Historical Society, the Berks County Historical Society, the State Library of Pennsylvania, the Maryland Historical Society, and the Enoch Peabody Library of Baltimore.

Grateful acknowledgment is also offered to the Pennsylvania Historical and Museum Commission which made possible the publication of this work.

University of Chattanooga   JAMES WESTON LIVINGOOD
March 6, 1941

TABLE OF CONTENTS

TABLE OF MAPS

TABLE OF APPENDICES

CHAPTER I

"A TALE OF TWO CITIES"

As the colonial anchorages of the thirteen British North American settlements developed into commercial centers and as pioneers pushed inland, the importance of direct communication with the interior revealed itself. Routes into the back country from coastal market towns gradually became longer and increased the trade area of the ports. Since the early eighteenth-century means of transportation was usually by river, the hinterland of a port generally comprised the valley in which it was located. But by the closing years of the colonial period, settlers had passed beyond the hills which formerly had walled in these economic cells. As the commercial spheres spread beyond their valley nucleus, frontier hinterlands sought by rival ports overlapped. A lively competition ensued for commercial supremacy in these areas which in many cases proved to be struggles involving the future pre-eminence or mediocrity of the port.

Directly in the path of Philadelphia's westward expansion was the large Susquehanna Valley with its potential wealth of diversified resources. Since the Quaker merchants of the Delaware River port apparently believed that trade and political units coincided, they were slow to realize that this valley was physio-geographically related with the growing port of Baltimore, which was located on the northern Chesapeake Bay water front, and that trading was profitable between central Pennsylvania and the Maryland city. The Philadelphians never expected any Pennsylvanian to trade with his southern neighbor after the bitter border dispute between the two colonies. But the settler in central Pennsylvania was willing to cast provincial patriotism aside for personal profits to be gained at a convenient market. Therefore, the Susquehanna Valley was destined to be the jousting ground for a spirited commercial contest. The tournament was waged between the Revolutionary War and the Civil War. It was an epoch of many experiments and countless mistakes, a struggle between two entrepôts for control of the buying and selling power of this vast region, and the use of it as a stepping-stone in gaining the trade of the fast-awakening West. It was a contest between the port of Philadelphia, whose supremacy had passed to ambitious New York, and the young, energetic town of Baltimore, which was just beginning to prosper. It was an encounter between Pennsylvania's commercial metropolis, fearful of becoming a commercial derelict left to the mercy of the ebb and flow of commerce, and the new port of Maryland which possessed all the enthusiastic enterprise of a growing community. The result of the tournament meant supremacy, prestige, and prosperity for the winner; the loser might suffer the fate of Perth Amboy, Gloucester, and Annapolis— ports whose histories were short because they failed to command an extensive hinterland.

Philadelphia became a commercial center almost from the day it was laid out by its founders in 1683. Its exports consisting of grain, salt provisions, and pipestaves during the early days, gradually gave way to flour, bread, lumber, iron, and flaxseed as the colony grew into a more mature state of civilization. From the first, the course of her trade remained almost the same. Since England offered a scant market for the products of the Middle Atlantic Colonies, Philadelphia's important purchasers were the West Indies.[1]

The early merchants of Philadelphia depended on the rich hinterland that composed the Delaware River economic region for the country products which they exported. The southern part of New Jersey and the Pennsylvania counties of Bucks, Berks, Philadelphia, and Northampton together with the eastern and northern parts of Chester and Lancaster were within this economic sphere.[2] The Lehigh, Schuylkill, and Delaware Rivers bore much of the produce of this area to Philadelphia, while short colonial roads carried some produce from regions not situated on the navigable streams. The proximity of Philadelphia to her rich interior soon made her the metropolis of the English North American Colonies.

The city was dominated by the Quakers who had, according to an early traveller, "given a tone to the manners of the people different from what is to be found in most places of equal extent. They are industrious and sober, and, though sufficiently commercial, they do not conduct their business in the same *dashing* style which is done by some commercial cities; but confine themselves within bounds, and secure what they gain."[3] The value and imperative need of extensive artificial connections with the interior did not seem to impress itself upon this group. They appeared to be satisfied with pioneer transportation conditions. In fact, they seemed to be much more interested in the possibilities of commercial expansion on the seas than development of a large commercial sphere in

---

[1] For a short time Philadelphia wished to export tobacco which could be sold directly to England, but by 1722 the Pennsylvanians were encouraged to raise wheat owing to the trade which had grown up with British colonies, especially the West Indies. Hanna, "Trade of the Delaware District before the Revolution" in *The Smith College Studies*, II, No. 4, 248-9.

[2] *Ibid.*, 242; Smith, "Sectionalism in Pennsylvania During the Revolution" in *The Political Science Quarterly*, XXIV, 220.

[3] Melish, *Travels in the United States of America, 1806-7, 1810-11*, I, 153.

the interior. Most of the merchants of Philadelphia invested in the import and export business. In 1753, when the frontier was about to become the battlefield for fierce Indian fighting, the commercial folk of the Delaware River port dispatched the schooner Argo in search of a north-west passage to India. The captain of this first voyage of discovery sponsored by one of the North American colonies failed in his efforts, but the Philadelphians encouraged him by rewards to renew his fruitless search.[4] Foreign trade was their chief interest.

By the year when the Argo weighed anchor in the port of Philadelphia, many German and Scotch-Irish settlers had landed at the same wharves and passed on into the interior. The German immigrants, as they sailed up Delaware Bay, seemed to scent the fertile limestone sections of Pennsylvania. They immediately sought out these regions for their homes; many of them, therefore, became residents of the counties in the vicinity of the Susquehanna River in the south central part of the colony. The Scotch-Irish settlers generally moved farther west into the small mountain valleys beyond the Susquehanna to make their homes along the colonial frontier.

The northern part of the great Susquehanna Valley did not attract the early pioneer since it was composed of rough, hilly country and was far removed from the settled part of the colony. In many sections the soil was not fitted for agriculture although the itinerant minister, Phillip Fithian, found that in certain places the earth was so rich that it was "almost oily."[5] Some few people dwelt in the northern Susquehanna Region—in northern Pennsylvania and southern New York—before the Revolution, but their business relations with colonial seaports were extremely limited.

The pioneers who settled in the Susquehanna Valley found themselves in a region apart from the Delaware River economic region. Settlement had been made overland from Philadelphia or New York because the Susquehanna River which "appears on the map like a large crooked tree, with numerous branches" was not navigable near its mouth. No Delaware River tributary reached westward into the valley far enough to make a route by water and a short portage possible. Therefore, the early immigrant interested in moving into the frontier belt was obliged to rely on land transportation.

After the first hewing, plowing, and hauling had been finished, the Susquehanna Valley pioneers began to realize that there was no market town in the valley. Unlike other Atlantic rivers, the Susquehanna was

---

[4] Trego, *Geography of Pennsylvania,* 133.

[5] *Phillip Vickers Fithian's Journal,* ed. Albion and Dodson, 44. Fithian spent some time about Sunbury.

not navigable near its mouth. The river valley had not become a colonial economic cell. The settlers also realized that they were not connected with the metropolis of their own colony by any economically profitable roads. Almost eighty miles of bad roads separated Columbia and Philadelphia, while Harrisburg was 105 miles from the Capital. The Quaker Assembly felt that the freight hauled by the "horse and ox marine" from the interior had to patronize Philadelphia despite road conditions, and so did nothing to help decrease the cost and danger of transportation from beyond the Delaware River watershed. The sedate Philadelphia merchants felt assured that none of Pennsylvania's produce went south into Maryland since that colony had passed legislation in 1704 prohibiting the importation of the staple products of her northern neighbor.[6] But the Maryland policy soon became more amiable; a friendly attitude grew up between Maryland and the settlers of central Pennsylvania. This change was unnoticed by the Philadelphians who continued to neglect road improvements.

Geographically the Susquehanna Valley faced southward. The Chesapeake Bay appeared like a giant wedge driven through the heart of Maryland to meet the river and was really a part of it. Simultaneously with the peopling of the lands in southern Pennsylvania which were watered by the meandering Susquehanna River, the town of Baltimore was chartered on the Patapsco River along the northern shore of the Chesapeake Bay. The pioneers of central Pennsylvania were politically, racially, and religiously like the inhabitants of colonial Baltimore. They differed from their fellow colonists in Philadelphia in all these characteristics. Moreover, the Quaker city merchants of the latter city lived in luxury which was very displeasing to the frontiersman. The high prices and monopolistic spirit of the merchant princes of Philadelphia added to the westerners' dislike for the Pennsylvania metropolis.[7] A well-defined prejudice existed between the sections of Pennsylvania which greatly harmed business relations and caused central Pennsylvania to turn toward friendly neighbors to the south who thought and lived much as they did.

Maryland was very much alive to the importance of the strained relations between the seaboard and interior of the colony of Pennsylvania.

---

[6] Lincoln, *The Revolutionary Movement in Pennsylvania, 1760-1776*, 55. This law prohibited the importation of "bread, beer, flour, malt, or other English or Indian grain or meal, horses, mares, colts or fillies, or tobacco from Pennsylvania and the territories there belonging."

[7] *Ibid.*, 57-60. For other accounts of this sectional rivalry see Boyd, ed., *The Susquehanna Company Papers*, IV, introduction; Smith, *op. cit.*, in *The Political Science Quarterly*, XXIV, 208-35; Root, *Relations of Pennsylvania with the British Government, 1696-1765;* Shepherd, *History of Proprietary Government in Pennsylvania.*

As early as 1739 a road was surveyed between the towns of the northern Chesapeake waterfront and the southern counties of central Pennsylvania; three years later Charles Town in Cecil County, Maryland, was founded to attract trade from the Susquehanna Valley.[8] Between 1750 and 1770 the network of colonial roads in Pennsylvania shifted from a general western direction to a southern one. This was especially true of the region west of the Susquehanna River which had eight roads toward the commercial town of Baltimore by the latter date.[9]

Not until Quaker fear of Romanism and the frontier's fear of the Indians caused the rival sections of Pennsylvania to work together did the Philadelphia merchants realize that the Susquehanna region was not dealing entirely with its own commercial metropolis. War-time traffic problems, which arose at the outbreak of the French and Indian War, presented rural conditions to the Philadelphians in vivid detail. But the cooperative spirit and common interest lasted only a short time; bitter feeling soon reappeared in the famous Paxtang riots. Sectionalism reawoke with its former bitterness and the Quaker Assembly elected to do nothing toward the improvement of roads into the back country.

Nevertheless, the need for internal improvements had been seen. Traffic to and from the interior of Pennsylvania had grown to such proportions that the old roads could not be kept in repair. Iron forges in Lancaster County were unable to send their products to Philadelphia and sell them there at a sufficiently low price to compete with iron brought from Europe.[10] Many people were beginning to trade with Baltimore or other Maryland centers. These facts gradually became known to the commercial folks of Philadelphia, and about 1769 one of their most progressive organizations, The American Philosophical Society, took up the question of transportation. Their surveyors reported, "The river Susquehanna is the natural channel through which the produce of *three-fourths of this province must* in time be conveyed to market for exportation, and through which a great part of the back inhabitants

---

[8] Griffith, *Annals of Baltimore*, 25; Johnston, *History of Cecil County*, 267. Johnston, in writing of this town asserts, "The fact that one of the streets was called Conestoga is indicative of a desire to cultivate the best feeling with the people of Lancaster County (Pa.) . . ."

[9] Turner, Commercial Relations of the Susquehanna Valley, Unpublished University of Pennsylvania Doctoral Thesis, 75-6. This student writes, "No such action can be explained only by pure, blind folly growing out of the niggardliness of a smugly complacent Quaker plutocracy with the reins of government in their hands and placed there by a manipulated charter which gave twenty-four members to the three eastern counties and eight to the four western." Also see Lincoln, *op. cit.*, 59-60, 62; Gibson, *History of York County*, 321-30.

[10] Meyer, ed., *History of Transportation in the United States before 1860*, 78.

will be supplied with foreign commodities."[11] Surveys were made of routes between the Chesapeake and Delaware Bays and between the waters of the Schuylkill and Susquehanna Rivers so that the waters of the central parts of Pennsylvania could mingle and minister to the prosperity of Philadelphia.[12]

The citizens of that city soon began to petition for better roads into the interior; the back country folk likewise took up the cry and added to the demand for improvements.[13] "A Friend of Trade" in "An Address to the Merchants and Inhabitants of Pennsylvania" called attention to the condition of the inadequate communication between the sea-board and the interior in 1771 and offered a solution to the colonial Assembly. He wrote:

"Baltimore town in Maryland has within a few years past carried off from this city almost the whole trade of Frederick, York, Bedford, and Cumberland Counties, its situation on the West side of the river Susquehannah and its vicinity to these counties will always be a prevailing inducement with the inhabitants of those parts to resort to Baltimore for trade, rather than be at the expense of crossing the river Susquehannah and afterwards to drag their wagons along a road rendered almost impassable by the multitude of carriages which use it, and the insufficiency of our road Acts to keep it in repair."

*   *   *   *   *

"By conversing with many experienced persons I find most of them are of the opinion that provided the ferries which lead over the Susquehannah to Carlisle and York were made free, and the road leading from Lancaster to this city, a turnpike or repaired by some other method that would keep it durably good, we should have a rational foundation to believe they would prove speedy and effectual remedies for they might be made to operate immediately by reducing the expense of carriage from those parts, both by saving of the ferriage and the advantage of carrying double the quantity in their wagons which they now do . . ."[14]

Pleas for improvements met with no response, but 1773 and 1774 saw a renewed effort for better routes to market. The dangers, expense, and difficulty of crossing the Susquehanna and Schuylkill ferries, together with the intolerable condition of the roads, were again revealed to the Assembly. Most of the complaints carried with them an account of Baltimore's influence in the region west of the Susquehanna River with

---

[11] American Philosophical Society, *Transactions,* I, 357-64.

[12] See Chapter IV, 81-83 and Chapter V, 101-102.

[13] Durrenberger, *Turnpikes,* 31-32; *Pennsylvania Archives,* IV, 362; Lincoln, *op. cit.,* 64-72; Turner, *op. cit.,* 82-84.

[14] A Friend of Trade, "An Address to the Merchants and Inhabitants of Pennsylvania," original in the Library of Congress, Pennsylvania Broadsides, Fol. 143; quoted in part by Lincoln, *op cit.,* 64 and Boyd, ed., *op. cit.,* IV, iv (introduction).

the hope of arousing Philadelphia's competitive spirit. A letter to Richard Penn written in 1773 clearly pictures the state of affairs:

"Our people are impatient & almost out of hope of obtaining their reasonable request. The Marylanders have indeed been among us. They do not only encourage us with the best Roads which they have measured, but lay before us the great advantages of a near navigation, which is to be found only the short distance of 30 miles from the best and most populated parts of our county. The people at present seem Avers to have any Intercoas with them, but what neglect & disappointment may soon produce in this matter needs no great penetration."[15]

But all efforts were in vain; even the appeal to Philadelphia through her own pocketbook failed. The interior was left to deal with Baltimore or struggle over miserable roads to the Pennsylvania metropolis, and as the storm of the Revolution began to blow, men turned their attention away from economic affairs to this many-sided controversy.

About the same time that road petitions were disseminated, another effort was made to improve the way to market by the settlers in the Susquehanna Valley. In 1769 the owners of land along the Juniata River petitioned the Assembly to improve that stream, since its navigability was essential to the residents of the valley. They pointed out that if they were not given this assistance, their produce would all be exported through Maryland. But the Pennsylvania Assembly could arouse only enough interest in this plan to postpone it from one sitting to another. Action on the petition finally gave way to a more extensive plan for river improvement when a "noble inclination of improvement" appeared in the colony. On March 9, 1771, a law was passed which declared the Susquehanna and its branches to be public highways. But in this legislation to improve the waterways of central Pennsylvania, the Assembly was very wary in not allowing the main Susquehanna River to be opened too near the Maryland Line; it was carefully provided that no money should be spent on the river farther south than Wright's Ferry lest Maryland should profit.[16] So Pennsylvania, after a long period of lethargy, awoke during the years just prior to the Revolution, at least, to the realization that she had a competitor for the trade of the Susquehanna Valley and that improved transportation routes were essential. During these years she formed a defensive policy to prevent a southern flow of produce

---

[15] Revolutionary Papers, II, 93, Letter, Joseph Ferrees to Richard Penn, January 11, 1773. There were many other petitions of similar type circulated about this time.

[16] Lincoln, op. cit., 71-2; Turner, op. cit., 90-93. The same protective idea was repeated in a law of 1773 in which the Assembly offered to expend £1000 on the improvement of the Susquehanna River providing that an equal amount would be raised by subscription and that none should be spent to improve the river south of Wright's Ferry.

which was to guide her commercial legislation during the next fifty years.[17]

After Washington had successfully steered the revolting colonies through the Revolution, he frequently gave suggestions and advice in regard to the material development of the country. Internal improvements, he believed, were fundamental if its potential wealth and power were to be realized. In 1784, this tireless leader noted, "The western settlers . . . stand as it were upon a pivot. The touch of a feather would turn them any way . . . smooth the road, and make easy the way for them, and see what an influx of articles will be poured upon us; how amazingly our exports will be increased by them, and how amply we will be compensated for any trouble and expense we may encounter to effect it."[18] Washington's pleas naturally attracted nation-wide attention, but in Pennsylvania improvements were not possible because of the reawakened feud between the older settlements and the interior. A disgusted Philadelphia editor commented in 1787:

"Happy would it be for Pennsylvania if her boundaries were comprised by the Susquehannah; we should then be more compact and more united. The back countries are a dead weight upon us; they pay very little towards the support of the government. . . . They seem to be so much attached to self-interest, and possess so little patriotism, that the real welfare of the community seems to be a feather in the balance."[19]

Tom Paine made the same complaint, claiming:

"The commerce and traffic of the Back Country members and the parts they represent goes to Baltimore. From thence are their imports purchased, and thence do their exports go. They come here to legislate and go there to trade. . . . If one part of the state is thus to go on in opposing the other, no great good can come to either."[20]

The post-Revolution sectional rivalry in Pennsylvania was merely one of the little whirlwinds of the changing pattern of political theory in America. Economic problems made the contest more bitter; the interior was especially aware of this condition. Finally in 1790 a constitution of more moderate cast was won and the bitter rivalry was mollified. The

---

[17] The frontier-seaboard rivalry which the economic situation helped to promote was not wholly caused by Quaker inaction. The pioneers were often too eager to find fault which caused the city merchants usually to disregard their demands. In Pennsylvania, the frontiersmen even went so far as to blame the Quaker government for the policy announced by the Proclamation of 1763, which they claimed the latter inaugurated in order to curtail the activities of the settlers.

[18] *Writings of George Washington* (Ford, ed.), X, 408-9.

[19] *The Independent Gazette*, March 12, 1787.

[20] *Ibid.*, March 7, 1787, as quoted by Smith, *op. cit.*, 222. An earlier article, dated November 29, 1786, in the same paper written by "A Friend to Property of both Sides of the Susquehanna" carries the same thought.

political differences which hindered cooperation during the colonial period and the years of early statehood of Pennsylvania disappeared for a time.

The economic depression which followed the Revolution also hindered the improvement of routes of transportation. But gradually this rounded into more prosperous times and the palsy which affected every type of trade, enterprise, and commerce, disappeared. "A desire of encouraging whatever is useful and economical" began to prevail.[21] Men who had begun to look at financial losses sustained during the war as the price of liberty found themselves with interest-bearing securities. The funding of the national debt, the assumption of state debts, and the restoration of public credit, called dollars, pounds, guineas, and joes from their hiding places. Since shipping interests suffered from the break from England, much of the ready money found its way into domestic enterprises. It appeared that internal improvements would be the economic feature of the last ten years of the eighteenth century.

Philadelphia, financial, commercial, and political metropolis of young America, having previously heard pleas for internal improvements, became very active in the awakened movement. In 1789 "A Society for Promoting the Improvement of Roads and Inland Navigation in the State of Pennsylvania" was founded in the city. Robert Morris served as its president. Meetings were held once a week during the sessions of the Legislature in order to suggest plans, information, and proposals for projects to the lawmakers.[22] These early lobbyists immediately attracted much attention to internal improvements; canals and turnpikes became the subject of discussion in the coffee-houses of the city. Newspapers eagerly supported the movement.

Much of this interest centered in the Susquehanna Valley, which was, in a certain sense, Philadelphia's West. The lower part of this valley was likened unto "the bottom of a great bag or sack, into the upper part of which natural and agricultural produce is poured from the north-east, from the north, and from the west."[23] It was the desire of the Philadelphians to tap this sack so that its lucrative contents would flow to their city. They maintained that once the produce flowed toward their city immense sums would not be able to divert it to any other port. Plans were accordingly made to connect the Susquehanna Region with the

---

[21] McMaster, *History of the People of the United States*, III, 461-2; Johnson, *History of Domestic and Foreign Commerce of the United States*, I, 127; Pickell, *A New Chapter in the Early Life of Washington*, 155.

[22] A photostatic copy of the constitution and minutes of the Society is housed in the Archives Division of the Pennsylvania Historical and Museum Commission. Also see Hazard, *Pennsylvania Register*, II, 119; McMaster, *op. cit.*, 11, 74.

[23] Coxe, *View of the United States*, 336. The original is in italics.

Delaware Valley. A canal across the isthmus separating the Delaware and Chesapeake Bays was proposed and work undertaken. The route from Middletown to Reading along the Tulpehocken and Quittapahilla Creeks was again brought before the public. To make the latter more practical for Philadelphia, another canal was begun to join the Schuylkill and Delaware Rivers just north of Philadelphia. Funds were also raised to improve the Schuylkill River. Work on the various sections of this Philadelphia, Reading, and Middletown route was begun and pursued with encouraging anticipation for several years. Meanwhile, other enthusiasts contemplated a canal connection between the Lehigh and Susquehanna Rivers where the distance was short but the terrain mountainous. Through the southern counties of Chester and Lancaster, where water communication was not practicable, the famous Lancaster Turnpike was surveyed and constructed.[24] The activity aroused by the society gave Philadelphia a legitimate claim to the title of inaugurator of internal improvements in the United States.

During this period of brisk business and internal improvement construction, Philadelphia continued to be the first city of the United States in commercial affairs. The aggregate exports of this city of about 42,000 people from 1791 to 1796 amounted to about fifty million dollars, while those of the whole country were valued at only $312,954,513. In 1796 Philadelphia's exports were abnormally high, reaching $17,513,866, which was one-fourth of the nation's export trade and 25% more than her closest rival.[25] Annalists and travellers noted that Philadelphia owed her supremacy to trade with the interior which, despite deplorable road conditions, forwarded its products to the port of Philadelphia. This was especially true of all the region east of the Susquehanna River which was an extensive granary. But the capital and prestige of the metropolis on the Delaware River also attracted trade with the West; Indian traders and fur trappers carried Philadelphia's credit 800 miles and more into the Ohio Valley.[26]

---

[24] *Journal of the Society for Improvement of Roads and Inland Navigation.* In following chapters all the various projects are discussed at greater length with the exception of the Susquehanna and Lehigh Canal. This scheme claimed the attention of friends of improvements for some time, but the region between the two rivers was too rough for canal construction.

[25] See Appendix I, 24-25. New York's exports in 1796 were $12,208,207.

[26] McPherson, *Annals of Commerce,* IV, 393; Weld, *Travels Through the States of North America and the Provinces of Upper and Lower Canada from 1795 to 1797,* I, 59.

But 1796 marked the peak of Philadelphia's prosperity; after that date New York moved boldly into first place as the nation's leading port. Moreover, Philadelphia soon lost her political importance. Both the national and state capitals were removed to new sites. The value of her exports dropped to less than $12,000,000 in 1800. Philadelphia's canal projects, born in speculative ardor, encountered the difficulties of technical mistakes, mismanagement, and general disapproval which come with innovations. Failure of the projects, after much capital had been expended, discredited internal improvements. Although a few enthusiasts kept the various canal organizations alive, Philadelphia made little effort to reach the Susquehanna River by canal until the construction of the Erie Canal aroused all America.

The only successful project of the era of the 1790's was the Lancaster Turnpike. This improved road, financed by a joint stock company, was constructed with a bed of stone and gravel distributed in such a fashion as to prevent the wheels of wagons and stages from cutting into the soil. It served Philadelphia well and did much to prevent that city from fading more rapidly into complete inactivity in the field of internal improvements. The success of the Lancaster Turnpike spurred on the construction of similar projects. Many improved roads were constructed to connect the city of Philadelphia or her Delaware Valley economic region with the Susquehanna Valley.[27] However, those which were constructed suffered from the limitations of expensive and definitely limited land transportation. The Lancaster road, itself, did not divert the produce of the Susquehanna River to Philadelphia to the extent which had been anticipated. By the time this highway was extended to the river at Columbia, pioneer settlers were descending the river to tidewater in crude, homemade boats, which were strong enough to ride the

---

[26] The chief articles exported from Philadelphia in 1796 were:

flour	bbls.	195,157	rice	tierces	6,265
rye flour	bbls.	50,614	tobacco	hhds.	3,437
Indian meal	bbls.	223,064	train oil	gals.	37,726
Indian corn	bu.	179,094	sperm oil	gals.	7,782
bread	bbls.	19,568	tea	lbs.	21,600
bread	kegs	6,010	pepper	lbs.	244,552
beef	bbls.	6,860	spices, value in		$116,086
pork	bbls.	12,029	sugar	lbs.	12,969.916
hams	lbs.	1,082,690	coffee	lbs.	21,002,300
timber, boards and lumber of all kinds			cocoa	lbs.	161,120
			cotton	lbs.	911,325
furs, value in dollars		47,713	indigo	lbs.	99,200

(from McPherson, *Annals of Commerce,* IV, 394.)

[27] See Chapter II, 39-47.

rapids in the portion of the stream which Pennsylvania's Assembly had stipulated should not be improved. At the mouth of the river, the fresh-water navigators were close to the rapidly growing town of Baltimore.

By the time that New York had passed Philadelphia commercially, Baltimore had grown to be a keen rival of the Pennsylvania metropolis. This youngest of the great commercial centers on the Atlantic seaboard was founded in 1729. It was laid out 200 miles (by the ship channel) from the ocean on a deep inlet or branch of the Patapsco River and was "nearest to the North, nearest to the South, nearest to the West in fact, so central on the seaboard as to be nearest all classes of industry and of production."[28] Although its location was not favorable for European or northern coastal trade, it was advantageous for southern coastwise shipping trade with the West Indies. Warm waters made the harbor practically free from ice.

The small village founded almost fifty years later than Philadelphia was destined to have a slow growth immediately after its charter had been granted; it made no pretentious claim to distinction. The geographic features of the Chesapeake region were not conducive to the growth of a colonial commercial center. No community had a sufficient hinterland to supply it with produce since each of the inland estuaries which fringed Chesapeake Bay was in a sea-lane for trans-oceanic ships. City middle-men were not needed to make commercial transactions. Moreover, the new town on the Patapsco was surrounded by older and jealous rivals and was obliged to contend with all the obstacles that could be put in her way.[29] By 1765 it was reported that Baltimore had no more than fifty houses and that her shipping was composed of one brig.[30] Three years later Baltimore was made a shire-town.

At this time conditions in Maryland had begun to change. Tobacco culture moved southward; wheat replaced the older crop along the shores of the Chesapeake and in the Piedmont.[31] Middlemen were needed to handle this new business. People of commercial and enterprising spirit moved into the town of Baltimore from all quarters so that they could

[28] Schoepf, *Travels in the Confederacy,* I, 326-7.

[29] *Hunt's Merchants' Magazine,* XXIII, 35; Pickell, *op. cit.,* 30.

[30] *Niles' Weekly Register,* III, 45.

[31] After 1750 grain exports from Maryland increased rapidly. The northern counties of Maryland raised little tobacco by 1760, but their wheat was becoming famous. Gould, "The Economic Causes of the Rise of Baltimore," in *Essays on Colonial History;* Craven, "Soil Exhaustion as a Factor in the Agricultural History of Virginia and Maryland, 1606-1860," in the University of Illinois *Studies in the Social Sciences,* XIII, 66-68; Kuhlman, *History of the Flour Milling Industry,* 39.

enjoy the facilities of its good harbor.[32] Many of them, like the famous Ellicott brothers, moved here from Pennsylvania. The habits of many of the newcomers had been influenced by the frontier. A spirit of enterprise was immediately born in Baltimore; the wilderness bowed and gave way to the prosperous commercial center. The extension of the staple wheat into the Chesapeake and Piedmont regions and the arrival of pioneers in both the port and the surrounding territory prepared Baltimore for a magical growth which the fast-brewing Revolution was to bestow on her.

The war operated as a great stimulus to the industry and commerce of Baltimore, whose port was free from the British blockade, and started her toward a position of maritime importance. During the colonial era most of the merchants of Baltimore were merely factors or agents using the funds of Philadelphia business men; after the War for Independence large supplies of local capital and the development of a banking business gradually made the Maryland city independent of outside funds.[33] In 1790 the first bank in the city was founded. Six others were incorporated by 1810. In 1773, the first newspaper was published in the growing town and her merchants no longer were dependent for information on the Philadelphia and Annapolis press.[34] During the same era, Baltimore became a port of entry. Up to 1780 all ships bound for her wharves entered at Annapolis. But the Revolution was detrimental to the standing of the Maryland capital. She was blockaded from the sea; her hinterland was small and the changing staples of Maryland left this rival of Baltimore with little business. On the other hand Baltimore was not blockaded. Another rival, Norfolk, in spite of its advantageous location, failed to gather in the trade of the Chesapeake Region; it lacked business enterprise and was therefore outstripped by Baltimore. Thus in a relatively short time Baltimore became the most important port of the Chesapeake Bay.[35] In 1790 the *Newport Mercury* in poetic meter told of her rise to commercial importance:

---

[32] Griffith, *op. cit.*, 29, 34, 37-8, 42-3; Scharf, *Chronicles of Baltimore*, 37, 202; Kuhlman, *op. cit.*, 28-9; Faust, *The German Element in the United States*, I, 163-4. About 1770 much of the rival town of Charlestown moved into Baltimore. "Many of the inhabitants who had erected substantial houses in Charlestown tore them down and shipped the materials to Baltimore." See Johnston, *op. cit.*, 265ff.

[33] Sparks, "Baltimore," in the *North American Review*, XX, 106; LaRochefoucauld, *Travels through the United States of North America . . . Performed in the Years 1795, 1796, and 1797*, II, 672-5.

[34] *Hunt's Merchants' Magazine*, XXIII, 35; Griffith, *op. cit.*, 53; Sparks, *op. cit.*, in *The North American Review*, XX, 103. This journal was the weekly, *The Maryland Journal and Baltimore Advertiser*.

[35] *Hunt's Merchants' Magazine*, XXIII, 35; Hall, ed., *Baltimore, Its History and Its People*, I, 455; Weld, *op. cit.*, I, 60.

"Torn from herself, where depth her soil divide,
And Chesapeake intrudes her angry tide,
Gay Maryland attracts the wand'ring eye,
A fertile region with a temp'rate sky;
In years elaps'd, her heroes of renown
From British Anna nam'd her favorite town
But lost her commerce, tho' she guards their laws,
Proud BALTIMORE that envi'd commerce draws;
Few are the years since there, at random plac'd
Some wretched huts her happy port disgrac'd:
Safe from all winds, and cover'd from the bay
There, at his ease the lazy native lay,—
Now rich and great, no more a slave to sloth
She claims importance from her hasty growth,
High in renown, her streets and homes arrang'd
A group of cabbins to a city chang'd
Tho' rich at home, to foreign lands they stray,
For foreign trappings trade their wealth away."[36]

Baltimore's spirit of industry and enterprise was already obvious by 1788 when the visitor Brissot de Warville noted that "a great deal of the trade of Philadelphia had passed there..."[37]

The traveller, Dr. John D. Schoepf, who as a surgeon accompanied some German troops to America during the Revolution, wrote about this time that Baltimore was a good market "for, Philadelphia excepted, there are nowhere in that country so many merchants gathered together and ready to take up what is offered."[38] In 1791, 746 vessels entered and 1049 cleared Baltimore customs. A vivid word picture of the growing town of this era reads:

"It was a treat to see this little Baltimore town just at the termination of the War of Independence, so conceited, bustling and debonair, growing up like a chubby boy, with his dumpling cheeks and short grinning face, fat and mischievous, and bursting incontinently out of his cloths in spite of all the allowance of tucks and broad salvages. Market Street had shot, like a Nuremberg snake out of its toy box, as far as Congress Hall, with its line of low-browed, hiroofed wooden houses in disorderly array, standing forward and back, after the manner of a regiment of militia with many an interval between files. . . ."

"In the day I speak of, Baltimore was fast emerging from its village state into a thriving commercial town. Lots were not yet sold by the

---

[36] *Maryland Magazine of History and Biography,* XIX, 196-7, quotes from the *Newport Mercury,* June 28, 1790.

[37] Brissot de Warville, *New Travels in the United States of America,* II, 260. In 1788 this traveller saw the importance of the Susquehanna to Baltimore. He wrote, "many foodstuffs go down there by the Susquehanna. When that river is navigable, Baltimore will be an important place."

[38] Schoepf, *op. cit.,* I, 326-7; Scharf, *History of Maryland,* II, 605.

foot, except perhaps in the denser marts of business; rather by the acre. It was in the rus-in-urbe category."[39]

Baltimore's importance grew principally because she had a market and vessels to carry the wheat of her interior. She was favorably situated to carry on trade with the West Indies. The product which they demanded was Baltimore's staple. The wheat raised in the Piedmont of Maryland, Virginia and parts of Pennsylvnia made flour which could stand the heat of the torrid zone and was eagerly purchased by the merchants of the West Indies and later by South American dealers.[40] Baltimore's fast sailing clippers, schooner-rigged craft possessing the advantage of sailing close to the wind, enabled the Maryland city to continue its commerce during the Revolution without much fear of risk. With the aid of the clipper, Baltimore's commerce continued to grow after the war "from absolute insignificance, to a degree of commercial importance, which brought down upon it, the envy and the jealousy of all the great cities of the union."[41] Colonel John May of Boston recorded in 1789 that flour "came to a quick market in Baltimore and so high the price, that the wagoners choose rather to bring flour there than to engage to go over the mountains."[42] Much wheat was also transported to Baltimore and its vicinity where excellent mill sites had encouraged the building of flour mills. In 1805, within eighteen miles of the city, there were "fifty capital merchant mills."[43] The millers of the Baltimore district exemplified the spirited enterprise of their fellow citizens by adopting the inventions of Oliver Evans which made milling easier and more profitable. Under these conditions the port of Baltimore soon became the leading flour center of America.[44]

---

[39] Scharf, *Chronicles of Baltimore,* 231.

[40] Rutter, "South American Trade of Baltimore," in Johns Hopkins *Studies in History and Political Science,* 15th series, part 9, 9-10. The West Indies trade of Baltimore was a stepping stone in the South American business which developed after the Portuguese Royal Family fled to Brazil.

[41] *Niles' Weekly Register,* III, 45.

[42] "Journal of Colonel John May of Boston" in *The Pennsylvania Magazine of History and Biography,* XLV, 151.

[43] Scott, *Geographical Dictionary,* article on Baltimore; Melish, I, 186. Melish, who passed through Baltimore about 1806, noted: "Upon the whole, I was highly pleased with the commercial importance of Baltimore and regretted that I did not fix upon this place for my commercial establishment, in place of Savannah."

[44] Evans used the power which drove the mill stones for all other milling processes. Elevators, conveyors, and other mechanical devices combined the different steps into one continuous process. Under these conditions milling became a large-scale business.

Growing Baltimore,[45] enjoying all the important requirements of a first-rate port, realized the importance of good communication with her hinterland. Situated at the base of the great Susquehanna system, she planned to win that region for her market. By taking advantage of the sectional rivalry within Pennsylvania, the citizens of Baltimore won much of the trade of the settlers west of the river by 1750. Maryland and Baltimore eagerly sponsored roads into this area and immediately after the Revolution turned to improving the Susquehanna River from the Mason and Dixon Line southward. The beneficent influence of the war on Baltimore made it possible for that city to turn to internal improvements before Philadelphia. The friends of trade of the Chesapeake city, in 1783, began the canalization of the lower Susquehanna in order to tap central Pennsylvania. Despite the costs and mistakes of this pioneer project, the canal from the mouth of the river to the Pennsylvania-Maryland Line was completed and Baltimore thus gained the first improved waterway into the Susquehanna Valley.[46]

Baltimore's policy of turnpike and canal construction was to extend improvements to the State Line and cross into Pennsylvania whenever permission could be obtained. The policy of the Pennsylvania Legislature, however, was to avoid the Maryland line and even to treat that border section of her own State as if it were defiled by its proximity to Maryland. Therefore, Baltimore's attempts to reach into the Susquehanna were more or less thwarted by her northern neighbor. Although Pennsylvania did not hold to this policy very rigidly in the case of roads, she did refuse to improve the Susquehanna River, which definitely limited the value of Baltimore's short canal.

Pennsylvania's defensive attitude to protect the trade of the Susquehanna Valley for Philadelphia and the failure of canals which Baltimore sponsored into other regions—especially the Potomac Company—caused the Maryland metropolis to doubt the value of canals. Like her Pennsylvania rival, Baltimore wearily gave up the idea of improved waterways.

---

[45] The population of the two rivals 1790-1860 (in thousands):

	1790	1800	1810	1820	1830	1840	1850	1860
Philadelphia	42	69	91	112	161	220	340	565
Baltimore	13	26	35	62	80	102	169	212

Sparks, *op. cit.*, in *The North American Review*, 99ff, gives five reasons for the rapid rise of the Maryland metropolis:

1. Nearness of Baltimore to the western country.
2. Fast sailing vessels.
3. The almost exclusive trade with San Domingo.
4. The two great staples, tobacco and wheat.
5. Energetic spirit of the people.

[46] See Chapter II, 34.

During the decade from the peace of Amiens to 1812, the commerce of America fluctuated with the times. The carrying trade of Europe was thrown into our ships only to be hindered by blockades, decrees, and orders-in-council. But earnings were so attractive that America invested heavily in foreign commerce and a merchant marine rather than in internal improvements. But the war trade demanded produce from the back country—especially wheat and flour. Producer and shipper were mutually interested in getting the country products to tidewater.[47] National discussion of the question of internal improvements brought forth on April 4, 1808, the famous Gallatin Report, which was an awakening influence on inland transportation. Although the Government granted no aid, the report was interpreted as a pledge for future Congressional assistance. Shortly afterwards, the Governor of Pennsylvania announced that political economy of the time seemed to concur with the general opinion that internal improvements were more important to a nation than external commerce even when pursued under the most favorable circumstances.[48]

The War of 1812 confirmed the belief of the Pennsylvania Governor. While the war turned the activities and thoughts of the people from improvements, it demonstrated most vividly the enormous cost involved in inadequate internal transportation. Moreover, the world's carrying trade was slipping from America's grasp; capital and business men sought new fields. The particular advantages which once made cities commercially important shrank into relative insignificance; commerce began to abandon its old haunts. Not only was the utility of public works much more clearly defined but the possibility of profits from them became more evident. Investors' money, which was more readily available than ever before, made a wide program for internal improvements possible, which, in turn, reawakened slumbering commercial rivalries.

During these early years of the nineteenth century, Philadelphia and Baltimore both sponsored turnpikes to gain the growing Susquehanna Valley trade. The Pennsylvania city, aided by State appropriations, dominated the eastern and northern portion of the valley with improved toll roads. Baltimore, on the other hand, improved her old roads into southern Pennsylvania; her turnpikes dominated the western and southern portion of the Susquehanna Valley. Baltimore also received a grow-

---

[47] Pitkin, *A Statistical View*, 373. The effect of heavy exporting caused prices to rise rapidly. From 1785 to 1793 the average price of a barrel of flour in Philadelphia was $5.41 while the average price from 1793-1807, exclusive of 1802, was $9.12 per barrel.

[48] *Pennsylvania Archives*, 4th series, IV, 732. Governor Snyder's opening message to the Legislature in 1810.

ing trade by the river itself. Although only descending navigation was possible, river "arks" carried cargoes of flour, wheat, whiskey, boards, and some iron to the Chesapeake, which threw a majority of the Susquehanna trade to Baltimore. Insurance men, traders, and merchants spent time and money in improving the river channel to make it more safe and dependable. Annually Baltimore became the market for more Pennsylvania producers, but because the Susquehanna afforded no ascending navigation, much of the return goods for the valley folk was purchased in Philadelphia. Thus a triangular trade was practiced which caused city rivalry to become more bitter because each was in a position to see either buying or selling pass to the other.

Financial evils created by the second war with England brought on a crisis, shortly after peace had been made, which caused a lull in the rivalry, and paralyzed the activity, of both Philadelphia and Baltimore. The expiration of the national bank charter, the suspension of specie payment, and a superficial paper economy caused the entire business world to halt. Baltimore suffered possibly more than any other city. Her merchants seriously lacked a working capital.[49] The spirit of enterprise which had done so much to build the city broke down after many of the commercial people, who were not of native families but who had come to Baltimore during the boom days of the Revolutionary era, were not able to cope with the crisis. Since no traditional ties bound them to Baltimore, many migrated. Active capital was drawn from its accustomed channels. Those who had escaped the storm of bankruptcies and mortgage foreclosures were terrified by the shock and became doubtful and hesitant. Commerce languished; internal improvements were paralyzed. The British consul reported on April 8, 1819, "The trade of this city was never more depressed, pecuniary embarrassment beyond anything ever before known, many failures, more expected and no one knows who to trust."[50]

Philadelphia also suffered greatly during the depression. The traveller, James Flint, who visited the city in 1818, reflected, "On approaching Philadelphia, I felt disappointed in seeing the shipping so very inferior to that at New York; and the houses fronting the river are old and irregularly placed, so that the idea of a port declining in trade immediately occurred."[51] To vindicate the traduced reputation of Pennsylvania and Philadelphia, gained to a certain extent from a seeming lack of interest in internal improvements, the Honorable Samuel Breck undertook to

---

[49] Fearon, *Sketches of America*, 341; Sparkes, *op. cit.*, in *The North American Review*, XX, 115-8.

[50] British Consular Reports, F. O. 5/144, Dawson to Planta, April 8, 1819.

[51] Flint, *Letters from America*, in Thwaites, *Early Western Travels*, IX, 53.

awaken interest in this field. In 1818, this New Englander, who had taken up residence in Philadelphia, published a pamphlet entitled, "A Sketch of Internal Improvements." By this medium he hoped to save his adopted city from a gloomy fate. To counteract the evils of the threatening conditions of a slump in trade, Breck suggested that the routes to the Susquehanna and the West should be improved. Briefly he presented the crux of the situation:

"Foreign commerce, during the golden days of neutrality, and a monopoly of the best share of the western trade, have heaped together in this small district, so vast a treasure. But our foreign commerce is less extensive and less gainful now, and rivals in the north and south are about to deprive us of our home trade. We must defeat their efforts; we must maintain, protect, and increase these riches. We can and will baffle the attempts of our neighbours. We have a *motive* in the defense of our *property;* we have the *means* in that *property* itself; and *nature* points out to us the *road;* a road, broad, fair, safe and interminable! If we follow it, we shall insure to ourselves, without the possibility of rivalship from any quarter, the most brilliant career and highest destiny. We may command at one and the same time, the trade of the Great Lakes— of the Ohio—half the Mississippi—the whole of the Missouri—these parts of Pennsylvania,—and one third of New York;—and in such event —an event in train to be realized—we shall see the expectations of the great founder of our city fulfilled. We shall behold storehouses and commercial streets lining the banks of the Schuylkill, and receding east, until they meet those of the Delaware, and thus cover the vast area marked out by Penn, as the ground-plot of his city of brotherly love."[52]

Breck's plan was most likely designed to rival the Erie Canal plan of New York; he wished to dominate more than the trade of his own state. But his advice was not heard. In 1824 the British consul stationed in Philadelphia reported to his Government that commerce was declining in the Pennsylvania metropolis and that "commercial men here seem to have lost all their accustomed enterprise."[53]

The statistics of Philadelphia's dilemma were too painful to be misunderstood. Her exports dropped from nearly eighteen million dollars in 1796 to little more than seven millions in 1821. In 1823 her domestic exports were slightly more than three million dollars worth, which was only one-ninth of the nation's total. That year her aggregate exports were 45% less than those of New York. Compared with Baltimore, Philadelphia's situation was really not bad, but it excited serious thought. The domestic exports of the Chesapeake metropolis in 1821 were more than two and one-half million dollars and increased 20% during the next

[52] Breck, *A Sketch of Internal Improvements,* 80-81.
[53] British Consular Reports, F. P. 5/189, Robertson to Canning, January 5, 1824.

two years while her Pennsylvania rival reported a 20% decrease.[54] Fear was officially expressed in the Pennsylvania House of Representatives that unless the state "awakes to a true sense of her situation . . . she will be deprived of the source of public prosperity . . . and instead of regaining the high commercial rank she once held, she will be driven even from her present station in the system of the Confederacy."[55]

Work on the Erie Canal caused every commercial center to reflect on the importance of a hinterland and the value of internal improvements. Citizens everywhere urged that the New York project should be imitated. Baltimore and Philadelphia were especially interested since this new route would draw away trade from the northern part of the Susquehanna Valley and they both realized that the Erie Canal would impair their chances of winning the great west. A Pittsburgh editor, interested in the prosperity of Philadelphia, wrote:

"Whenever we hear of the New York canal a kind of tremor seizes our frames. Whenever we hear any of Mr. Clinton's speeches or reports, we can hear old Cato's *delanda est Carthage* thundering in our ears, and not unfrequently (sic) when we are thinking of the future situation of Philadelphia does the idea of *Old Sarum, the rotten borough* come to us. We leave it to the 'Academy of Fine Arts' to account for the association."[56]

Spurred on by necessity both Philadelphia and Baltimore began improvements to gain supremacy in the Susquehanna Valley. Its own growing importance together with the possibility of using this area as a stepping-stone to the West excited keen interest and bitter rivalry. In December 1824, "A Society for the Promotion of Internal Improvements" was organized in Philadelphia.[57] Members subscribed funds, sent an engineer to England to study British railroad experiments, and

---

[54] The domestic exports for 1821, 1822, and 1823 of New York, Philadelphia, and Baltimore were (in millions of dollars):

	1821	1822	1823
New York	7.8	10.9	11.3
Philadelphia	2.8	3.5	3.1
Baltimore	2.7	3.4	3.1*

* Hunt gives this figure while the general table of Homans gives 4.1. *Hunt's Merchants' Magazine*, I, 186, 187, 365; Homans, *History and Statistical Account of the Foreign Commerce of the United States*. These two sets of figures agree except for Baltimore, 1823.

[55] Meyer, ed., 237-8, quotes from the *Pennsylvania House Journal*, 1823-24, 163-70.

[56] *Pittsburgh Gazette*, XXXIII, July 7, 1818, New Series, No. 15, quoted by Croll, "Rivalry Between Pittsburgh and Wheeling" in the *Western Pennsylvania Historical Magazine*, XIII, 240.

[57] *First Annual Report of the Society for the Promotion of Internal Improvements;* McMaster, *op. cit.*, V, 140; Meyer, ed., *op. cit.*, 312; Ringwalt, *Development of Transportation Systems in the United States*, 70.

reawakened interest in western routes. The Chesapeake and Delaware Canal and the Union Canal projects were revived so that Philadelphia could tap the Susquehanna River traffic, most of which was floating to tidewater at Port Deposit and then passing on to Baltimore. A railroad was also chartered in 1823 by Philadelphians who pledged to assist the inventor John Stevens to construct a line to the Susquehanna River at Columbia.

Baltimore, on the other hand, entertained gigantic plans to win the trade of both the Susquehanna Region and the West. After deliberating on the merits of each, the Chesapeake metropolis staked her immediate future on the canalization of the lower Susquehanna. The Chesapeake and Ohio Canal, which had been Baltimore's hope of reaching the West, was found to be too far south to be of great value to Baltimore. The Susquehanna Region demanded attention since Philadelphia had revived her projects to tap its trade. The hope of gaining the return trade of the valley also beckoned the Baltimore commercial people to turn their attention northward.[58] Plans were therefore made for a canal from the mouth of the Susquehanna to the falls at Conewago, which impeded river traffic, and for a second canal from Havre de Grace to Baltimore.

Philadelphia's railroad venture, which appeared to be out of place in the era of canal-mindedness, was a miserable failure; her canals were slow in being completed. Baltimore's canal plans were obstructed by the defensive policy of refusal to grant a charter to any Maryland project, which the Pennsylvania legislature again displayed. Meanwhile, the trade of the Susquehanna Valley appeared to the rivals as only of secondary importance and both thereon turned to more Herculean projects in order to gain the trade of the West. In this larger field both saw an opportunity to gain wealth and prestige; a safe monopoly of this trade would topple New York from her commercial throne. In 1826 Pennsylvania inaugurated her system of State Works which was to cross the Susquehanna Valley, win the trade of Pittsburgh and the Ohio, and rebuild Philadelphia's export trade.[59] The next year Baltimore chose to stake her future on railway transportation and procured a charter for the Baltimore and Ohio Railroad. The rivalry was "marvelously" bitter during this era; each city tried to outdo the other with a more radical type of innovation. America's obsession for speed was being born.

[58] See Chapter III.

[59] A study of the State Works has not been included in this volume. The Main Line of the Works was primarily constructed to win the trade of the West. The lateral canals, born in political bargains, were often impractical and unnecessary. For the history of the construction, business, and sale of the State Works, see Bishop, *The State Works of Pennsylvania* in the *Connecticut Academy of Arts and Sciences,* XIII, 149-298.

Sanguine enthusiasm revived Philadelphia's hope for commercial importance and intensified her dislike for her rivals. "The internal improvements of this state," wrote the British consul in 1827, "are carried on with great vigor. Canals are opening in every direction and the produce of the distant districts will come direct to this city which at present find their way to New York and Baltimore."[60] Before 1830, the Union and the Chesapeake and Delaware Canals were finished; the State works promised early completion; and Philadelphia was busy sponsoring short lines of railroads to tap the rich sections of the Susquehanna Valley.[61]

However, the great business boom which Philadelphia anticipated did not mature. Although her coastwise trade flourished, its importance was principally due to the anthracite coal trade. Flour exports were practically stationary between 1831 and 1845 and below the totals for the colonial period.[62] Exports from Pennsylvania showed no sign of a boom during these years. The internal improvements sponsored by the State of Pennsylvania and by Philadelphia merchants and capitalists were unable to divert all the Susquehanna Valley trade from Baltimore, or successfully compete with the Erie Canal for the business of the West. The Chesapeake and Delaware Canal was forced to share the business of the Susquehanna River (and later the Susquehanna and Tidewater Canal) with Baltimore. The Union Canal was physically unable to handle the traffic of a through waterway. The State Works proved to be a dissipation of capital and energy which almost forced Pennsylvania into bankruptcy. The failure of these Philadelphia canals and railroads caused that city to again assume a Rip Van Winkle attitude toward improvements. Her many investments had not won for the city "the Golden Fleece" of the Susquehanna Valley or the more extensive West. Only the Pennsylvania Railroad marched on to future greatness.

In Baltimore, a new spirit was awakened by the Baltimore and Ohio Railroad. One year after its charter had been granted the Chesapeake City, thoroughly convinced of the practicability of railroads, decided to construct another line. The Baltimore and Susquehanna Railroad was

---

[60] British Consular Reports, F. O. 5/128, Robertson to Bidwell, January 2, 1827. In 1831 he again wrote of Philadelphia's activity, "Philadelphia will in a short time become again one of the most important commercial cities in the Union." F. O. 5/267, Robertson to Bidwell, No. 1, February 8, 1831.

[61] See Chapter VII.

[62] Kuhlman, op. cit., 67.
Flour averages for five-year periods from 1831-55 were (in thousands of barrels):

1831-35	146
1835-40	130
1840-45	176
1845-50	254
1850-55	331

planned to reach northward into the Susquehanna Valley. Philadelphia displayed her feeling of commercial insecurity by stubborn opposition to this plan. Pennsylvania's Legislature, under the influence of Philadelphia, fell back upon her defensive policy of refusing to grant a charter giving the Maryland project a right of way within the Commonwealth of Pennsylvania.[63] However, political rivalries within Pennsylvania itself— rivalries which had been partly born in opposition to the State's own internal improvement policy—finally gave Baltimore victory.

Almost immediately after this success, the Maryland metropolis began another campaign to construct a canal along the lower Susquehanna from a junction with the Main Line of the State Works at Columbia to the mouth of the Susquehanna River. Again Philadelphia assumed the defensive; the Pennsylvania metropolis could not allow any canal to divert all the traffic of the Pennsylvania State Works. Since the eastern division, which began at Columbia, was the Philadelphia and Columbia Railroad, a canal to tidewater at this point seemed especially bad. However, the presence of the Chesapeake and Delaware Canal south of the Maryland terminal of the proposed canal removed the graver dangers of such a waterway. The legal struggle was bitter but shorter than that waged for the chartering of the Baltimore and Susquehanna Railroad.

By 1840 both Baltimore's canal and railroad had been completed to Wrightsville, on the Susquehanna River opposite Columbia; both had connections with the Pennsylvania State Works. But Baltimore was not satisfied; a new goal beckoned her onward. Although the Maryland port still claimed to be one of the largest flour markets in America, Baltimore also wished to become a coal center. She wished to make the Susquehanna Valley her Lehigh or Schuylkill region; she desired to be mistress in more than one field. So anxiously did Maryland push her improvements through the Susquehanna Valley to Harrisburg and then to Sunbury that the projects soon became financially weak and thereby lost much of their effectiveness.

From the day when the two colonial marts of Philadelphia and Baltimore discovered that their economic interests overlapped in the Susquehanna Valley, rivalry for the control of this region grew. Each new type of transportation with which young America experimented these two rivals tried to apply in this overlapping hinterland in an effort to gain supremacy. Although nature seemed to point to Baltimore as the most convenient market, Philadelphia's political control over Baltimore projects constructed within the Commonwealth of Pennsylvania counterbalanced this advantage. The years before the Civil War saw the two cities

[63] Chapter VI, 119-130.

still striving to divert trade their way, but each had to be satisfied that it must share the trade with its rival.

APPENDIX I

Table of the exports from Maryland and Pennsylvania from 1791-1856. Since Baltimore and Philadelphia did most of the shipping in these two states, the figures may be judiciously used to represent the exports of these two ports. The following table is in millions of dollars.

TOTAL EXPORTS OF

YEAR	MARYLAND	PENNSYLVANIA
1791	2	3
1792	2	3
1793	3	6
1794	5	6
1795	5	11
1796	9	17
1797	9	11
1798	12	8
1799	16	12
1800	12	11
1801	12	17
1802	7	12
1803	5	7
1804	9	11
1805	10	13
1806	14	17
1807	14	16
1808	2	4
1809	6	9
1810	6	10
1811	6	9
1812	5	5
1813	3	3
1814	.2	..
1815	5	4
1816	7	7
1817	8	8
1818	7	8
1819	5	6
1820	6	5
1821	3	7
1822	4	9

YEAR	MARYLAND	PENNSYLVANIA
1823	5	9
1824	4	9
1825	4	11
1826	4	8
1827	4	7
1828	4	6
1829	4	4
1830	3	4
1831	4	5
1832	4	3
1833	4	4
1834	4	3
1835	3	3
1836	3	3
1837	3	3
1838	4	3
1839	4	5
1840	5	6
1841	4	5
1842	4	3
1843*	2	2
1844	5	3
1845	5	3
1846	6	4
1847	9	8
1848	7	5
1849	8	5
1850	6	4
1851	5	5
1852	6	5
1853	7	6
1854	11	10
1855	10	6
1856	11	7
1857	13	7
1858	10	6
1859	9	5
1860	9	5

* Nine months to June 30. Fiscal year for 1843 and following began July 1.

Compiled from *Hunt's Commercial Magazine,* I, 365 and Homans, J. S., *An Historical and Statistical Account of the Foreign Commerce of the United States.*

Baltimore Flour Inspections 1798-1843. (In thousands of barrels.)

1798....256	1814....156	1830....598
1799....274	1815....388	1831....555
1800....273	1816....395	1832....527
1801....360	1817....399	1833....534
1802....370	1818....444	1834....489
1803....407	1819....466	1835....527
1804 ...261	1820....582	1836....401
1805....335	1821....484	1837....399
1806... 351	1822....430	1838....430
1807....490	1823....442	1839....561
1808....258	1824....544	1840....780
1809....423	1825....510	1841....629
1810...364	1826....596	1842....548
1811....530	1827....573	1843...566
1812... 553	1828....546	
1813....291	1829....474	

Compiled from Hazard, *United States Register,* IV, 134 and *Hunt's Merchants' Magazine,* IV, 195. Sparks, *Baltimore,* in *The North American Review,* XX, 122 gives table for years from 1798 to 1823.

APPENDIX III

Table comparing the amount of flour inspected at New York, Philadelphia, and Baltimore from 1820-30. (In thousands of barrels.)

	1820	1821	1822	1823	1824	
New York	267	258	342	347	360	
Philadelphia	400	396	271	302	301	
Baltimore	577	485	429	442	544	

	1825	1826	1827	1828	1829	1830
New York	446	527	625	722	670	827
Philadelphia	294	342	351	333	297	473
Baltimore	510	596	572	546	473	597

From Albion, *New York and Its Rivals,* in the *Journal of Economic and Business History,* III, No. 4, 613, as adapted from *Niles' Weekly Register,* XXXIV, 238; XLII, 149. Note that some of the figures for inspections at Baltimore differ in the two tables given above.

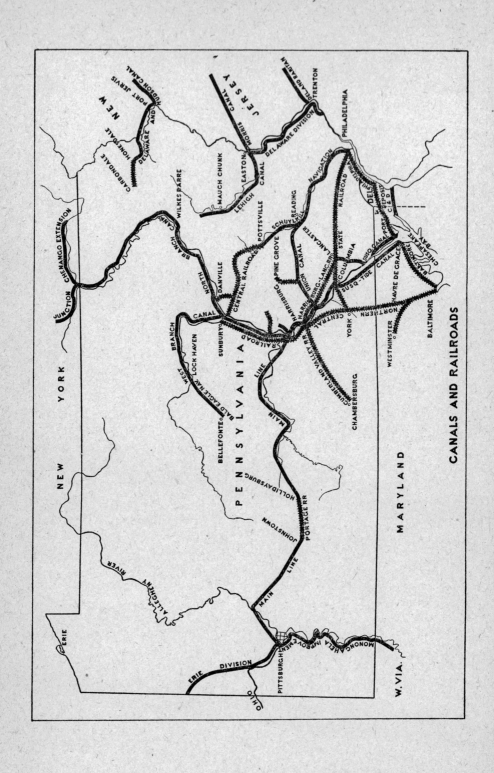

CANALS AND RAILROADS

CHAPTER II

PIONEER ARKS AND WAGONS

The crooked, meandering Susquehanna River appeared pointed out by nature to be the highway for the expansive valley through which it flowed. However, since its lower course flowed over crystalline rock reefs and secret snags, the navigation of this wide, shallow river of "limpid" waters was dangerous and hazardous. Only navigable when spring freshets filled its capacious bed, the river's value as a waterway was limited. Baltimore, situated near the mouth of the river, gave much attention to improvements in the channel of the Susquehanna River and encouraged producers of interior Pennsylvania to do likewise. Philadelphia, on the other hand, believed that the lower waters of the river were treacherous by nature so that the produce of the residents of Pennsylvania would not be carried to the commercial metropolis of a "foreign" state. Since the Susquehanna flowed transversely to Philadelphia's avenue of western expansion, her only hope of gaining the Susquehanna Valley trade, at an early date, was placed in roads.

As the eighteenth century drew to a close, the volume of business in the more densely settled southern portion of the Susquehanna Valley grew rapidly. Gradually the northern part of the valley, far into New York State, also began to seek a market. Philadelphia improved her roads to receive the growing traffic, her famous Lancaster Turnpike penetrated to the river in 1803. Many later connections were made by turnpike between the Delaware and Susquehanna Rivers to carry the valley trade to the Pennsylvania metropolis. Baltimore saw the success of these turnpike roads; she realized that the river was not a satisfactory highway. Its descending trade was dangerous and of short distribution; return trade was impossible. Nor was the river convenient for the farmers in the rich farm lands which were not situated near the stream. Therefore, Baltimore also financed turnpikes into the Susquehanna Valley hoping to duplicate the success of the Lancaster Turnpike. The Baltimore roads dominated the trade of the western part of the valley; Philadelphia monopolized the wagon trade of the eastern and northern sections. From the Revolution to about 1820 the trade of the Susquehanna Valley was a pioneer trade which favored the Baltimore market, while the return trade of merchandise, sugar, coffee, tea, and manufactured goods came mainly from Philadelphia.

The winding Susquehanna River, which had seen the canoes of the Five Nations, had carried Conrad Weiser and his German followers from their New York settlement into Pennsylvania, and had been a highway for Revolutionary armies, rises in central New York State, which in colonial days was far in the interior and separated from Albany and New York City by a dense wilderness. At Tioga Point a junction is formed between the waters of the so-called East Branch and the Chemung River, which stretches its branches far into the famous Genesee Country of western New York. Turning southward at Tioga Point, the river passes through the romantic mountains of northern Pennsylvania into the Wyoming region. Instead of following a natural valley, the stream in this section breaks through successive ranges of hills, whose escarpments tower high above the water, into their intervening valleys. The breadth of the river is very unequal, sometimes exceeding a mile, then contracting between rocky cliffs to less than one-quarter of that width. Finally, after passing about half way through Pennsylvania, the large West Branch meets the main river. This mountainous stream cuts its way through the rugged hills of central Pennsylvania until it reaches far to the west, where its source waters almost intermingle with those of the Allegheny River. From the junction of the North and West Branch the river flows almost due south until it is met by the circuitous Juniata, another western branch which flows through the "Mohawk Valley" of Pennsylvania. Turning at this point, the main river takes a southeastern course and passes through the Blue Mountains, whose rocky ridges form a fall in the river which the tortuous stream was unable to chisel away. These falls, known as the Conewago Falls, were the first obstruction to navigation met from the source of the Susquehanna. North of this point the twisting river with all its main branches was navigable for descending and ascending keel and Durham boats.

From the falls southward, the stream is of a different character. Instead of being a river of moderate descent and bordered with extensive ranges of bottom or flat lands, the Susquehanna River below the fall line is swift, shallow, and rocky. Many rock shelves are hidden under the surface of the water, which flows with "prodigious velocity". From the falls to tidewater, a distance of some fifty miles, the river drops about 150 feet and for most of the distance washes the base of precipitous rugged hills varying from one hundred to three hundred feet above the surface of the water. Although there are no perpendicular falls, long rapids make the water very swift and treacherous. The lower course of the Susquehanna was "ill adapted to navigation"; the "embarrassments at its mouth" made the river a poor highway for commercial purposes.[1]

Since the Conewago Falls marked the beginning of rough water, the early boatmen did not pass below this point. Here the village of Middletown was laid out in 1755 just half way between Lancaster and Carlisle on the great highroad to the West. It soon became an important river port, since it was the lowest port of entry on the river. Middletown's founder, a Philadelphia Quaker, built up a lucrative trade with the Indians, western fur trappers, and Susquehanna rivermen before the Revolution.[2] But during the years of Indian troubles and those of the Revolution, much of the upper Susquehanna was utterly forsaken and destitute of inhabitants;[3] for a long period no boatmen plied the river. Internal trade in this region was negligible. However, in 1789 boards and scantling were floated down stream to Middletown,[4] and, the following year, 150,000 bushels of wheat came down the Susquehanna to Middletown in canoes and keel boats. Limited amounts of pig and bar iron along with some castings also came down the Juniata River to Middletown from the small, scattered ironworks of the Juniata Valley.[5] In a few years wheat was received from the rich, distant Genesee Country[6].

Middletown forwarded most of these shipments to Philadelphia over approximately 100 miles of poor roads at an estimated cost of 5s. 3d. per

[1] For descriptions of the river see: *A Description of the River Susquehanna;* Gallatin, *Report of the Secretary of the Treasury on Public Roads and Canals,* Appendix E., Mr. Latrobe's communication, 93-5; Weld, *Travels through the States of North America . . . from 1795 to 1797,* I, 127; *Philip Vickers Fithian's Journal,* ed. by Albion and Dodson, 38-9; Gilpin, "A Tour from Philadelphia," in the *Pennsylvania Magazine of History and Biography,* L, 75; Melish, *A Description of the Roads of the United States,* 169; American Philosophical Society, *Transactions,* I, 276-7.

[2] Day, *Historical Collections,* 287; Egle, *History of Pennsylvania,* 649-50; *Phillip Vickers Fithian's Journal, op. cit.,* 39. Fithian writing from Sunbury in 1775 notes, "Here are a Number of Boatmen imployed in going up & down the River to Middleton."

[3] Higgins, *Expansion in New York,* 100, 110; Parkins, "Development of Transportation in Pennsylvania," in *The Bulletin of the Geographical Society in Philadelphia,* XIV, 110.

[4] Letter, Alex Graydon to Mr. Jedediah Morse from Lewisburg, March 5, 1789, in answer to a list of queries on Dauphin County, reprinted in *The Pennsylvania Magazine of History and Biography,* VI, 115-6.

[5] *An Historical Account of the Rise, Progress, and Present State of the Canal Navigation of Pennsylvania,* 11. Bining, *Pennsylvania Iron Manufacture* in *The Eighteenth Century,* 40, 61.

[6] O'Callaghan, ed., *Documentary History of the State of New York,* II, 649.

hundredweight.[7] Because of this expensive freightage, much of the wheat received was reduced to a concentrated form and Middletown became the seat of an important flour milling business.[8] On the opposite shore from the thriving river port of Middletown some river boats discharged their cargoes. Milling establishments financed by Baltimore capital were erected at the little town of York Haven located here, and the Chesapeake metropolis about eighty miles away began to receive flour by wagon from this center.[9]

Merchandise for the settlers in the Susquehanna Valley was conveyed to the Conewago Falls from Philadelphia and to a less extent from Baltimore in the returning wagons. From the falls the merchandise was distributed throughout the upper valley by the returning boatmen. Seldom did a river craft of any weight attempt to pass up stream from a point below the falls, since this "required 30 to 40 men a great part of the day, and an expense of £5 or £6 at least, to accomplish this work; for the men are obliged to perch and scatter themselves (as it has been humorously expressed) like *black-birds* on the rocks, and to drag their burden shifting from rock to rock through the whole length of the falls."[10]

Such conditions could not be tolerated as trade increased; enterprising business men soon began to consider the question of avoiding the falls. In order to utilize more of the free river current and avoid slow, costly land transportation, river folk thought it best to improve the river southward from the Conewago Falls so that they could reach the new Schuylkill and Susquehanna Canal, which was to be constructed, or the turnpike from Columbia to Philadelphia. As early as 1789, meetings were held for discussion of this plan. A committee was appointed to survey the river

---

[7] Ringwalt, *op. cit.,* 42. Ringwalt estimates that the charge amounted to about $14.66 per ton in Pennsylvania currency. *American State Papers, Miscellaneous,* I, 858. In a comparative statement of the cost of land and water carriage made in 1794 it was estimated that the cost of land transportation from Middletown to Philadelphia was 5s. 6d. per cwt. or 20 tons for about £100. Kelsey, ed., *Cazenove's Journal,* 54. In the same year (1794) this traveller found that the cartage from Harrisburg to Philadelphia was the same as the estimate given between Middletown and Philadelphia (5s. 3d. per cwt.). He added that because of the passage of the army through this town, en route to the scene of the Whiskey Rebellion, rates had temporarily jumped to as much as 8s. per cwt.

[8] Kuhlman, *History of the Flour Milling Industry,* 22-3; *A Description of the River Susquehanna; Cazenove's Journal, op. cit.,* 52; La Rochefoucauld, *Travels through the United States of North America in the years 1795, 1796, 1797,* I, 90-91; Brissot de Warville, *New Travels in the United States,* 154-6; Letter, Alex Graydon to Mr. Jedediah Morse, in *The Pennsylvania Magazine of History and Biography,* VI, 117.

[9] Day, *op. cit.,* 701; *Niles' Weekly Register,* XXXI, 4; Gibson, *History of York County,* 333.

[10] *Account of the Conewago Canal, on the River Susquehanna.*

from Wrightsville Ferry to the Head of McKees Half Falls, and also the Juniata River as far as Aughwick Falls, and to estimate the expense necessary to remove obstructions.[11] They reported on January 30, 1790, that *"Conewago Falls,* about 14 miles above Wright's Ferry, *the great obstruction and barr to the wealth and population of our Western Country,* is at present the grand object. We are clear that a *CANAL* is the *sure* and *safe way* of effecting a good navigation for boats to pass and repass."[12]

On April 13, 1791, the Legislature of Pennsylvania appropriated £5250 to improve the Susquehanna River from Wright's ferry to the mouth of the Swatara creek which was to be the western terminus of the canal that Philadelphia planned. Governor Mifflin indorsed this policy of river improvement. Although the natural difficulties were great and although "some objections in point of policy" might be made against the principle of opening the river to the Maryland boundary, the Governor maintained that the Susquehanna should at least be cleared as far as Columbia.[13]

Overtures were made to Governor Mifflin by various contractors who wished to make the improvements as stipulated by the Legislature. The appropriation measure, which this body had passed, required the construction of a short canal without locks to be built and operated free of toll for the small sum granted by the act.[14] However, some of the Managers of the Schuylkill and Susquehanna Canal Company, which was organized to construct a canal between the two rivers named in its title, after viewing the Swatara Creek and the Conewago Falls, decided that every part of the great river improvement should be connected with their project and under their management. They knew that "the success of *one* would aid the *other.*"[15] These men volunteered, as a company or as individuals, to make a canal around the Conewago Falls according to their own plans which provided for locks. They even agreed to make up any possible deficit that might be incurred from their funds.[16] Their offer

---

[11] *Ibid.,* 1; Gibson, *op. cit.,* 332; Landis, "Jasper Yeates and His Time," in the *Pennsylvania Magazine of History and Biography,* XLVI, 214-6. The committee was composed of Samuel Boyd, Bartram Galbraith, and Thomas Hulings.

[12] *Account of the Conewago Canal, on the River Susquehanna,* 2; Gibson, *op. cit.,* 331. Gibson quotes from the committee report, but the wording is not the same as the report which is signed by the committee and published in the *Account . . .*

[13] *Pennsylvania Archives,* 4th series, IV, 196-7.

[14] *Letter Book of the Secretary of the Commonwealth, Dec. 24, 1790-Mar. 3, 1794,* III. Letter, A. J. Dallas, Sec. of the Commonwealth to Robert Morris, John Nicholson, and William Smith dated June 29, 1792.

[15] This was undoubtedly true from the canal officials' point of view since their route was to meet the river at the mouth of the Swatara Creek which is below the Falls.

[16] *Account of the Conewago Canal, on the River Susquehanna,* 6.

was, indeed, attractive; and on July 3, 1792, Governor Mifflin contracted with seventeen of these men, most of whom were prominent Philadelphians and interested in the Schuylkill and Susquehanna Canal Company,[17] to cut a canal around the falls. The ditch was to be at least forty feet wide and four feet deep with two "safe and commodious" locks; it was to be operated by the company, after construction, as a public highway without toll charges.

Finally in 1797, after spending more than $100,000, the company declared the canal finished. On November twenty-second a great opening ceremony was held; the first canal in Pennsylvania was duly dedicated. Five hundred enthusiastic citizens braved the cold rain of the late November day to hear Governor Mifflin's party saluted by "amature cannon."[18]

In the meantime, work on the canal from the Schuylkill River to the Susquehanna River had been suspended and Philadelphia's hope of gaining the Susquehanna trade by a water route was temporarily thwarted. However, once past the Conewago Falls, boats could reach Columbia where they were in the vicinity of the turnpike which had just been completed from the city of Philadelphia to Lancaster, which soon began to receive freight from the new river port at Columbia. Immediately Middletown lost its former importance; Columbia became Philadelphia's port of entry on the Susquehanna.

The canal around the falls, however, was not destined to play an important role in river navigation. Even before it had been completed, there appeared on the Susquehanna a new type of craft which was capable of running the falls in safety. About 1794 an enterprising German miller from the vicinity of Huntington on the Juniata River appeared at Conewago in a boat "in the shape of an ark" fully freighted with flour which he planned to deliver to Baltimore.[19] This miller skipper passed the

---

[17] The members of the group were Robert Morris, William Smith, Walter Stuart, Samuel Meredith, John Steinmetz, Tench Francis, John Nicholson, John Donaldson, Samuel Miles, Timothy Matlock, David Rittenhouse, Samuel Powel, A. J. Dallas, William Bingham, Henry Miller, Abraham Witmer, and Robert Harris.

[18] *Account of the Conewago Canal, on the River Susquehanna,* 11-13; Gibson, *op. cit.,* 333; Gallatin, *op. cit.,* 32; Harlow, *Old Towpaths,* 15.

[19] *A Description of the River Susquehanna,* 19; Hazard, *The Register of Pennsylvania,* II, 300; Jones, *History of the Early Settlement of the Juniata Valley,* 173; Johnston, *History of Cecil County, Maryland,* 379; Day, *op. cit.,* 287; *Cazenove Journal,* ed., Kelsey, 53.

Various accounts of this ingenious German spell his name differently and give varying dates for his first trip. His name appears as Cryder, Kryder, and Breider. Cazenove, the General Agent of the Holland Land Company, reported that arks were on the river when he made his journey through eastern Pennsylvania in 1794; others give the date to be as late as 1797.

Conewago Falls in safety; he floated past Wrightsville in the morning and was at Havre de Grace in time to transfer his cargo to a bay shallop so that it could be delivered in Baltimore the next day. The Maryland city was greatly pleased with skipper Kryder's success; merchants of the city gave him premiums for his trail-blazing voyage. The accomplishment of the ark was soon known throughout the Susquehanna Valley; in a short time many similar craft were floating downstream during the river freshets when the flood waters would carry these flat-bottomed boats safely over snags and rocks. The settlers of the far away Genesee Country turned to Baltimore as the most "advantageous" market; prices of lumber, fat cattle, butter, and cheese were reported to have been 50% higher at the Chesapeake port than at Albany.[20] Baltimore was immediately recognized as "the natural sea port" of central Pennsylvania and southern New York.

Some rivermen devoted time and energy in rendering the river safer and easier to navigate. In dry seasons driftwood was piled around rocks and burnt until the rocks were very hot. Water was then thrown over the rocks splitting them and making their removal possible. Much of the bad water was between Columbia and the Maryland line, the stretch which Pennsylvania wished to keep unimproved so that the river trade would turn to Philadelphia rather than hazard the trip south to the Mason and Dixon line. This policy, beginning as early as 1771, enraged Baltimore. A friend of that city wrote that her neighbor's attitude "results from that ever existing principle, which to all eternity will influence the body politic as well as the individual, that of making itself the first object of solicitude and care."[21] In 1799, Pennsylvania reenacted her former policy in a law which read that, "Any individual or company, who shall without proper authority from the governor of the commonwealth, remove or attempt to remove, the obstructions in the river Susquehanna, between Wright's ferry and the Maryland line, shall be fined in a sum not less than two hundred dollars, nor more than two thousand dollars, with such imprisonment as the court before whom they are prosecuted in their discretion may direct, not exceeding six months." This law prevented improvement in the stream below Columbia until 1801 when, in return for the right to construct the Chesapeake and Delaware Canal, the Susquehanna River was declared a public highway by the State of Pennsylvania.

To assist Baltimore in securing the prospective trade of the Susquehanna River, the General Assembly of Maryland passed an Act in 1783

[20] O'Callaghan, ed., *op. cit.*, II, 668-9; 1146, 1149, 1150, 1153-54, 1159-62, 1177.

[21] *Reflections on the Proposition to communicate by a Navigable Canal the Waters of the Chesapeake with those of Delaware Bay* . . ., 27-8.

granting a charter to a company for making a canal from a point known as Love Island, just south of the Pennsylvania-Maryland boundary, to tidewater. The organization, composed of some forty men, mostly from the city of Baltimore, promised to raise twenty thousand pounds and finish construction of the canal by 1801. Their company was thereupon incorporated as "The Proprietors of the Susquehanna Canal";[22] their undertaking was one of the first of its kind in the United States.

Work on the canal progressed slowly. The magnitude of the construction was much greater than had been anticipated. At numerous times supplementary laws were passed by the Assembly extending the time of completion and increasing the capital stock of the company. Other acts allowed the company to spend $5000 in opening and clearing the bed of the river, which was parallel to the canal, with the stipulation that half-tolls could be charged. This move was bitterly attacked by Pennsylvania since Maryland had formerly declared the Susquehanna a public highway. Although Maryland soon relinquished the right to collect tolls on river traffic, the argument did much harm in regard to the establishment of friendly relations between the two states and their commercial centers.[23]

By 1802 enough water could be kept in the Susquehanna Canal to make an official inspection possible and the Governors of Pennsylvania and Maryland were taken through the new waterway. "In the course of the Excursion," the canal managers reported, "they were able to demonstrate to the entire satisfaction of all persons present that the Canal will afford a safe, easy and expeditious navigation of more than nine miles up and down the most difficult and dangerous part of the River."[24] Reports of the inspection were widely disseminated. The purpose of the entire proceedings was to interest Pennsylvania in extending the canal northward at least as far as Columbia but this proposed cooperation did not mature, since it would cause a reversal of Pennsylvania's policy toward rendering the Susquehanna navigable without any compensation for such a move. The market price of the canal stock fell from £1000 to £500.

The next year the canal managers announced that the route was officially finished. It was a rough course of irregular breadth and depth.

---

[22] Excerpts from the Original Minute Book of The Proprietors of the Susquehannah Canal, owned by J. Alexis Shriver, corresponding secretary of the Maryland State Historical Society. Also see Scharf, History of Maryland, II, 524; Scharf, Chronicles of Baltimore, 208; Johnston, op. cit., 376-7; Griffith, Annals of Baltimore, 101.

[23] Letter Book of the Secretary of the Commonwealth, October 17, 1799-October 14, 1812, V, 89-91. Letter from Governor McKean to Governor Mercer, Lancaster, October 25, 1802.

[24] Excerpts from the Original Minute Book of the Proprietors of the Susquehanna Canal.

The engineers made a fatal mistake in making the bottom circular, which was not suitable for arks and other wide, flat-bottomed craft. Premiums were offered to promote navigation up and down the canal, but few claimants for these prizes actually appeared though "Mr. Henry Putt a respectable inhabitant of the waters of the Juniata did make one complete voyage down and up and down a second time" for which he received $50 prize money.[25]

The Baltimore sponsors of the canal continually tried to get Pennsylvania to clear the Susquehanna River for safe navigation from Columbia to the Maryland line; the Pennsylvanians, who were influenced by Philadelphia, persistently turned a deaf ear to any active cooperation with the Marylanders.[26] The canal officials attempted to remove some obstructions at their own expense in Pennsylvania territory, but they were stopped by the authorities of that State who acted under the law of 1799 forbidding such action.[27] The legislators at Harrisburg feared that by smoothing the bed of the Susquehanna River they would prune Philadelphia's tree of commercial fortune. They maintained that it was their patriotic duty to aid their own metropolis against the advances of a "foreign city." In view of this situation, the Baltimore canal enthusiasts planned to open a road from the head of their project at Love Island into Lancaster County in order to tap that region without having to rely on the uncertain river.[28]

In spite of state aid, assessments on stock-holders, and tax exemptions, the canal was not profitable. Expenses grew, construction was faulty, and revenues could not be collected. Passage through the canal was slow because of the many locks. Then, too, the canal had been constructed as much with a view to the erection of mills run by water power as for navigation purposes. The current in the channel, therefore, had to be fairly strong. Alluvium of the river was carried into the canal by this current; the banks were washed, and resulting bars of silt made navigation difficult. The canal was almost as dangerous as the river itself and its tolls were avoided whenever a river passage seemed possible.[29]

In 1804 the Legislature of Maryland gave the canal company the right to operate lotteries to supplement their elusive revenue. The benefit from

---

[25] *Ibid.*

[26] *Letter Book of the Secretary of the Commonwealth,* October 17, 1799-October 14, 1812, V, 85. Letter from Thomas McKean, Governor of Pennsylvania, to Robert Gilmore, Governor of the Susquehanna Canal Company at Baltimore.

[27] *Excerpts from the Original Minute Book of the Proprietors of the Susquehanna Canal.*

[28] *Ibid.*

[29] Gallatin, *op. cit.,* Answer to the queries by Gallatin submitted by Robert Gilmore of the Susquehanna Company, 33.

this right was apparently slight, for in 1817 the canal was sold, by the sheriff of Cecil County at a great loss to the original owners. The purchasers immediately executed the bold measure of extending the wing dam of the canal at Love Island so as to obstruct the entire eastern channel of the river.[30] This dam was constructed on the "plea of necessity" but there was a possible sinister purpose of making this "a sure means to force upon the public the use of the Canal." This move embittered the valley folk, who formerly were accustomed to use the canal only when river navigation was impossible. This action of the new owners increased the friction between Pennsylvania and Maryland and created a great demand for Pennsylvania to interfere in the situation[31] as well as a fine opportunity for Philadelphia to advise the use of her port.

To the merchants of Baltimore, the little canal was obviously a keen disappointment. The owners, after 1817, were openly operating for personal profit; they did not appreciate the great value of this project as an avenue from the Pennsylvania hinterland to the Baltimore market. Instead of befriending the rivermen, they embittered them by mean, tricky policies. One staunch Baltimore supporter claimed that in the hands of the new owners the canal had *"become tributary to the interests of Philadelphia."*[32]

Meanwhile, after a few trial runs in their home-made boats, the inhabitants of the Susquehanna Valley regarded the river as a great artery for their commerce. Keel boats, with their durably built hulks shaped like canal boats, and with heavy timbers extending the whole length of the bottom of the boat to serve as keel and shock absorber, continued to ply the upper waters of the Susquehanna with their ascending and descending cargoes.[33] Giant arks of the roughest and strongest construction, mere "cast, rough, and unweildy" boxes with flat bottoms and perpendicular sides called boats because they floated, appeared on the river with every freshet.[34] From 60 to 90 feet long, 15 to 20 or more feet

---

[30] *Niles' Weekly Register,* XXII, 178.

[31] MS. Petition signed by more than 800 persons of Union County, Pennsylvania, in 1820, in the Archives Division of the Pennsylvania Historical and Museum Commission; *Pennsylvania Archives,* Fourth Series, V, 163-6. The Governors of the canal claimed, "to take it (the dam) away, will destroy the utility of a work calculated to facilitate navigation and to improve the property and interest of the Canal Company, without reason or necessity."

[32] *Address to the Mayor and City Council of Baltimore on the trade of the Susquehanna & the Rail Road to that River,* 6. Author's italics.

[33] Dunbar, *History of Travel in America,* 1, 281.

[34] *Cazenove Journal,* ed., Kelsey, 54. The Dutch traveller noted that arks "are a kind of ferryboat, with high sides, triangular in the front and back." Dunbar, *op. cit.,* I, 282; Ringwalt, *op. cit.,* 12.

wide, 3 to 5 feet deep, drawing about two feet of water, these rude craft were capable of carrying about fifty tons of goods. Each of the two tapered ends of the ark was equipped with long sweeps which two men manipulated to govern the boat's course, as the ark had no rudder. They bounced and tumbled over falls and rapids, propelled by the current and steered by the fresh water sailors who manned them.

Arks were absolutely helpless against the current and therefore could not ascend the Susquehanna. They were sold at the mouth of the river for about $15 and torn apart to be sold for lumber. Besides the great amount of rough lumber which reached tidewater in this fashion, many huge rafts of logs and sawed lumber were floated downstream. Tightly fastened together with saplings, they were piloted southward to Port Deposit at the mouth of the river by the venturesome rivermen. Most of this lumber was consigned to Baltimore and was often collected at tidewater into giant rafts and towed through the Chesapeake to the wharves of the city.[35]

The invention of the ark revolutionized transportation on the Susquehanna; Baltimore was in a very favorable position to contest for the entire central Pennsylvania hinterland. Grain, flour, whiskey, country products of all descriptions, iron, bituminous coal, plaster-of-Paris, salt from New York State, and lumber in all forms passed downstream to the Baltimore market. Each year the amount increased. Although no accurate figures can be given on this trade, it was estimated that in 1817, $1,870,000 worth of goods passed York Haven;[36] from the first of April to the fifth of July of the same year, 343 arks and 989 rafts were seen on the river below Columbia.[37]

Despite this descending river trade, the Susquehanna cannot be said to have afforded a satisfactory highway to market. Viewed in its whole

---

[35] Ringwalt, *op. cit.*, 13; *Niles' Weekly Register*, XXXVI, 299; Defebaugh, *History of the Lumber Industry of America*, II, 572; Hough, *Report Upon Forestry*, 404. It is claimed that rafting on the Susquehanna River began on a fairly large scale about 1807.

[36] *Niles' Weekly Register*, XII, 320.

[37] *Ibid.*, XII, 159; Hazard, *The Pennsylvania Register*, VI, 406; *Observations on the Improvement of Navigation of the River Schuylkill for the Purpose of Connecting it with the Susquehanna*, 16. At this time Philadelphia was interested in improving the Schuylkill River for they deemed it "invaluable to Philadelphia" as a link in a system of canal and river navigation by which Philadelphia hoped to gain the growing Susquehanna trade.

extent, its ascending navigation was extremely limited and difficult.[38] Its descending navigation was dangerous and unsatisfactory. Arks and rafts could descend the shallow river only at time of high water, which rarely occurred except in the spring. The consequence was that nearly the whole trade of the valley descended at about the same time. The market, which was at all times uncertain, became glutted; prices fell almost as soon as the country farmer-sailors began to arrive on the freshets. The owners of the produce had incurred expenses which they could not meet without sale and were obliged to dispose of their goods at ruinous sacrifices. Many were wrecked by the swift currents of the floods and were forced to abandon their products, which had been raised, harvested, and partly manufactured during the year, or sell them to some salvaging agent who often traded with blind horses and watches without works. Then too, perhaps there was no spring freshet sufficient for descending navigation and the producer lost heavily since he had no other means of reaching market with his products which deteriorated over the summer months.

Since the only type of water craft that could navigate the lower Susquehanna was sold at tidewater by the rivermen, Baltimore did not sell much return merchandise. The country above the Wyoming Valley was supplied from either New York or Philadelphia while south of that region Philadelphia did most of the return business. This meant that Baltimore made profit on only one transfer; it meant that the Maryland metropolis had to have a large supply of capital on hand to pay the rivermen when they arrived with their wheat, flour, whiskey, and lumber. Baltimore was, therefore, not satisfied with this inconvenient method of trade; she wished to eliminate the triangular nature of business in the Susquehanna Valley by improving the conditions of ascending navigation so that she could gain the return trade for herself. Philadelphia, too, was dissatisfied with the triangular trade since she had a big demand for country produce and begrudged Baltimore's close relations with her own fellow-citizens of Pennsylvania. The Delaware River metropolis tried to hinder the opening of the lower Susquehanna River to thwart her rival, and projected roads and canals eastward from the Susquehanna in an attempt to divert the descending trade.

---

[38] Maryland and Pennsylvania could not agree on the dangers of the river. Maryland said it wasn't bad; Pennsylvania claimed it was very treacherous. Of the ascending trade a Pennsylvania commission reported: "That although the ascending navigation, may by towing, and perhaps in one or two places, short canals with locks, be considered improved, it must always remain tedious and dangerous, and if even free from toll, more expensive and less eligible, than the present land carriage from Baltimore, or even Philadelphia." *Observations on the Importance of Improving the Navigation of the River Schuylkill for the Purpose of Connecting it with the Susquehanna.*

The pioneer settlers in the Susquehanna Valley relied on roads as their avenue to market before the ark came into use, because of the natural obstructions in the river. Roads were especially important in Lancaster, Dauphin, York, Adams, Franklin, and Cumberland Counties, where fertile soil and the friendly Indian policy of the Penns enabled early settlers to have a marketable surplus of products. Although the Pennsylvania Assembly refused to see the importance of improved roads, the settlers east of the Susquehanna River were inclined to deal with the metropolis of their own Province. West of the river the settlers at an early date began to deal with Baltimore. They were "very intent on ye thing and have opened a road to Patapsco" on the Chesapeake Bay; such was the word Thomas Penn received from the southern counties which lay west of the Susquehanna in 1743.[39] By 1770 eight main roads crossed the Pennsylvania-Maryland border in this area,[40] which fact in itself caused a movement within the colony of Pennsylvania for better roads "to keep the growing and flourishing trade of Pennsylvania's western counties from being carried off to enrich the inhabitants of another Province."[41]

In 1791 Governor Mifflin recognized the fact that the Susquehanna River was acting as a dividing line between the commercial spheres of Philadelphia and Baltimore. In his annual message that year, the Governor said:

". . . the circumstances of our inland trade, will probably suggest the idea of making a reasonable compensation to the holders of certain ferries on the Susquehanna, and other rivers, in order to give a free passage to waggons transporting produce to the market, and returning with the merchandise to Philadelphia. This, it has been conceived, would be the means of preventing the trade of several counties from centering in other states, as experience has shown, that when the Susquehanna is frozen over, many farmers convey their produce to this city, which, in other seasons, they dispose of in Maryland."[42]

Despite the need of good roads, those of colonial days remained unrepaired. The responsibility for making and maintaining roads rested with the local governments[43] which were not capable of any extensive ways of construction or repair. Not until 1782 when a lottery was authorized to

---

[39] Letter from John Logan to Thomas Penn dated 1743, quoted by Gibson, *op. cit.*, 514.

[40] Turner, *op. cit.*, 75-6; Duane, *Letters addressed to the People of Pennsylvania respecting the Internal Improvements of the Commonwealth by means of Roads*, 7.

[41] Thomas Barton, Lancaster, Pa., April 28, 1793, to Thomas Penn, in Spring Gardens, London, MS., Historical Society of Pennsylvania, quoted from Plummer, *The Road Policy of Pennsylvania*, 40.

[42] *Pennsylvania Archives*, 4th series, IV, 198.

[43] Plummer, *op. cit.*, 19-20, 26.

raise funds to improve the Schuylkill River and the leading public roads from Philadelphia to the western part of Pennsylvania, was any provision for funds authorized by higher officials.[44]

Despite petitions, legislation, and messages, the main roads to Philadelphia remained unrepaired and were so bad that "Carriages of Burthen" could scarcely pass. The road leading from the important river port of Middletown was "very bad & deep even upon the Hills, & the whole of it is very stony & Hilly," reported people of that vicinity in 1792.[45] In spite of the fact that appropriations were granted for the repair of this road, nothing was done. The prominent Middletown miller, George Fry, wrote in 1793 complaining of the miserable condition of the road from that town leading toward Philadelphia:

"The consequences are of Importance to the Public in General and to this, neighbouring Places & the Settlements up Susquehanna & Juniata Rivers in particular, because the large Quantities of Wheat & other Produce which are brought to this Town by Water, and the Flour & c. manufactured about here, and which are to be forwarded by Land, remain on Hand for want of Teams which are terrified by the bad and dangerous Roads over Connowago & other Hills. . . . This occasions that Such Produce will often came too late to Market and be Subject to Suffer during the Warm Season by laying in crowded Storehouses, not to mention that by such Delay the Credit of many People may be hurt for want of Cash which they expect to draw from their Property as soon as they could get it delivered at the Place of its Destination."[46]

Nor was the main road from Philadelphia to the West via Lancaster much better. By 1766 traffic on it had become so heavy that the road could not be kept in repair.[47] Giant wagons plowed the natural earth until it appeared bottomless; heavy expenses made the transportation of produce over such a road practically profitless. But pre-Revolutionary agitation for improvements met with no success in the Pennsylvania Assembly, although the Rev. Thomas Barton of Lancaster forecast that "Pennsylvania will literally become a happier land than even that de-

---

[44] *Ibid.,* 26-8. This plan was not very successful as the act contained "disadvantages and discouragements" in the sale of tickets.

[45] "State Roads," MSS., No. 8 Archives Division of the Pennsylvania Historical and Museum Commission.

[46] *Ibid.,* Letter written by George Fry dated May 13, 1793.

[47] Turner, *op. cit.,* 71; Landis, "History of the Lancaster Turnpike," in *The Pennsylvania Magazine of History and Biography,* XLII, 28. This road was a King's highway laid out in 1733 and known as the Lancaster Road or the Provincial Road. After the Revolution it was called the Continental Road.

scribed in the 8th Chapter of Deuteronomy" if road improvements were made.[48]

After the Revolution the subject of road improvement was again taken up. The increased interest in roads in America was contemporaneous with advances in the science of road building in Great Britain, where turnpike trusts were formed to improve the highways by surfacing them with stone and gravel. The ideas of Telford and Macadam, two British experimenters in road construction, had great influence in the United States. The former stressed the desirability of a foundation of large stones covered with a layer of smaller ones. Macadam, however, advocated the use of an earthen roadbed topped by small broken stones closely bound together.

In 1791 the Society for Promoting the Improvement of Road and Inland Navigation in Pennsylvania endorsed a plan for road improvements. Governor Mifflin, a friend of internal improvements, that year announced that he was aware of the situation and pointed out that "the want of a good and permanent road is, at present, the principal defect in the communication between the middle counties and the metropolis."[49] A special commission, appointed to study the situation, reported that a road from Lancaster to Philadelphia would have a prosperous future. They were of the opinion that the great amount of heavy traffic plying between these two cities would require an artificial road. Since the construction of such a thoroughfare would be very expensive, the commission suggested that a stock company be formed to finance and manage the new road.[50]

On April 2, 1792, when the country was in the grip of a great epidemic of "scriptophobia", the Pennsylvania Assembly passed an Act enabling the Governor to incorporate "a company for making an artificial road from the City of Philadelphia to the Borough of Lancaster." The preamble to the act read:

[48] See pages 6-8; Plummer, *op. cit.,* 46-7. In 1772 the citizens of Lancaster County suggested to the Assembly that a turnpike be made. Their petition claimed, "that the Inhabitants of the Western Counties labour under the greatest Difficulties in transporting the produce of the Country to the City of Philadelphia, the Grand Mart of the Province, owing to the extreme badness of the Roads, which are sometimes almost impassable, and at all times dangerous, and attended with great Delays and Losses That a great Part of this Produce is already lost to the city of Philadelphia, etc. That a Turnpike Road would soon restore the valuable and increasing trade of York and Cumberland Counties, secure the trade of Lancaster County, and be an easy Mode of transporting the Products, not only of those Counties, but of the newly settled country, to the Metropolis of our own Province." This petition appeared in *The Pennsylvania Gazette,* February 20 and March 5, 1772.

[49] *Pennsylvania Archives,* Fourth Series, IV, 198.

[50] Landis, "The First Long Turnpike in the United States," in *The Lancaster County Historical Society Publications,* XXII, 16.

"Whereas, the great quantity of heavy articles of the growth and produce of the country, and of foreign goods which are daily transported between the City of Philadelphia and the western counties of the State requires an amendment of the highway which can only be effected by artificial beds of stone and gravel, disposed in such a manner as to prevent the wheels from cutting into the soil, the expense whereof will be great; and it is reasonable that those who enjoy the benefits of such a highway should pay a compensation therefor and there is reason to believe that such highway will be undertaken by an association of citizens, if proper encouragement be given it by the Legislature."[51]

No attempt had systematically been made to fit roads for extensive wagon traffic before this time; no project of internal improvement had ever involved such a great expenditure. Philadelphia was extremely interested in the turnpike, and one of her leading citizens, William Bingham, became the first President of the Company.

The capital stock of the Philadelphia and Lancaster Turnpike Company was 1000 shares at $300 each. Six hundred of this number were allotted for sale in Philadelphia, while the remaining four hundred were reserved for Lancaster purchasers. In the city of Philadelphia, "a very great number of citizens, far exceeding the number of shares, met with the purpose of subscribing thereto—that all having an equal right to subscribe we found ourselves (the managers) at a loss in what manner to receive subscriptions without undue preference to any person present. Whereupon the citizens there assembled agreed to determine by lot who should be the 600 persons who should subscribe for the said shares, and having themselves appointed eight respectable citizens, 2,276 persons delivered in their names with thirty dollars each, to the said eight persons, who having delivered to us $1800 and a list of 600 persons who by the aforesaid agreement were entitled to subscribe the shares—we thereupon admitted them to subscribe accordingly."[52] The demand for shares by the

---

[51] *American State Papers, Miscellaneous,* I, 894-7.

[52] *American Daily Advertiser,* April 27, May 19, and June 7, 1792, quoted by Plummer, *op. cit.,* 48; Durrenberger, *op. cit.,* 52, 105-6; McMaster, *History of the People of the United States,* II, 75, 554; Davis, *Essays in the Earlier History of American Corporations,* II, 218-20; Landis, "The First Long Turnpike in the United States,"34; Landis, "History of the Lancaster Turnpike," in *The Pennsylvania Magazine of History and Biography,* XLII, 133-4. Landis quotes a letter written from Philadelphia in June, 1792, by Edward Burd to Edward Shippen in which Burd wrote, "There was great confusion in this city about ye subscription to the Turnpike Road. I intended to have subscribed a few shares by way of encouraging the object, but finding that unnecessary I gave myself no further trouble about ye matter. My office was deserted the whole day by Mr. Davis and my apprentices, they having been infected with the Turnpike Rage. Everything is now turned into Speculation. The quiet Quaker who attended for ye purpose of joining in ye Subscription, and encouraging the road, finding such an uproar, withdrew."

citizens of Lancaster was also keen, but not so great as in Philadelphia
for the books did not close the first day and some persons received two
shares of the stock. Nevertheless, shares sold readily and one observer
wrote, "I have never seen men so wet with sweat in an harvest field, as
some were in the crowd to-day, to subscribe to the Turnpike Road. Most
of them did not think that the worst of it, for many did not get in for a
prize, which warmed their minds as well as their bodies."[53]

This wave of enthusiasm was a part of a general speculative movement
in which the prospect of increasing the value of the back-country, the
hope of great dividends, and the fascination of speculation played a large
part. After the stock had been taken and the company organized, a
movement of opposition arose. The people along the way did not wish
to surrender their lands for a road; the cry of monopoly was heard. The
farmers near Philadelphia opposed the venture; they feared the competition of the produce of the western farmer. Meetings were held and protests made against this act to incorporate a few men of wealth to violate
the right of property. Embittered orators repeated that the turnpike was
dangerous and unjust to the rights of the people as granted by the constitution.[54] Nevertheless, construction was begun and the turnpike was
practically finished by 1794, although even as late as 1796 the newspapers
spoke of "the almost completion" of the Lancaster Turnpike. A traveller
who passed over this road, which had cost almost half a million dollars,
only a short time after its completion noted, "There is, at present, but one
turnpike road on the continent which is between Lancaster and Philadelphia, a distance of sixty-six miles, and it is a masterpiece of its kind; it is
paved with stone the whole way, and overlaid with gravel, so that it is
never obstructed during the most severe weather."[55]

When finished, many people refused to use the turnpike which was "by
no means relished by the people at large, particularly the waggoners."[56]
However, they soon began to realize that it was cheaper to use the
smooth toll road than the free dirt roads bounded by ruts and inter-
spersed with tree stumps. The trade of the West, the traffic of the Susquehanna Valley, and the produce of the counties along the turnpike soon
began to find their way to Philadelphia over this improved highway. The
Irish traveller, Weld, reported, "It is scarcely possible to go one mile on
the road without meeting numbers of waggons passing and repassing be-

---

[53] Landis, *op. cit.*, in *The Pennsylvania Magazine of History and Biography*,
XLII, 235; Durrenberger, *op. cit.*, 106.

[54] McMaster, *op. cit.*, II, 553-6; Plummer, op. cit., 49-50.

[55] Bailey, *Journal of a Tour in the Unsettled Parts of North America in 1796
and 1797*, 107.

[56] Weld, *Travels through the States of North America and the Provinces of
Upper and Lower Canada from 1795 to 1797*, 110.

tween the back parts of the state and Philadelphia."[57] Tavern keepers along the turnpike grew rich; their sheds and stables were crowded with loaded wagons and fine horses. The rumble of the enormous wheels of the great Conestoga wagons as they lurched forward was a familiar sound. These giant canvas-covered wagons with their capacious, concave wagon-beds, painted in the conventional red and blue, carried three or four tons.

The amount of tolls received by the toll-gatherers in 1799, after their own salaries had been deducted, amounted to more than $14,000. In 1803 this total had risen to almost $25,000, while four years later the business for the first six months amounted to more than $19,000.[58] However, dividends to the 1st of January, 1803, did not average two percent. One of the reasons for this small return was the fact that much of the money was "plowed back" into the turnpike. Elliston Perot, President of the Turnpike Company, claimed in 1807 that continually more people were using the road and that he confidently believed that the Turnpike would thereafter yield higher dividends. From 1825 to 1829 inclusive, the tolls on the road amounted to $148,741, while repair bills devoured more than one-third of this amount.[59] From the time of its completion the prosperity of the Philadelphia and Lancaster Turnpike was nationally known; its dividends were usually liberal.[60] But the pressing need for cheaper and faster transportation caused the construction of a rival in the Philadelphia and Columbia Railroad, which diverted traffic from the Conestoga wagon to the small-burden cars of this early railroad.

The success of the Lancaster Turnpike stimulated Pennsylvania to extend her road improvement program. Public sentiment was in favor of turnpikes, and soon many new companies were chartered to construct toll roads. The Lancaster Turnpike immediately called for an extension to the Susquehanna River; this ten-mile link was authorized by law on

---

[57] *Ibid.*, 115.

[58] There were thirteen toll gatherers whose salaries were from $250 to $350 per year. The tolls received on the Lancaster Turnpike from 1799-1807 after the salaries of the toll gatherers had been deducted were (in thousands):

1799	$14.4	1804	$20.1
1800	17.6	1805	22.9
1801	21.2	1806	22.8
1802	20.3	1807	19.0
1803	24.9	(for only the first six months)	

This information was submitted by Elliston Perot, President of the Turnpike Company, on September 7, 1807, upon the request of Albert Gallatin. *American State Papers, Miscellaneous*, I, 893.

[59] Hazard, *The Pennsylvania Register*, V, 399.

[60] Hulbert, *Paths of Inland Commerce*, 90. Hulbert says that the dividends reached fifteen per cent. This is extremely high and must be erroneous.

April 22, 1794, but its construction was rather slow. The end of the speculative era caused the issuance of letters patent to be postponed for two years and commencement of construction until 1801.[61] Two years later the "viewers" reported the road completed according to the contract and ready for business.[62] In 1807, Robert Fulton stated that a barrel of flour (200 pounds) carried over the turnpike from Columbia to Philadelphia paid one dollar for this 74-mile haul. A broad-wheeled wagon carried thirty barrels or three tons and paid three dollars toll.[63] In 1822 it was officially reported that the Susquehanna Turnpike was paying dividends amounting to about 5⅓% and that the average annual toll received since 1803 was about $5226.[64]

Three other important turnpikes were completed to points on the lower Susquehanna. In 1796, two companies were chartered to construct roads from Lancaster to Middletown and from Middletown to Harrisburg which were to serve as a short cut from the latter city to Philadelphia. In their years of greatest prosperity these turnpikes paid 8% and 3¾% dividends respectively.[65] Another company was incorporated in 1803 to build a turnpike from Downingtown on the Lancaster Pike to Harrisburg. This route was a bit shorter than the main Lancaster road and was used principally by loaded wagons. However, its history was not prosperous; in 1822 it was about one half a million dollars in debt and had not paid any dividends.[66] The third road was the "Berks and Dauphin Turnpike" which was chartered in 1803 to connect Reading and Harrisburg. This turnpike was not finished until 1817, and its claim for future prosperity was stolen ten years later with the completion of the Union Canal which practically paralleled the turnpike.

[61] Durrenberger, *Turnpikes*, 106; Plummer, *op. cit.*, 53; Ringwalt, *op. cit.*, 29; Davis, *op. cit.*, II, 220.

[62] "State Roads," No. 13, MSS. in the Archives Division of the Pennsylvania Historical and Museum Commission.

[63] *American State Papers, Miscellaneous*, I, 917-9. Fulton continued by comparing this charge with that of water communication. He estimated that if a canal from Columbia to Philadelphia were constructed, it might receive $6 for toll per ton instead of $1 received by the road and still deliver the flour at Philadelphia for $7 per ton instead of $10 which was the total freightage by land.

[64] *Pennsylvania Senate Journal*, 1821-22, "Report on Roads, Bridges, and Canals."

[65] Durrenberger, *op. cit.*, 52, 114. A short local turnpike was incorporated from Falmouth on the Susquehanna River to Elizabethtown on the Middletown-Lancaster Turnpike in 1810 to accommodate persons who came down the river by boat to this point. However, when the river trade began to pass southward beyond this little town, the turnpike was abandoned and was locally called the Pumpkin Vine Turnpike because of all the vines which grew over it. See Klein, *History of Lancaster County*, I, 114, 291.

[66] *Pennsylvania Senate Journal*, 1821-22, "Report on Roads, Bridges, and Canals"; Durrenberger, *op. cit.*, 53-4.

Philadelphia's connections with Sunbury and other communities in the northern part of central Pennsylvania and southern New York also depended on roads. After this area had been resettled at the close of the Revolution, the citizens petitioned:

"That in Order to promote the Commerce, Agriculture and true Interest of Pennsylvania the Public-Roads from the West and North West which lead to Philadelphia, ought to be rendered passable for Travellers and for Teams, as soon as possible, and before our Rival-Neighbours, on one side, engage too securely, the Trade of Cumberland & York Counties; and on the other Side, they increase the Population of their Frontiers, with Persons, who would rather live on the Lands near the Susquehanna, if the Roads were made well and kept in good Order; and Peace and good Government fully established in this County.

"Since a Number of Judicious Persons, who have travelled from Pittsburg to Sunbury, have made it appear so very clearly, that a good Waggon Road may be easily made, from Philada to Pittsburg, through a Gap of the Allegany Mountain, by the Course; and much shorter and better than the present used Waggon-Road . . . Although we have a Communication by Water to and from Harrisburg and Middletown, yet the Course from Philadelphia by these Places is circuitous, and the Arrivals of our Supplies are irregular and uncertain. . . ."[67]

Again in 1805 citizens in this area were petitioning for a turnpike to Reading. The old road was practically impassable at this time and occasioned "a difference of one third to one half in the Price of wheat at Sunbury and Reading."[68] This year their memorial was answered by the incorporation of the Centre Turnpike Company which was chartered to construct a turnpike from Reading to Sunbury. This route was completed shortly before 1812 and appears to have been a fairly successful highway. By 1830 its dividends amounted to three percent.[69] Samuel Hazard, writing in the *Pennsylvania Register,* stated that few turnpike companies were as prosperous as this one.

A long road projected far into the northern part of the Susquehanna Valley also led toward Philadelphia. This route composed of the turnpikes of two companies extended from the Lehigh River to Elmira, New York. The first section, from Lausanne on the Lehigh to Nescopeck on the Susquehanna River, was chartered in 1804 as the Susquehanna and Lehigh Turnpike with the definite hope of diverting the trade of southern

---

[67] "State Roads," MSS. No. T, No. 25. Petition of the citizens of Northumberland to the House and Senate, 1787.

[68] MS. Petition from Lycoming County found in the Archives Division of the Pennsylvania Historical and Museum Commission.

[69] Montgomery, *Historical and Biographical Annals of Berks County,* I, 32; Hazard, *The Pennsylvania Register,* VI, 32.

New York State to Philadelphia.[70] The second section was the eighty mile turnpike from Nescopeck to Newtown (Elmira) on the Tioga River which was the property of the Susquehanna and Tioga Turnpike Company.[71] Several other turnpikes were laid out and constructed between points on the Delaware and Susquehanna Rivers in the northern part of Pennsylvania. One connected Easton and Wilkes-Barre, a second extended from Great Bend to Coshecton, while a third ran from Milford to Owego, New York. Still another long road was planned to join Philadelphia and the Great Bend on the Susquehanna River. All these turnpikes were constructed with the hope that goods from the Susquehanna Valley would be carried over them by wagon or sled to the Delaware River, where they would be forwarded to Philadelphia by boat.[72]

New York State, impressed by the flow of goods by river and road from her own interior to Philadelphia and Baltimore, also took an interest in turnpike construction. In 1802 the Catskill Turnpike was incorporated to construct a road to the Susquehanna River at a point where the use of boats was possible. By 1812, it was maintained that five turnpikes connected the villages of Newberry, Kingston, and Catskill with points on the Delaware or Susquehanna Rivers. By these turnpikes New York cut off some of the trade of the southern part of her state and so pared down the size of the hinterland for which her two southern rivals contended.[73]

West of the Susquehanna River two important roads led toward the Ohio during the colonial days. Even before they were improved these roads served as important lanes to the West. The trade of the frontiersmen travelled over these roads and some of the local products from the Susquehanna Valley found their way to Philadelphia along these routes. However, most of the products of local origin went to a nearer market. By 1770 Baltimore had become the hub for many roads which extended northward into the counties of Pennsylvania which lay west of the Susquehanna. From the main roads to Baltimore a network of by-roads radiated in all directions. Maryland had always been aware of the importance of her road connection with central Pennsylvania. In 1787, before the Lancaster Turnpike was chartered, the Legislature of Maryland passed laws providing that several turnpikes be laid out in Balti-

---

[70] *American State Papers, Miscellaneous,* I, 733, 891-2; Pearce, *Annals of Luzerne,* 443; O'Callaghan, ed., *Documentary History of New York,* II, 1177.

[71] *American State Papers, Miscellaneous,* I, 892; *Pennsylvania Senate Journal,* 1821-22, "Report on Roads, Bridges, and Canals."

[72] Hazard, *The Pennsylvania Register,* IV, 50; Pearce, *op. cit.,* 442; *Pennsylvania Senate Journal,* 1821-22, "Report on Roads, Bridges, and Canals."

[73] McMaster, *op. cit.,* III, 463; Flick, ed., *History of New York,* V, 265; Dunbar, *op. cit.,* I, 319-20; Hulbert, *Historic Highways of America,* XII, Chapter 6.

more County. One of these improved roads was to extend in the direction of Frederick, Maryland; a second toward Reisterstown, branching there in one direction toward Westminster and in another toward Hanover, Pennsylvania; a third turnpike was to lead toward York, Pennsylvania.[74] These roads were to have the same physical characteristics as the later turnpikes, but were not to be financed by incorporated companies. They were to be managed by officials appointed by the court of Baltimore County and were to be open to the public.[75]

Little progress was made by the Baltimore County officials on their turnpikes, but the settlers west of the Susquehanna in southern Pennsylvania continued to send their produce to the Chesapeake Bay metropolis and made some new connections to the old roads leading southward. In 1789 there were not enough wagons available to carry the trade over the road from Shippensburg, Pennsylvania, to Baltimore.[76] A few years later, a frantic road contractor was hurrying to complete a road from Shippensburg Gap to York so that "a midling team can hall twenty five hundred without deficulty. . . ."[77] The dashing Dutch commercial agent, Theophile Cazenove, who represented a group of Dutch bankers and whose duty it was to report on the economic prospects and conditions of the districts in which his employers were interested, passed through this region in 1794. He found that all the towns west of the Susquehanna River did a major part of their trading, especially in wheat and flour, with Baltimore.[78] He noted that the cost of carting a barrel of flour from Carlisle to Baltimore was one dollar, while the rate to Philadelphia was ten shillings. To transport merchandise from Philadelphia cost one dollar and twenty-five cents a quintal.[79]

The county turnpikes of Maryland proved a failure, and it was not until 1804 and 1805 that legislation was enacted which provided for the chartering of Turnpike Companies. Companies were then organized to construct turnpikes through Reisterstown toward Hanover and through Westminster to the Pennsylvania line, and from Baltimore to the State line in the direction of York.[80] Another, "The Fall Turnpike Company",

---

[74] Sioussat, Highway Legislation in Maryland, 144, 163; Davis, op. cit., II, 217-18.

[75] Sioussat, op. cit., 163.

[76] "Journal of Colonel John May of Boston," in The Pennsylvania Magazine of History and Biography, XLV, 109.

[77] "State Roads," MSS., No. 22 in the Archives Division of the Pennsylvania Historical and Museum Commission.

[78] Cazenove Journal, Kelsey, ed., 60-68.

[79] Ibid., 60.

[80] American State Papers, Miscellaneous, I, 901-7; Sioussat, op. cit., 166-7; Durrenberger, op. cit., 66.

was incorporated to construct a road directly toward Hanover and Carlisle with the expectation of uniting the "trade of the North with Baltimore."[81]

Pennsylvania encouraged the Marylanders in their road making by incorporating companies to extend the Maryland turnpikes far into the Susquehanna Valley. The York and Maryland Line Turnpike and the Conewago Turnpike provided an improved highway from the Conewago Falls to Baltimore. The latter company was supported by Maryland funds and had a Baltimore man as its president. This route gave the Chesapeake Bay city an advantage over Philadelphia in the competition for the trade collected at this important point.[82] Other turnpikes extended from the Mason and Dixon Line northward through Hanover and Carlisle into the rich Cumberland Valley.[83] Farther west turnpikes were constructed through Gettysburg from points on the State line which had connections with Baltimore.[84]

Over these roads in their covered wagons passed Pennsylvania Dutch farmers, who have left colorful verse like the following to the memories of bygone days.

> "Nooch Baltimore geht unser Fuhr
> Mit dem bedeckte Waage; . .
> Der Turnpike zeicht uns die Geschpurer
> Die Gäul sin gut beschlaage,
> En guter Schluck, Glück zu der Reisz
> Der Dramm, der schteight un fallt im Preisz—
> So blooze die Posauner—
> Hot, Schimmel, Hot! ei, Brauner!

---

[81] McMaster, *op. cit.*, III, 463. McMaster says, "Maryland, in the hope of turning aside to Baltimore some of the rich trade which came down from the Genessee country and passed through Carlisle to Philadelphia, had chartered three roads to extend from Baltimore to points on the Mason and Dixon line . . ." *American State Papers, Miscellaneous*, I, 900; Sparks, "Baltimore," in the *North American Review*, XX, 132.

[82] Gibson, *History of York County*, 329; Durrenberger, *op. cit.*, 57-8; "State Roads," MSS. No. W-Y, No. 4 in the Archives Division of the Pennsylvania Historical and Museum Commission.

[83] *Pennsylvania Senate Journal*, 1821-22, "Report on Roads, Bridges, and Canals"; Gibson, *op. cit.*, 328. From its completion in 1809 until 1821 the seven-mile Hanover and Maryland Line Turnpike averaged tolls amounting to $3,460.

[84] Bates and Richards, *History of Franklin County*, 220. The Gettysburg road extended from that town to Petersburg while the important Chambersburg Turnpike led to Hagerstown, Maryland.

"Den Dramm, den, heir mer jetzr ferkaaft.
Un's Gelt isch in de Tasche;
Jetzt fahre mir fergnuzt zu
Haus, uns leres in die Kaschte.
Ein guter Schluck! Glück zu der Reisz!
Der Dramm der Schteigh un fallt im Preisz—
So blooze die Posauner
Hot, Schemmel! Hot, ei Brauner!"

Travelling through the fertile country west of the Susquehanna River in 1809, Joshua Gilpin, resident of Philadelphia and great friend of internal improvements, noted:

"All our route today [he reached Chambersburg that evening] was nearly parallel to the dividing line between Pennsylvania & Maryland about 25 miles northward of it & the roads from Baltimore are numerous so that the whole produce of this country goes direct to that town & not to Philadelphia . . . such is the zeal with which the Marylanders are improving the carriage from this State that the produce of this part of it will undoubtedly centre in Baltimore."[85]

But the fact that so many turnpikes were being constructed toward the Maryland boundary escaped the attention of most Philadelphians until the question of the permanent location of the State capital came up in 1810. When the Pennsylvania metropolis heard that Harrisburg was proposed as the new seat of government, she looked with an unpropitious eye at Baltimore. Philadelphia immediately lamented the fact that she had not tried to prevent the incorporation of the turnpike companies which connected with Maryland roads. "A Citizen" wrote for the columns of *The Aurora*:

"I have looked with astonishment at the wayward and mistaken policy of Pennsylvania, which has for several years past been pursued by the different legislatures,—professedly, for the extension of her own internal commerce, by the improvement of the great natural resources which she possesses—but in fact, this policy is perverting the benefits which providence has kindly bestowed upon her; by directing them, so as to promote the interests of another state, and the foreign commerce of a rival capital, in preference to her own. I advert more particularly to the improvements made and making westward of the river Susquehanna."[86]

The very thought of moving the capital to Harrisburg made this correspondent feel that Philadelphia was being made the target of finesse, deception, and subterfuge. His message to the public continued:

"If this bill should eventually become a law, I pronounce without hesitation, that, Pennsylvania as a state, will have passed the meridian of her prosperity—her resources, instead of being collected, will be dispersed— her commercial capital which has received several severe wounds, will

---

[85] Gilpin, "A Tour from Philadelphia in 1809," in *The Pennsylvania Magazine of History and Biography,* L, 169.

[86] *The Aurora,* February 2, 1810.

receive one more severe, more destructive in its consequences. Pennsylvania was once the first star in the constellation of the union; the commerce of Philadelphia was the source of her splendor, and that commerce was fed from her internal resources. About ten years ago, Philadelphia paid the highest amount of revenue into the treasury of the U. States; but by the adoption of the present mistaken line of policy, which commenced about that time, New York exceeds her by some hundreds of thousands of dollars, and Baltimore is fast approaching to an equality, and if it is adhered to, will soon be in advance of her."[87]

Philadelphia was greatly disturbed by the situation. Harrisburg was twenty-four miles closer to Baltimore than to their own city. The supporters of the Delaware River port believed that the network of roads west of the Susquehanna River which led southward was the result of malicious practices on the part of the Marylanders. The Philadelphians believed that the friends of Baltimore tampered with the small towns in this area and, by high pressure methods, convinced them to help pass the laws necessary for turnpike construction.

Despite Philadelphia's protests, the State capital was moved to Harrisburg, and the Legislature refused to do anything to help the city improve trade lanes into the interior. True, they continued to incorporate companies, but no State funds were available to supplement the capital obtained from the fluctuating stock sales. Many of the companies which were chartered were impeded in their construction; some failed altogether. Finally, in 1811, William J. Duane, editor and Chairman of the Committee on Roads and Internal Navigation, tried to destroy the indifferent attitude of the Legislature toward giving financial assistance to improvements. In a series of letters addressed "to the People of Pennsylvania," Duane drove out former apathy. In seeking information for his committee, this Legislator had been astonished by the languid attitude of not only the representatives but also the people at large. In his public messages, Duane called attention to this deplorable situation and urged the people to be more careful in their selection of men to represent them in the Legislature.[88]

The enthusiasm of the following meeting of the Legislature proved that Duane's denunciations were not in vain. That year the state appropriated $825,000 to be used to support various turnpike and bridge enterprises. Between 1812 and 1816, in spite of the war and currency disorders, $817,000 were appropriated; by 1821 the State subscription to turnpike stock amounted to $1,861,542.[89] This tendency continued

---

[87] *Ibid.*

[88] Duane, *Letters addressed to the People of Pennsylvania respecting the Internal Improvement of the Commonwealth by Means of Roads and Canals.*

[89] *Pennsylvania Senate Journal,* 1821-22, "Report on Roads, Bridges, and Canals."

until the State took an active interest in canal and railroad transportation in 1824.

During the years when Baltimore and Philadelphia were both relying on turnpikes as the best method of attracting trade to their respective cities, the volume of trade in the Susquehanna Valley grew rapidly. Goods estimated at a value of almost two millions of dollars were shipped each year by river craft; Conestoga wagons were always to be seen on the turnpikes leading to Philadelphia and Baltimore. Although it is impossible to estimate the amount of trade carried over the turnpikes, the business of the valley has a good index in the number of good roads constructed. While Philadelphia dominated the northern and eastern sections of the valley, Baltimore was the center for traders of the western part of the Susquehanna Region. The turnpike served as a main artery of trade until canals and railroads dominated the area, whereupon the function of the road changed to that of a local highway or feeder to a trunk canal or railroad system.

APPENDIX IV

Turnpike Roads of the Susquehanna Valley

Mi.	Date	Name	Letters Patent	Finished
62	1792, Apr. 9	Philadelphia and Lancaster	1792, June 21	1794
10	1794, Apr. 22	Lancaster and Susquehanna	1796, Feb. 24	1803
60	1803, Feb. 11	Easton and Wilkes-Barre	1803, Dec. 28 (47½ done)	1815
67¾	1803, Mar. 24	Downingtown, Ephrata, and Harrisburg	1803, June 21	1819
26	1804, Mar. 5	Lancaster, Elizabethtown and Middletown	1805, Apr. 1	1812
11½	1804, Mar. 19	Susquehanna and York	1808, May 16	1810
30	1804, Mar. 19	Susquehanna and Lehigh	1804, May 16	1806
50	1804, Mar. 29	Coshecton and Great Bend	1805, Apr. 22	1811
75	1805, Mar. 25	Centre (leading from Reading to Sunbury)	1808, May 10	1814
80	1806, Mar. 28	Susquehanna and Tioga	1806, Oct. 10	not yet
18	1807, Mar. 31	York and Maryland Line	1807, June 3	1809
7	1808, Feb. 22	Hanover and Maryland Line	1808, June 27	1809
11	1809, Mar. 2	York and Conewago	1809, July 27	1812
30	1809, Mar. 25	Hanover and Carlisle	1812, Feb. 29	not yet
9¼	1810, Mar. 19	Middletown and Harrisburg	1815, June 14	1818
10	1811, Feb. 6	Berlin and Hanover	1811, Sept. 23	1817
41	1805, Mar. 2	Berks and Dauphin	1816, Feb. 16	not yet
48½	1814, Mar. 9	Harrisburg, Carlisle and Chambersburg	1816, Feb. 8	1818
63*	1819, Mar. 16	Philadelphia and Great Bend	1820, Dec. 21	......

*None finished yet, but work began in 1821.

(Taken from *Pennsylvania Senate Journal*, Vol. 1821-22, Report of the Committee on Roads, Bridges, and Inland Navigation.)

CHAPTER III

BALTIMORE DURING THE "CANAL RAGE"

About 1820 the country fell under the influence of grandiose schemes for internal improvements. Each trading center felt that it had to improve communication with its hinterland. This exhibited the sensitiveness of trade centers which became evident whenever their rivals for commerce encroached on what they considered their own territory.

Baltimore, visioning the Susquehanna as *"our river,"* felt that it could be made more profitable for producer and merchant if the channel were improved for ascending trade. Although the amount of produce that hazarded a trip downstream was growing annually, Baltimore realized that if the river trade could be of both descending and ascending character, the Maryland port would divert much of Philadelphia's wagon trade. In the early twenties Maryland authorized a canal northward along the Susquehanna River to Conewago, but Baltimore was unable to finance the project at this time. The novelty of steamboat navigation then turned commercial people of Baltimore to a trial attempt to use five-mile-an-hour giants of sheet iron on the Susquehanna. Meanwhile Philadelphia began a campaign to thwart Baltimore's potential advantage in the Susquehanna Valley. The Pennsylvania metropolis revived her Union and Chesapeake and Delaware Canal projects; the State-financed and managed system of public works to Pittsburgh was begun. In constructing the mongrel canal and railroad route to the west, Pennsylvania brought forward a new problem which revealed the crux of the bitter feelings between Philadelphia and Baltimore. Artificial obstructions in the Susquehanna River to provide water for the State canals hindered "arking" on the river. Philadelphia held that these dams were essential to an improved trading era; Baltimore maintained that their sole purpose was to force the trade of the Susquehanna Valley into unnatural channels. However, as the Pennsylvania State Works neared completion, Baltimore realized that complaining was getting her no trade and so the Maryland city turned again to her original plan of canalizing the lower Susquehanna. By means of a canal, at this time, she could now not only provide ascending and descending passage for riverboats but could also tap the expensive western route just completed by her northern neighbor for the benefit of her commercial rival. The future looked bright; but Pennsylvania refused to grant a charter to a Baltimore company to construct a canal within her jurisdiction. After much contesting, the Pennsylvania

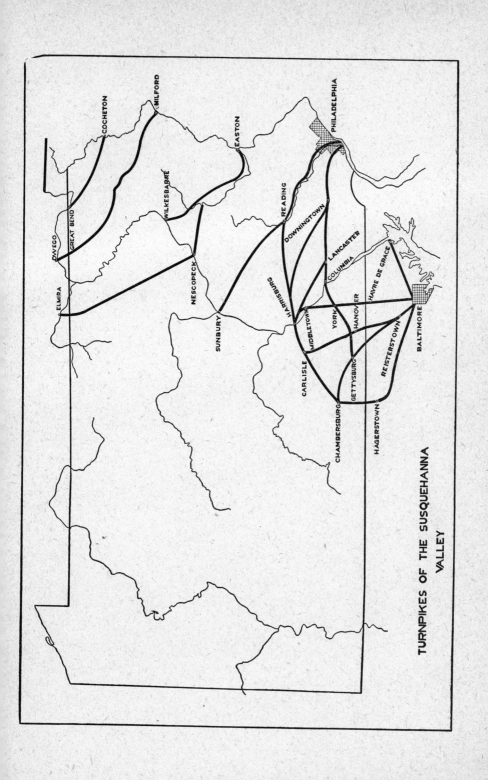

TURNPIKES OF THE SUSQUEHANNA
VALLEY

Legislature finally consented to grant canal privileges to Baltimore. This privilege was, however, not given until Philadelphia's Chesapeake and Delaware Canal had been officially opened. The Maryland city was, therefore, again thwarted in her attempt to gain an advantage over Philadelphia since the canal merely moved the lowest port of entry on the river and the point of trade competition south of Havre de Grace. Plan as she might, Baltimore did not succeed in gaining the project of her early dreams without the constant presence of her lifelong rival.

Although Susquehanna Valley trading conditions had been hampered by expensive overland hauling and dangerous river navigation, the settlers annually became more numerous and their marketable surplus much larger. Regardless of the fact that no noticeable improvements had been made in the river channel, the valley folk preferred to brave its dangers rather than pay ruinous freight charges for wagon and teamster. Arks, keelboats, and rafts waited every spring for the freshet; several men established a return service from tidewater to Columbia by keel boat with the aid of ropes, windlasses, and much patience.[1] In 1821, from the opening of spring navigation until December, products valued at $1,121,000 were reported to have reached Port Deposit in 925 rafts and 535 arks.[2] By 1822, a great number of arks and rafts descended the Juniata River to augment the regular Susquehanna trade. In that year some $1,337,925 worth of goods descended the river to Port Deposit from which port most were transshipped to Baltimore. For the whole year the reported losses amounted to only $12,000. The 537 arks which descended the river carried flour, wheat, whiskey, clover seed, butter, lard, harness, calfskins, corn, flaxseed, tallow, pork, beef, rye, oil, plank, potatoes, potash, apples, buckwheat, bark, staves, oars, poles, coal (450 tons), tobacco, slate (100 tons), ten dozen wool hats, twenty French pots, and twenty bake ovens.[3]

---

[1] *Niles' Weekly Register*, XX, 387. "The Lady Lightfoot" carried goods from the tide to Columbia at 40 cents per barrel or 20 cents per cwt. On one occasion she carried northward six and one-half tons of plaster, seventeen barrels of herring, nine barrels of shad, and one-half ton of groceries. Also XXVII, 332, tells of the "General Jackson" which ascended the Susquehanna with sixteen tons of plaster and twenty-five barrels of herring. This boat was equipped with poles, oars, windlass and two lines.

[2] *Ibid.*, XXIII, 22, of supplement; XX, 303, 225. By June of that year 8,000,000 feet of lumber, 40,000 barrels of flour, and 200,000 gallons of whiskey were reported to have been received at Baltimore.

[3] Lightner, *Susquehanna Register of Arks, Rafts, &c., arriving at Port Deposit in the year 1822*. Besides the arks some 514 board and timber rafts went downstream. Most of the river business for this year was done at the usual time—in the month of April. *Niles' Weekly Register*, XXIII, 97-8, estimates one value of the Susquehanna trade for 1822 at $1,168,954. Niles continues, "The *descending* trade naturally centers around Baltimore, but this city has only a small part of that which ought to *ascend* this great artery of our country."

By this time, Baltimore's rivals in the North were very active in the pursuit of internal improvements. New York was Erie Canal-minded; Pennsylvania's old canal projects were reawakened. This activity made the Baltimore merchants nervous; Maryland business men were much alarmed over the future. Besides the dangers created by Philadelphia's energetic move to imitate New York, the old Potomac Company, which was to connect the Chesapeake Region with the West, was reported to be hopelessly insolvent and unable to carry out the purposes of its incorporation. In 1821 a board of investigators declared this project a miserable failure. This probe gave birth to a new project, the Chesapeake and Ohio Canal. Baltimore, at first, gave its support to this improvement but soon decided that the branch canal, by which Baltimore was to be linked with the main route, was a poor investment for the city. The Chesapeake and Ohio Canal was designed to throw its traffic into the southern part of the Chesapeake Region far out of Baltimore's reach. Therefore, notwithstanding her interest in internal improvements, Baltimore began to oppose the western canal.

Thus aroused, the metropolis of Maryland saw the need for a better navigation with the Susquehanna Valley. Not only did she wish to make the transportation of the standard forest and agricultural products safer and cheaper, but Baltimore also was becoming interested in the developing coal and iron regions of central Pennsylvania. City leaders determined that the magnificence of the Chesapeake and Ohio plan should not dominate the Maryland Legislature. In this the Baltimore people were successful and by a resolution passed February 18, 1823, commissioners were appointed "to lay out, and survey a route for a canal, which will connect the waters of the Susquehanna with the city of Baltimore, beginning at the Conewago falls, or on a point of said river which the commissioners may deem the most practicable. . . ."[4]

After some bickering, permission was finally granted by the Pennsylvania authorities allowing the commissioners from Maryland to make surveys within the Pennsylvania Commonwealth.[5] The commissioners then visited the Erie Canal and there hired James Geddes, who was employed on the Erie, to survey their proposed route. In New York, the Maryland men were convinced that "the great advantages of canal navi-

---

[4] *Report by the Maryland Commissioners on a Proposed Canal from Baltimore to Conewago; Niles' Weekly Register,* XXV, 19. The members of this commission were George Winchester, John Patterson, and Theodorick Bland.

[5] *Pennsylvania Archives,* 4th series, V, 446-7. The Archives contain correspondence concerning the Maryland Commissioners' desire to conduct a surveying party within Pennsylvania.

gation are no longer a matter of speculation and theory"[6] and determined that Baltimore should have one. To acquaint themselves with the Susquehanna system above the northern terminal of their proposed canal, and to show the possibilities of a water route from Baltimore to northern Pennsylvania and southern New York, the commissioners returned from the Erie Canal via Lake Cayuga and the Susquehanna River on which they floated in an open boat to Harrisburg.

This Maryland delegation estimated that the cost of navigating a forty-ton ark from Oswego, New York, to Conewago, a distance of 250 miles, was about fifty dollars, while from Conewago to tidewater, a distance of between 60 and 70 miles, by the river channel, the expenses were from fifty to seventy dollars. The trip from the Conewago falls to tide, independent of insurance, which amounted to about one-half per cent above the falls but which was as high as seven to ten per cent of the value of the cargo below the falls, cost more than half the expense of the entire trip from the highest point up the river.[7] The commissioners learned that a large amount of trade was diverted from the Susquehanna at Columbia to Philadelphia since producers found it cheaper to carry their goods by wagon to the latter city at a cost of ten dollars per ton than to hazard the swift, shallow rapids of the river. The return goods for most of the valley, the commissioners reported, came from Philadelphia to river towns from which they were conveyed upstream in keel or Durham boats.[8]

The Maryland investigators were certain that these facts warranted a canal; their surveys satisfied them that a practical one could be constructed along the river. By means of this proposed avenue, the commissioners informed the merchants of Baltimore, they would gain access to a region three times as large as the state of Maryland with a population larger than that of their whole state. As *their natural and only sea-port,* Baltimore would gain the whole ascending trade of this vast region and would no longer have to trade *"in money"* with the rural shippers.[9]

The proposed canal was also seen as a possible link to the West. With a short canal to connect the Juniata and Allegheny Rivers, the commissioners believed a continuous water route could be opened between Pittsburgh and their own metropolis. Such a connection was seriously needed by the Chesapeake port, as river streamers had come into active service

---

[6] *Report of the Maryland Commissioners on a Proposed Canal from Baltimore to Conewago,* 4-8.

[7] *Ibid.,* 30-31.

[8] *Ibid.,* 25-6.

[9] *Ibid.,* 42, 45-8.

on western streams about 1817, and much of the former wagon traffic to Baltimore had been diverted into the well-known triangle of the West to New Orleans to New York. The possibility of this connection was also a good debating point to be used in arguments with the friends and backers of the Chesapeake and Ohio project.

The Baltimore Commissioners were not satisfied merely to build a canal from the falls of the Susquehanna to tidewater; their plans called for a continuous canal from Conewago to Baltimore. River craft and canal boats, they maintained, were "utterly unfit to contend with the wind and waves of the exposed deep waters of the tide." The continuous route would avoid this danger and would cut the cost of the trip, as it would eliminate the transshipment at Havre de Grace. But most important of all was the fact that "no other market whatever can, with any thing like the same advantages, come in competition with that of Baltimore; because, to reach any other seaport would require transshipment at Port Deposit, additional tolls, exposure, delays, and the travelling a greater distance by canal and navigation." Baltimore was especially anxious to have a continuous canal, because of the growing possibility that the Chesapeake and Delaware canal would be completed, thus giving Philadelphia access to the goods received at the mouth of the Susquehanna or the terminal of a canal which would extend only to tidewater. So important did the Maryland commissioners regard the Susquehanna canal plan that they suggested the project should not be entrusted to the hands of a chartered or joint-stock company, but that the state of Maryland should own it exclusively.[10]

The report of the commissioners aroused interest in internal improvements to a fever pitch in Baltimore. Opinion was seriously divided on whether the Susquehanna project or the Chesapeake and Ohio plan was the more advantageous to the city, providing a lateral canal should be constructed from the Chesapeake and Ohio Canal to Baltimore. Newspapers carried articles to educate the public and acquaint them with the facts about each route.[11] Early in December, 1823, General Robert Goodloe Harper and a number of prominent citizens of Baltimore waited on the mayor and requested him to call a meeting of the citizens at the "Exchange" for the purpose of taking into consideration the expediency of promoting a connection between the Ohio and the Chesapeake at Balti-

[10] *Ibid.*, 65. Most likely the Baltimore committeemen got this idea from the New York policy of state improvements. However, the unfortunate policy followed by the owners of the short Susquehanna Canal to Love Point probably caused a distrust of private ownership of improvements.

[11] Newspaper clipping. Box on the Susquehanna and Tidewater Canal in the Maryland State Historical Society.

more, by a canal through the District of Columbia.[12] The mayor readily agreed and a meeting was called for the thirteenth of the month. When notice of this meeting appeared, some citizens requested that it be postponed until the twentieth of December, at which time the Chesapeake and Ohio project and the Susquehanna Canal plans could be jointly considered. The meeting was so arranged and a large assembly gathered on the appointed day.

General Harper addressed the meeting in terms highly favorable to the Chesapeake and Ohio plan. He noted that the Susquehanna navigation was important, but that the Chesapeake and Ohio Canal would be of a more national character, serve more people, rescue the western trade, and elevate Baltimore to the highest place among the commercial cities of the country. In supporting his favorite project the General said, "you now enjoy the downward trade of the whole country watered by the Susquehanna and its branches, in which you have no successful rival." He maintained that the Commissioners who surveyed the Susquehanna, like Philadelphia merchants, over-emphasized the hazards of the river traffic of which actual losses were less than one per cent of the total goods conveyed by the current.[13] The speaker then turned his attention to the Philadelphia projects which were being sponsored at the time to tap the Susquehanna trade. Harper prophesied that the Union Canal would most likely lack water and that the Chesapeake and Delaware Canal would necessitate expensive transshipment. "I think myself warranted in the conclusion," continued the speaker, "that Baltimore cannot be deprived of the downward trade of the Susquehanna, even when the two canals projected by the people of Pennsylvania shall be finished: events which are certainly not very near, perhaps not quite certain."[14]

The subject of gaining the ascending trade of the tortuous Susquehanna River was the next point considered by the General. He held that Philadelphia's Chesapeake and Delaware Canal would be in the same situation as Baltimore with regard to this traffic. Until the Union Canal is finished, Harper claimed, all return goods and merchandise must be hauled overland. Viewing the course of wagon trade at the time, the speaker held that Baltimore suffered no handicaps in competing with Philadelphia for the overland business. He asserted that the distance from Baltimore to the Conewago Falls was only 58 miles "over an excel-

---

[12] *General Harper's Speech To the Citizens of Baltimore on the Expediency of Promoting a connection between the Ohio, at Pittsburgh, and the waters of the Chesapeake at Baltimore, by a Canal through the District of Columbia with his Reply to some of the objections of Mr. Winchester;* Scharf, *Chronicles of Baltimore,* 408; *Niles' Weekly Register,* XXV, 257.

[13] *General Harper's Speech* . . ., 12.

[14] *Ibid.,* 16.

lent turnpike," while that from Philadelphia to Columbia "over a road
not so good" was 74 miles with an additional ten miles to the falls. The
General warmed to fever heat on this topic. He charged the merchants
of Baltimore themselves for the loss of the ascending or return trade.
He asked what gave Philadelphia superiority, "It is your own supine-
ness; your want of attention to the proper means of advancing . . . your
own interest; the erroneous principles on which you conduct the trade;
and believe me, that while you continue in the same course, the canal to
which you look with such fond expectations, would afford you no relief."[15] In conclusion, the orator presented the resolution "That the
measure in question (the Susquehanna Navigation), although highly
interesting in its character, and deserving to be steadily kept in view by
the citizens of Baltimore, and the whole state, is not of pressing or
immediate exigency."

For a moment it appeared that the commercial people of Baltimore
would give up the rivalry with Philadelphia for the Susquehanna Valley
for a struggle with the southern Chesapeake Bay ports in a quest for
western trade. But then George Winchester, one of the commissioners
who surveyed the Susquehanna and a firm believer in the canalization
of the lower Susquehanna, presented his opinions to the meeting. With
much feeling and eloquence Winchester asserted that the salvation of
the city of Baltimore must, in a great measure, depend upon the Susquehanna Valley. "The great importance which it contemplates with the
very extensive trade which the proposed canal will lay open to this city,
with the fairest portion of the United States," he argued, "certainly presents a prospect which no good citizen can look upon with indifference."
He maintained that it would be premature to consider a western project
such as the Chesapeake and Ohio; but that the canal along the Susquehanna should receive the unanimous and undivided support of the city.[16]

In rebuttal, General Harper refuted Winchester's statements at great
length. However, when the question was taken, Mr. Winchester's resolutions favoring the Susquehanna project were carried by a great majority.[17] Baltimore saw its future in the Susquehanna Valley. The city
hoped to end the post-war period of depression which had gripped it for
such a long time[18] by opening the door into the Susquehanna Valley,
and in accordance with this desire the Maryland Assembly authorized
the construction of a canal from Baltimore to Conewago.

---

[15] *Ibid.*, 17.
[16] *Ibid.*, 60.
[17] *Ibid.*, 72.
[18] See page 18.

The favorable audience which had so heartily endorsed the plan at the December meeting, however, did not suffice to bring it into execution. Financial conditions were still extremely precarious; the outlook for a canal to the north was very poor at this time.[19] But the merchants of the city realized that they either had to keep pace with their commercial rivals or starve. In 1824 and 1825, reports were made by the Susquehanna Commissioners in an attempt to keep the project alive and to cultivate Pennsylvania's favor[20] so that that State's cooperation might be relied on.

It was the opinion of a majority of the active citizens of Maryland's commercial metropolis that a canal along the lower section of the Susquehanna River was vital. However, as it began to appear that the Chesapeake and Delaware Canal leading to Philadelphia would be completed, an improved connection with the mouth of the Susquehanna assumed paramount importance in the Baltimore mind. The people of the city had no doubt that the Chesapeake and Delaware Canal was planned to carry the trade of the Susquehanna Valley and give Philadelphia a commanding control in the central Pennsylvania hinterland. Since the construction of the canal to Conewago from Baltimore appeared too burdensome for the Marylanders' pocketbooks at this time, the idea of a still-water canal from Baltimore to Havre de Grace was brought forward to counterbalance Philadelphia's Chesapeake and Delaware Canal.[21]

Meanwhile, the river continued to pour products into the markets of Baltimore. This fact continually kept the Maryland city awake to the growing need for improvements. During one week in 1826, 7438 barrels of flour, 99 hogsheads and 1271 barrels of whiskey arrived at the Chesapeake port from the Susquehanna Valley via the river, while the total value of goods descending the river for the year was estimated at $1,528,-000.[22] But this important trade also aroused Philadelphia to a new desire to divert it to the Delaware port. Two canals and a railroad were planned[23]; no innovation seemed too radical for the awakening Pennsylvania metropolis. The Maryland commercial center, although it was interested in improvements and realized that something had to be done, disagreed over the minor details of their various projects. Dimensions, terminals, and locations were street corner subjects. In this state of mind

---

[19] Scharf, *Chronicles of Baltimore*, 445.

[20] *York Recorder*, January 27, 1824.

[21] *Report of the Commissioners to Explore and Survey the Route for a Canal and Still Water Navigation.*

[22] *Niles' Weekly Register*, XXX, 153; XXXI, 283.

[23] The Union, and Chesapeake and Delaware Canals were being constructed at the time. Pennsylvania had also chartered a railroad from Philadelphia to Columbia to be built by John Stevens. For a discussion of the later see Chapter VII.

nothing constructive could be done and it was finally deemed advisable to call a public meeting to promote "concert and unity of action" among the citizens. This assemblage appointed a committee to study the situation and "to place before the public the object to which the city's single attention should be brought."[24]

With lynx-eyed accuracy the committee sorted out the main issues and reported to their fellow citizens in January, 1827.[25] They maintained that after forty years of planning and spending for internal improvements, Baltimore was "still in the wilderness." Before the days of the canal transportation their city could compete with Philadelphia, but in 1827 those days of "generous competition" were passed.[26] Since their rival on the Delaware had begun to experiment with new methods of transportation, Baltimore's life hung in the balance; but she had done nothing to save herself. Since Pennsylvania had turned to a system of State Works which would give Philadelphia a path directly to the West, the committeemen claimed that Baltimore must make "instant exertions" to cope with the new situation. The investigators said that Baltimore must make a canal at once, for, if Philadelphia ever diverted the Susquehanna trade, it could never be regained by Baltimore. Baltimore could not grow rich feeding upon the gleanings of her rival. In descriptive language the Baltimore probers said that "the desert daily advances upon the city, and in such cases the very spirit of pestilence seems to have driven from its streets *the busy hum of industry*."[27] The committee had discovered that Baltimore needed a Susquehanna Canal; but a number of years had to elapse before Pennsylvania, who held the trump card, would tolerate such a Baltimore enterprise on her soil.

During this era, the "canal rage" also struck the inland town of Lancaster, a fact which seemed very important to the people of Baltimore. Lancaster, which had been dependent on turnpike transportation to Philadelphia, now turned toward the Susquehanna River with the construction of an eighteen-mile canal and river navigation to Safe Harbor.[28]

---

[24] "Diary of Robert Gilmore," in *The Maryland Magazine of History and Biography*, XVII, 245-6.

[25] *Report and Resolutions relative to Internal Improvement and the Susquehanna Canal*.

[26] *Ibid.*, 8.

[27] *Ibid.*, 13.

[28] Barnes, "Organization and Early History of the Conestoga Navigation Company," in the *Lancaster County Historical Society Publications*, XXXIX, 49-60; Clark, "Early Conestoga Navigation," in the *Lancaster County Historical Society Publications*, XII, 315-329; Tanner, *Canals and Railroads of Pennsylvania and New Jersey*, 19. As early as 1806 plans for a canal were made but did not mature. Again in 1820 a slack-water canal was authorized, but this project likewise miscarried. On March 3, 1825, a new act was passed by the Pennsylvania Legislature and construction was soon begun.

Tired of the expensive land carriage, Lancaster desired the smooth waters of a canal. Disgruntled by labor combinations, for which Philadelphia was a hotbed, and by trade regulations in which the country folk had no voice, Lancaster merchants bitterly complained of their reception at the markets in Philadelphia.[29] Lost in a dream of marine significance, Lancaster vainly adopted the name, "The Port of Lancaster". Baltimore encouraged the construction of the Conestoga Navigation, since it would turn regions which had formerly been within Philadelphia's economic sphere towards the Chesapeake Bay.[30] The town of Lancaster advertised that it alone manufactured one hundred hogsheads of liquor a day; the surrounding territory was known as "the garden of America". The gain of this trade seemed a valuable acquisition to the Baltimore merchants.

In 1829, the Conestoga Navigation was completed. However, within a few weeks it was rendered impassable because of flood damages, and the channel was not open for business for some time. In 1830, tolls amounting to $1500 were collected, while the next year they increased to $2243. Trade, however, did not center in Baltimore as had been expected when the Conestoga Navigation was chartered. The Chesapeake and Delaware Canal began operation the same year as Lancaster's canal; and, instead of carrying on trade with Baltimore alone, Lancaster now had a water route to either the Maryland city or her own State metropolis.[31] Although the financial status of the Conestoga Navigation was always a great handicap to the company officials, it continued to play a part in commercial affairs of Lancaster until the opening of the Columbia and Philadelphia Railroad rudely broke the enchanting spell of marine fame.[32] Baltimore was thereby forced to relinquish the Lancaster trade—especially whiskey and flour—which this canal had forwarded to her.

Meanwhile, the reawakening interest in internal improvements had caused men again to consider the improvement of the channel of the river itself. Committees representing Baltimore and Lancaster met to discuss this improvement. They agreed on the importance and necessity of river navigation and decided that the two states which they represented should be asked to share all incurred expenses. Memorials were immediately drawn up and presented to the Legislatures of Pennsylvania and Maryland. Maryland, in turn, authorized the city of Baltimore to raise $50,000

[29] *The Aurora,* July 20, 1821. Reprints article from the *Lancaster Gazette.*

[30] *Niles' Weekly Register,* XXXI, 203, 400; Hazard, *The Pennsylvania Register,* III, 254. Hazard reprinted an article from the *United States Gazette* which read in part, "We rejoice at the prosperity of the city and county of Lancaster and only regret the Conestoga . . . did not find its way into the Schuylkill, instead of a more southern embouchment."

[31] Hazard, *The Pennsylvania Register,* III, 254; V, 256.

[32] *Ibid.,* XVI, 72.

for river improvements, which the city officials immediately did.[33] On March 31, 1823, the Legislature of Pennsylvania passed an act appropriating $50,000 for a similar purpose with the stipulation that $10,000 were to be spent annually and the commissioners from Baltimore could expend such part of their appropriation as they deemed proper within the Commonwealth of Pennsylvania.[34] With one eye on the Chesapeake and Delaware Canal which was under construction, the Pennsylvania Legislature allowed the channel below Columbia to be improved.[35] By 1826 the commissioners reported that little work remained to be done to meet the needs of descending navigation on the Susquehanna from Columbia to tidewater.[36]

That same year Hezekiah Niles estimated that 1037 arks, 164 keel-boats, and 1090 rafts carried produce valued at $1,528,000 down the Susquehanna Valley to tidewater. The Pennsylvania Canal Commissioners, however, placed the value of this traffic at a much higher figure. They claimed the Susquehanna business reached $5,000,000 in 1826.[37] Shipments continued to increase; in 1827 it was reported by a citizen of Harrisburg that between the last day of February and the twenty-third of June of that year, 1631 rafts, 1370 arks, and about 200 keel-boats descended the river. It was estimated that the rafts contained 40,775,000 feet of lumber; that 200 arks carrying 55 tons each were loaded with anthracite coal; and that the remaining 1170 arks carried mostly flour and whiskey.[38] The improvements in river navigation and the increased skill of the freshwater sailors reduced the cost of transportation so that in 1827 wheat was only twelve and one-half cents less per bushel at Columbia than the market price in Baltimore.[39] Insurance on wheat from

---

[33] *Niles' Weekly Register*, XXII, 48.

[34] *Ibid.*, XXIV, 82; XXIX, 399-400, contains the Report of the Susquehanna Commissioners appointed by Act of Legislature of Maryland; Hazard, *The Pennsylvania Register*, II, 300; Egle, *History of Dauphin County*, 319. The Baltimore Commissioners were allowed to spend only $5,000 per year. The difference in annual funds available to the two sets of Commissioners caused some delay in cooperation between them. This situation was finally remedied by a change in the Baltimore Ordinance.

[35] In 1825 further appropriations were granted by Pennsylvania to the amount of $30,000, for improving the river from Conewago to Northumberland. See *Niles' Weekly Register*, XXVIII, 66; Armroyd, *A Connected View of the Whole Internal Navigation of the United States*, 83-4.

[36] *Ibid.*, 87; *Niles' Weekly Register*, XXIX, 399-400.

[37] *Ibid.*, XXXI, 283.

[38] *Niles' Weekly Register*, XXXII, 290; Ringwalt, *op. cit.*, 13.

[39] *Niles' Weekly Register, op. cit.*, XXXII, 113. In 1811 wheat was fifty cents a bushel more in Baltimore than at Columbia.

the same town to Baltimore was between one and two cents a bushel. Annually, conditions for descending trade become better, and Niles reported that the business for 1831 would possibly amount to $10,000,000.[40]

The improvement of the river channel caused some of the leading citizens of Baltimore to try another scheme for gaining the return trade of the Susquehanna Valley. In 1824 a company was formed to test the practicability of using steamboats on the Susquehanna.[41] The next year the small steamer *Susquehanna* was launched at Port Deposit but the swift current and the crooked channel made an ascent of the river impossible. Another boat was contracted to be built by a York firm for $3,000. This boat, the sheet-iron *Codorus,* was completed in 1825 and arrived at Harrisburg as "the cry of the steamboat filled the shores of the river with delighted spectators." The *Codorus* weighed about five tons but drew only six and one-half inches of water when loaded. She progressed at the rates of five miles per hour against the current.[42]

The next year the *Codorus* ran to Binghamton and Elmira in New York State, and returned successfully to York Haven. Although the skipper was not satisfied with the trip, Baltimore believed that "scientific power had obtained a splendid victory over the natural impediments to a rapid and safe ascending navigation." In 1826 a third steamboat[43] was put on the Susquehanna River by the Maryland sponsors. After a successful first run, the career of this steamer came to a rude halt; someone, it was reported, held down the safety valve as the boat tried to pass the Nescopeck Falls. The boilers exploded and steamboat navigation on the Susquehanna River came to a sudden stop.[44]

---

[40] *Ibid.,* XL, 149.

[41] *Ibid.,* XXXVII, 258-9; Armroyd, *op. cit.,* 84, 112-3; Egle, *History of Dauphin County,* 319; Parkins, *op. cit.,* in *The Bulletin of the Geographical Society of Philadelphia* XIV, 112; Prowell *History of York County,* 609. Prowell says that most of the Baltimore promoters were identified with the Merchants Flouring Mills at York Haven.

[42] *Niles' Weekly Register,* XXIX, 215; Prowell, *op. cit.,* 609; Armroyd, *op. cit.,* 84-5.

[43] This was either the old *Susquehanna* or another steamer of the same model and christened *Susquehanna and Baltimore.* Prowell, *op. cit.,* 609, claims that another vessel, the *Pioneer,* was built for service on the Susquehanna, but that it was too heavy for successful use.

[44] The idea was reawakened in 1833 by a Harrisburg editor on a new and tremendous scale. It was planned to get Congressional support for "A Grand National Sloop and Steamboat Navigation for the Atlantic Ocean by way of the Chesapeake Bay, Susquehanna River, Seneca or Cayuga Lake and Lake Erie." Baltimore gave only tacit encouragement to the plan, which did not remain long before the people. The death of the Army Engineer who was sent to survey the route and the failure of pecuniary assistance from the Federal Government were the death blow of this grandiose plank in the American system platform. Hazard, *The Pennsylvania Register,* XII, 198-200, 213, 252, 261-3; XIV, 106-8.

During the years of Baltimore's experimentation in steamboating on the Susquehanna, Pennsylvania had decided to embark on a plan in order "to save face" and to regain some of her former prestige. In 1826, the Pennsylvania State Works were commenced; a through route from Philadelphia to Pittsburgh was planned. However, scarcely one year after the Main Line had been projected, the original plan was supplemented by another which, when finished, provided the State with an expensive and disconnected system of internal improvements. The members of the Legislature absolutely refused to vote appropriations for the Main Line unless their own local interests were answered. Therefore, the counties not bordering on the trunk line would not grant funds unless State canals were built through their territory. "The legislative halls became a market-place, wherein canals were to be bartered. . . ." Log-rolling was the pastime of the day; Pennsylvania ruined her opportunity to compete with her commercial rivals as she dissipated her funds on unneeded, unproductive, lateral canals.

Among the branch canals constructed by Pennsylvania were routes to thread the Susquehanna Valley along the North and West Branches, and from Sunbury to Harrisburg along the main river. In constructing these branch canals, Pennsylvania uncovered a new problem for the commercial rivals, Philadelphia and Baltimore, to wrangle about. Great dams from eight to ten feet high were constructed across the Susquehanna River at Sunbury, Nanticoke, and Duncan's Island to secure water for canal feeders. Although a chute or rafting gap was provided in each, these sluiceways increased the peril of river navigation. Ascending navigation was wholly destroyed; descending navigation was made treacherous; steam navigation was impossible. Philadelphia claimed these structures were aids to better communication with the interior; Baltimore saw them as obstructions placed in the river to force all the river shipping into the Pennsylvania State Canals and on to Philadelphia.[45]

The constituents of the legislators who had sponsored the lateral canals were greatly disturbed by the new situation. In 1829 it was claimed that two out of every three arks that passed the Shamokin dam were torn to pieces. "These things are wholly insufferable," they cried, "but will soon be remedied, for it is pretty certain that the spring freshets will again level this hopeful structure (the Shamokin dam)."[46] Their forecast was correct; however, the State not only repaired the dam but built the two others as planned.

Meetings of protest were called by the rivermen. At Port Deposit it was resolved that all impediments to the natural navigation of the Sus-

---

[45] *Niles' Weekly Register*, XXXIX, 72; Parkins, *op. cit.*, in the *Bulletin of the Geographical Society of Philadelphia*, XIV, 113.
[46] *Niles' Weekly Register*, XXXVII, 275.

quehanna River were a usurpation of a power inconsistent with the fundamental principles of government.[47] Seventeen New York towns sent delegates to a convention at Owego in 1831. They petitioned their governor to appeal to Pennsylvania to remove the dams. They maintained that Pennsylvania's policy was "an act of force, condemned by the judgment of mankind."

Baltimore stood shoulder to shoulder with her rural producers and river navigators. *Niles' Weekly Register* in sarcastic vein took up the cry against Philadelphia. Its Baltimore editors wrote:

"Now—as in this matter, there is no power to adjust the dispute between 'sovereign' Pennsylvania and 'sovereign' Maryland—We advise that an *army of Marylanders* shall be stationed at the northern line of the state to fire upon and kill any person 'feloniously' descending the Susquehanna from the 'nation' of Pennsylvania; and that a detachment of SOLDIERS should be located on the Maryland side of the Chesapeake and Delaware Canal, to cut through the banks and let off the water, at the very first moment when the present frosty weather will allow it to run away: which, together, would afford a *magnificent* specimen of the '*sovereignty' of the state*,—either named having the right to *nullify* the blessings of PROVIDENCE, or render useless the work of art! Let us go the 'whole hog' and *enquire* into the right and reason of things by loud huzzars!"[48]

The citizens of Maryland petitioned their government to study the situation and take a definite stand against Pennsylvania's policy. The two houses of the legislature thereupon appointed a joint committee to investigate this subject "of particular importance."[49] When this committee probed into their subject, it discovered that an act passed by the Maryland Legislature in 1799 stipulated that it would consent to the construction of a canal connecting the Chesapeake and Delaware Bays, if Pennsylvania in turn would declare the Susquehanna River a public highway and authorize the removal of obstructions to navigation from the bed of the stream. After due consideration, the Pennsylvania Legislature acted in compliance with this request.

The investigating committee immediately seized upon this agreement as a solemn contract. The dams built by Pennsylvania were an open breach of the contract agreed upon by the two states more than twenty-five years before. A copy of the findings of the committee was sent to the Governor of Pennsylvania for presentation to his Legislature; coopera-

---

[47] *The York Gazette*, May 4, 1830.

[48] *Niles' Weekly Register*, XXXIX, 425. A little later, the same journal again took up the question. Bitterly the editors claimed, " 'Sovereignty' has no limits—so we will shut up the Susquehanna, 'nullify' the Chesapeake and Delaware canal, and *hurrah* for 'State rights!' " *Ibid.*, XL, 46-7.

[49] *Ibid.*, XXXIX, 421-2; Hazard, *The Pennsylvania Register*, VII, 121.

tion was asked of New York and Delaware. Three commissioners were
appointed by the Maryland Legislature to remonstrate against the conduct of Pennsylvania at Harrisburg.[50] These gentlemen relied chiefly on
the argument that Pennsylvania had broken a contract agreed to in
solemn faith. Their presence at Harrisburg caused a committee to be
appointed by the Pennsylvania Legislature to study the situation. This
group, in turn, decided that the canal commissioners, who had sole control of the Pennsylvania State Works, "not as arbiters, but as agents, of
the state", should examine the dams and ascertain whether the law of
1801 had been violated and report their findings for the future action of
the State, if any was necessary.[51]

The procedure was by no means pleasing to the Maryland Commissioners. They complained that the whole matter had been referred to the
"wrong-doers themselves." The Marylanders insisted that the 1801 law
was a contract and protested in the name of their state against the proceedings of the committee which they maintained were merely to produce
delay. They also complained that the committee had submitted the question to "an ex parte tribunal itself implicated as authors of the inflicted
injury."[52]

Baltimore was raving mad when she heard the news of Pennsylvania's
elaborate trick of mock justice. Hezekiah Niles in his *Weekly Register*
again made caustic remarks about Pennsylvania's demand for State rights
and again pointed to the Chesapeake and Delaware Canal saying:

"If Pennsylvania dams the river to *promote* her interior trade, we may
dam Back Creek to *keep* the trade that descends! The other day twenty-
three vessels, fully laden, arrived at Philadelphia from Port Deposit.
Now, if Back Creek were dammed, their cargoes would have reached
Baltimore! Every good rule works both ways—and the happiness of
society depends on mutual and just concessions."[53]

As the Marylanders had anticipated, the Pennsylvania Canal Commissioners reported that they believed the law of 1801 had not been violated
by the construction of the dams. Although they confessed that a great
deal of damage had been caused to river shipping, they reported that
"such improvements have since been made as will for the future render
the descending navigation entirely safe."[54]

---

[50] *Pennsylvania Archives,* Fourth Series, V, 932-6; *Niles' Weekly Register,*
XXXIX, 421-2; Hazard, *The Pennsylvania Register,* VII, 121. The commissioners who were detailed to present Maryland's case at the Pennsylvania capital
were Robert Goldborough, John Mercer, and Samuel Sterett.

[51] *Niles' Weekly Register,* XL, 129-30; Hazard, *The Register of Pennsylvania,*
VII, 260-1.

[52] *Niles' Weekly Register,* XL, 130; Hazard, *The Register of Pennsylvania,*
VII, 261.

[53] *Niles' Weekly Register,* XL, 130.

[54] *Report of the Canal Commissioners,* December 15, 1831.

The following year the question again came to the fore; during the spring thaw the dams had been partially destroyed and Maryland asked Pennsylvania to reconsider her appeal before reconstruction was commenced.[55] Resolutions were again passed by the Maryland Legislature and the Governor was authorized to take such measure as he thought "proper and expedient" to prevent reconstruction of the obstacles. However, before acting, the Governor turned to his Attorney General for advice in the matter. After a thorough study of all the particulars, Attorney General Bayly reported that remonstrance to the government of Pennsylvania was the only measure that legally could be taken. Coercion or compulsion in a question of this character, he maintained, was not constitutional.[56]

Pennsylvania reconstructed the dams, but trouble with the rivermen soon resulted. After a number of arks had been demolished at a fourth dam constructed at Muncy, the navigators took matters in their own hands and wrecked a portion of the dam so that their crafts could pass. "Thus while the legislature appropriated millions to construct *useless* canals along our navigable streams, the people are *nullifying* their acts by tearing down their work," wrote a Harrisburg newspaper.[57]

Having used her press and lungs to no avail, and seeing that the western trade would soon be flowing toward Philadelphia over the Pennsylvania State Works, Baltimore returned to her original policy of canalization of the lower Susquehanna. Her need was no longer for a canal to the Conewago Falls but for one to Columbia where the Main Line of the new Pennsylvania State Works turned eastward toward Philadelphia. Baltimore was greatly handicapped in this plan because such a canal had to be partly constructed on Pennsylvania territory. However, certain groups of Pennsylvanians were eager to support their Maryland friends and were willing to exert great efforts to win charter privileges for a canal. In the southern tier of counties in central Pennsylvania, the bitter feeling toward Philadelphia had continued from colonial days. This animosity was reawakened when the State embarked on its system of public improvements. Although lateral canals were extended to many remote corners of the State, the southern counties had received no benefits. The Main Line was in direct competition with the through western roads which passed through this area. The conservative

[55] *Niles' Weekly Register*, XLII, 81; Hazard, *The Pennsylvania Register*, X, 404.

[56] Hazard, *The Pennsylvania Register*, XI, 77; *Niles' Weekly Register*, XLVIII, 258. Reprint of a letter from the Attorney General to the Governor of Maryland relative to the obstruction of the river traffic in the Susquehanna River by dams built by Pennsylvania.

[57] *Ibid.*, XLIV. 98; Hazard, *The Pennsylvania Register*, XI, 224.

Germans of this region were angered by the thought that they would
have to pay taxes to build internal improvements which would not pass
near their own doors. Therefore, when Baltimore announced her plan to
pave a smooth route to the Chesapeake, the citizens of Lancaster, York,
Adams, Franklin, and Cumberland Counties became interested. Many of
them were members of the Anti-Masonic Party which opposed the administration's internal improvement platform.[58] Their representatives
thus became spokesmen for Baltimore in the Pennsylvania Legislature.

A number of up-state coal and lumber people soon joined the Baltimore
followers in support of a canal to tidewater. The coal men claimed that
their product could not reach market at a price comparable to Schuylkill
or Lehigh coal without a canal; they maintained that no extensive business could be done with arks, even if the Susquehanna River were in
good navigable order.[59] The iron and lumber merchants announced the
same necessity for a direct and continuous canal to tidewater. The Philadelphia and Columbia Railroad (the eastern link of the State Works)
could not handle bulky coal, iron and lumber; the Union Canal from
Middletown to Philadelphia's Schuylkill Navigation was too small for
the canal boats of the Pennsylvania canals and this necessitated transshipment.[60]

As early as 1834 Baltimore began to feel the effects of the Pennsylvania improvements,[61] and the clamor of her merchants for a canal along
the lower course of the Susquehanna River became much louder.
Although the Chesapeake and Delaware Canal was open and afforded
Philadelphia a means of tapping any canal to tidewater at Havre de
Grace, nevertheless Philadelphia spokesmen condemned Baltimore's
machinations at Harrisburg in their effort to get a charter. The Philadelphia representatives opposed the canal because its very inception was
"inimical to the interest of their city."[62]

---

[58] McCarty, "Anti-Masonic Party: A Study of Political Anti-Masonry in the
United States, 1827-40," in The American Historical Association Annual Report,
427-30.

[59] Hazard, The Pennsylvania Register, XIII, 291, 294. Reprints Packer's Report
on the coal industry. Little coal could be carried by the river arks. Business
could not expand as coal demands a regular carrier and could not depend on
spasmodic spring freshets.

[60] Ibid., XV, 103-4. Hazard reprints a petition for the extension of the Pennsylvania Canal from Columbia to the Maryland Line. Many of the supporters
of Baltimore in the charter fight were not especially anxious to reach the Baltimore market; their chief interest was to get a through, continuous canal to
tidewater.

[61] The Columbia Spy, September 27, 1834; The York Republican, December 31,
1834. These Valley papers claimed that Baltimore was just beginning to appreciate the Susquehanna Valley trade now that it was beginning to escape her.

[62] Poulson's Daily Advertiser, March 30, 1835.

After many petitions had finally aroused the Pennsylvania Legislature, a bill chartering a company to construct a canal along the lower Susquehanna passed the Senate and from all appearances was destined to become law. Philadelphia, however, would not permit such action without a final stand. The leading citizens of the city gathered in town-meeting and drew up resolutions which they hurriedly forwarded to their representatives at Harrisburg. They viewed the proposed charter as "completely subversive to the principles" of Pennsylvania's expensive State Works; they knew that it would make *our public works tributary to a rival state.* In emphatic tone, they instructed their legislators to use all "honourable means" to defeat the bill.[63]

Despite Philadelphia's resistance, the measure became law on April 15, 1835. The act authorized a chartered company to construct a twenty-six mile canal along the eastern shore of the Susquehanna River from Columbia to the Maryland Line where it was to connect with a Maryland-incorporated canal.[64] Although the Pennsylvania commercial metropolis had fought a losing battle, she was able to modify the outcome. A qualifying section of the act of incorporation gave the Delaware River port some safety and security. It stipulated that charges on the canal could not be less than the rates on the Philadelphia and Columbia Railroad with the exception of lumber, iron, and coal freightage. The charges on the enumerated articles were to be uniform with the tolls charged on the State Canals.[65]

In spite of this protection and the fact that the Chesapeake and Delaware Canal offered Philadelphia a connection with the southern terminal of the proposed canal, the passage of the act caused considerable excitement in the Pennsylvania city. *The Philadelphia Herald* cried, "this measure strikes a deadly blow at the prosperity of Philadelphia." The capitalists of the Quaker City shook their heads in disgust to think that an internal improvement investment of thirty-two millions of dollars, largely supported by the tills of Philadelphia, would soon carry all the profits of the West and of the Susquehanna Valley into the lap of a rival.[66]

The Marylanders, on hearing the news of the passage of the bill, were happy and "almost ready to illuminate." The Maryland portion of the

---

[63] *Niles' Weekly Register*, XLVIII, 135-6.

[64] *Acts of Incorporation and Supplements . . . in Reference to the Susquehanna and Tidewater Canal Companies,* 5-15.

[65] *Ibid.,* Section X.

[66] *Niles' Weekly Register*, XLVIII, 136, 205. It was roughly estimated that the Pennsylvania canals and railroads cost $25,000,000; the Ohio canals, $5,000,000; and the canals, planned to connect the systems of the two states, about $2,000,000.

canal had already been incorporated as the Tidewater Canal Company,[67] and Baltimore believed that she was now in a commanding position to take advantage of the whole internal improvement system of Pennsylvania. The commercial men of Baltimore eagerly anticipated the opening of new, extensive hinterlands where wealth and prestige could be gleaned. In satirical tone *The Baltimore Gazette* remarked, "Philadelphia has gained the passage of this bill, she has acquired information which perhaps could not have been obtained in any other way and which may prove of infinite service in the future, it has taught her that a portion of the State of Pennsylvania lies west of the Susquehanna."[68] *The Baltimore American* enjoyed "sincere gratification" in disseminating news of the Baltimore triumph.[69]

Thus a struggle of more than fifty years was brought to a close. Baltimore was enthusiastic; she failed to notice that the days of the "canal rage" were passing. Philadelphia was nervous when the bill first passed; however, this city showed less apprehension of injury than was expected. She now had the Chesapeake and Delaware Canal to tap the new Susquehanna Canal; the center of competition for the Susquehanna Valley trade was merely to be moved south as a result of the proposed canal.

But even before construction was commenced, the canal officials stumbled into their first difficulty. The charter provided that the canal should be dug along the eastern shore of the river. It was planned to use the old Susquehanna Canal from Love Island to Port Deposit as the route for the lower part of the new canal. But on entering into negotiations to buy this canal, the sponsors of the new waterway to tide found the exorbitant demands of the owners of that waterway very unreasonable. All attempts toward reaching an understanding failed.[70]

---

[67] *Acts of Incorporation and Supplements . . . in Reference to the Susquehanna and Tidewater Canal Companies,* 23-5.

[68] *The Baltimore Gazette,* April 25, 1835.

[69] *The Baltimore American,* April 18, 1835. Two other editors, who had followed the charter struggle, predicted results which differed from the Philadelphia and Baltimore views. Niles in an editorial said the construction of the canal would "give to commodities descending the Susquehanna their natural direction to the tide—from whence, by the Chesapeake and Delaware Canal, or to Baltimore, they will seek a market as circumstances, or the wishes of parties, may direct." *Niles' Weekly Register,* XLVIII, 36, 113. The editor of the *Columbia Spy* had the same opinion. He wrote that both Philadelphia and Baltimore would prosper together with his own little "city in miniature." *Columbia Spy,* April 25, 1835.

[70] Committee of the Company, *Reasons why the Supplement to the Act Incorporating the Susquehanna Canal Company should pass; Niles' Weekly Register,* XLIX, 2; Hazard, *The Pennsylvania Register,* XVI, 153, 343. The Baltimore papers also carried many comments on this situation; they spoke in indignant terms of the conduct of the Maryland Canal officials for retarding the work on the new route. The price asked for the old canal company's rights was $375,000 while the highest offer made by the new company was $50,000.

After a long delay, it was decided to ask for an amendment to the charter granting the privilege of crossing the Susquehanna River at Columbia by means of a dam and towing bridge and routing the canal along the western shore of the river.[71] The request was granted in 1836, on condition that the State of Maryland should authorize a Pennsylvania connection by railroad from the State Line to the Baltimore and Ohio Railroad at or near Hagerstown or Williamsport, Maryland.[72] Maryland agreed to this new demand, but only after she had fully protected the interests of the much condemned proprietors of the old Susquehanna Canal, who were to receive, on the completion of the new canal, $2000 worth of stock in the new company for each share they owned in the old organization. Since this sum was much less than had been demanded when bargaining over a sale price, and since the Baltimore and Ohio Railroad welcomed branch lines, all conditions were accepted and agreed upon.

Excavation of a canal of the same size and design as the Pennsylvania Canals was immediately begun.[73] Hundreds of brawny men from the Emerald Isle worked under the direction of the construction engineers. But completion was not as early as expected.[74] The high wages during the boom period of the thirties disturbed labor conditions. Construction and repairs on the extensive Pennsylvania State Works caused a scarcity of labor. The difficulties of the money market hindered progress. The financial condition of the company was unsteady from its beginning. Under the Pennsylvania charter the capital stock of the Susquehanna Canal Company was placed at $1,500,000.

When the Tidewater Company of Maryland was organized, the Pennsylvania Company subscribed the entire stock of the Maryland Company. This step was taken in order to insure one ownership and one direction for the entire forty-five miles of canal. The stock of the Tidewater Company was therefore held by the Susquehanna Canal Company, but the latter organization gained no capital with which to construct the Maryland section of the route. Financial aid was, therefore, needed at once. In pursuance to requests of Baltimore friends of the enterprise, the state

[71] Gibson, *History of York County*, 334. When built, the dam cost the company $220,000, while the cost of tow-path bridge, including the right to attach it to the Columbia Bank and Bridge Company's structure, amounted to $10,000.

[72] *Acts of Incorporation and Supplements . . . in Reference to the Susquehanna and Tidewater Canal Companies*, 15-18.

[73] Tanner, *Description of Canals and Railroads in the United States*, 113. This 45-mile canal had a total lockage of 233 feet. The locks were 170 feet long and 17 feet wide; the number of lift locks amounted to 29. The channel, five feet in depth, was 50 feet wide at the water's surface.

[74] Susquehanna and Tidewater Canal Company, *Annual Report*, 1839.

of Maryland, in 1838, loaned one million dollars in state bonds to the company to straighten out its financial status.[75]

By the late fall of 1839 water was turned into the channel. A huge celebration commemorated the event. The nationally known Nicholas Biddle addressed the crowd assembled at Havre de Grace on the subject of "Internal Improvements."[76] Biddle said that he, like other Philadelphians, had feared the consequences of this project during its early stages, but that their anxiety was only momentary. Philadelphia had soon realized that the canal was a benefit to both cities. Old rivalries were put aside, at least for that day, to the extent that a toast was given to Philadelphia "whose public spirit so largely aided in the completion of the work we meet to celebrate."

Before the enthusiasm of the celebration had waned, nature dampened the immediate prospects of the canal with heavy rains and floods which ruined much of the embankments and some of the masonry of the $3,500,-000 canal.[77] Hurried repair work made a reopening of the canal possible in the spring of 1840.[78] Baltimore's great plan had been effected; the Chesapeake metropolis now had an ascending as well as a descending navigation into the Susquehanna Valley. Her route tapped Philadelphia's western trade and brought her into contact with the far away Erie Canal Region. Wheat, flour, whiskey, coal, lumber, and country products passed to Baltimore from every section of central Pennsylvania. But the Maryland metropolis did not have a monopoly on the commerce carried by the Susquehanna and Tidewater Canal; Philadelphia would never have allowed her rival to be so blessed. A report early in the first year of the canal's operation said that the trade was fairly evenly divided between the two cities.[79]

Four years after the opening of the canal, the managers reported that "half of the Western produce shipped from Pittsburgh seeks Baltimore

---

[75] Pamphlets on Canals in Maryland, No. 4, *The Susquehanna and Tidewater Canal, A Memorial to the Maryland Legislature for an appropriation; Hunt's Merchants' Magazine*, XX, 486; Susquehanna and Tidewater Canal Company, *Annual Report*, 1839; *Niles' Weekly Register*, LVI, 102. It is interesting to note that the Maryland act authorized the issuance of 5% sterling or 6% currency bonds so that they could be disposed of either in Europe or America.

[76] *Niles' Weekly Register*, LVIII, 144, 415.

[77] *Ibid.*, LVIII, 144, 167.

[78] *Ibid.*, LVIII, 136, 167; Hazard, *The United States Register*, II, 318 (article entitled, "New Era in the Commerce of Baltimore"). The first boats to reach Baltimore, towed through the bay by the steamboat *Patapsco*, were the *Judge Burnside* from Bald Eagle with wheat, the *Judge Porter* from Lewistown with wheat, the *Triumph* from Northumberland with wheat and furniture, and the *Tidewater* from Harrisburg.

[79] *Niles' Weekly Register*, LVIII, 160.

for a market . . . and about a third of the merchandise shipped through the Pennsylvania Canal for the west is also forwarded by this city."[80] A great amount of the traffic of the Pennsylvania Canals destined for Philadelphia also sought this channel and was forwarded from the southern terminal of the Susquehanna and Tidewater Canal through the Chesapeak and Delaware Canal. The distance to the Pennsylvania metropolis from Havre de Grace was only 74 miles, while from the same river port to Baltimore the distance of twenty miles less. A steam tow-boat service was immediately established by Philadelphia to assist her to win the traffic of the Susquehanna and Tidewater Canal. The number of boats towed by this organization rose from 961 in 1841, to 4806 in 1847.[81] Statistics for the years 1849-1856 show that Philadelphia received more than half of the boats towed from Havre de Grace. In the year 1850, Baltimore received 1640 boats, while Philadelphia attracted 2576.[82] Up to 1860, the trade to and from the southern terminal of the Susquehanna and Tidewater Canal passing through the Chesapeake and Delaware produced more than one-fourth of the revenue of the latter.[83]

However, a great amount of shipping from the canal did find its way to the wharves of Baltimore. Although one thousand more boats were towed to Philadelphia than to Baltimore from Havre de Grace in 1849, the difference decreased annually. By 1857 Baltimore received 2317 boats from the canal which threaded the lower Susquehanna Valley, a few more than entered Philadelphia in that year.[84] Although the lumber and wheat trade was, to a certain extent, diverted to Philadelphia, Baltimore grew in importance as a coal market, causing Virginia to grow nervous in fear that the bituminous coal received at Baltimore over the Susquehanna and Tidewater Canal would ruin her coal trade.[85] Coal which passed southward through the canal in 1845 amounted to only a little more than 70,000 tons while, in 1860, tonnage had increased to almost 230,000 tons, much of which must have gone to Baltimore.[86]

---

[80] Susquehanna and Tidewater Canal Company, *Annual Report*, 1840.

[81] *Niles' Weekly Register*, LXXIII, 255.

The figures given for the tow-boat business both to and from Havre de Grace are:

1841	961	1845	3,593
1842	1,380	1846	3,593
1843	1,908	1847	4,806
1844	2,474		

[82] See Appendix V, 78.

[83] Meyer, ed., *History of Transportation before 1860*, 225.

[84] Appendix V, 78.

[85] Hazard, *The United States Register*, IV, 24.

[86] See Appendix VIII, 80.

Providing transportation to the two markets for country products, coal, lumber, and iron, and to the interior for manufactured goods and necessary commodities, appeared to be a profitable undertaking for the canal company. Tolls rose from $41,558 in the first year to almost four times that amount in 1850. The Union Canal and the Philadelphia and Columbia Railroad suffered a great drain on their business.[87] Although the river continued, during navigable weather, to carry whiskey, flour, grain, etc., to tidewater, the days of river traffic were about over. Fifty or more years of "arking" and rafting had denuded the hills along the river of their best timber; the era of the riverman began to pass by the middle of the nineteenth century.[88] Annually the Susquehanna and Tidewater officials announced larger tolls until 1855 when a peak of $211,141 was reached. About three-fourths of the tolls were collected on the passage of freight from the interior; then the enlargement of the Union Canal after 1855 resulted in a marked decrease in the revenues of the Susquehanna and Tidewater Company.[89]

But these years of growing trade really tell only one side of the company's history; in spite of the picture they portray, one wonders that the canal ever survived. The year the Susquehanna and Tidewater Canal was completed, the Wrightsville division of the Baltimore and Susquehanna Railroad was put into operation; this gave Baltimore a direct railroad line to the Pennsylvania State Works at the same junction as the Baltimore Canal.[90] Although early railroads were not equipped to carry the heavy, bulky goods of the interior, this road did cut down the amount of business which the Susquehanna and Tidewater Canal had anticipated and later waged a rate war against the Canal.

The Philadelphia and Columbia Railroad, which served as the eastern link in the mongrel Pennsylvania system of improvements, also terminated in the thriving little town of Columbia. This railroad soon felt the diverting effects of the Baltimore Canal. The Pennsylvania Canal Commissioners, thereupon, tried to save this expensive section of the Main Line. Relief was sought through the State Legislature. A law was passed permitting a drawback of 75 cents per ton on most articles of western production shipped from Pittsburgh, if they went directly to Philadelphia via the State Works. Although this plan did not continue in effect very long,[91] it frightened the canal officials and demonstrated

---

[87] See pages 112-113.

[88] Pearce, *Annals of Luzerne,* 470; Klein, *op. cit.,* 35. About 1850, Canadian lumber began to appear on the market.

[89] See Appendix VI, 79.

[90] See pages 134-135.

[91] Susquehanna and Tidewater Canal Company, *Annual Report,* 1844; Meyer, ed., *op. cit.,* 225.

to them that they were vulnerable, at all times, to the Pennsylvania lawmakers.

But the big worry of the managers of the Susquehanna and Tidewater Canal was the financial condition of the company. Like a giant storm cloud ready to drench and flood the canal into an unredeemable state of insolvency, it hovered over the company from its very birth. With an actual capital of one and one-quarter millions of dollars, the directors of the company undertook to construct a route which cost more than three and one-half millions.[92] The cost of construction was about $80,000 per mile, which made the Susquehanna and Tidewater Canal the third most expensive canal to be constructed before the Civil War.[93] In 1842, the company reported that it could not pay its debts. Scrip, damage claims, and unpaid bills made the threat of *writs of sequestration* of tolls and revenues a probability.[94] Nevertheless, the company officials still maintained that the bad financial condition of their organization was only temporary.[95] They maintained that the causes for its present condition were the general depression which gripped the country, the fact that the coal and iron of Pennsylvania had not yet been developed, and the lack of proper connections with the anthracite coal fields.

In answer to the petitions of her citizens, Pennsylvania threatened to close the outlet lock to the Pennsylvania State Works and isolate the Susquehanna and Tidewater Company, if that organization continued to refuse to redeem its scrip or meet its obligations.[96] But, as general conditions improved, the company was able to satisfy its creditors by a gradual liquidation of the preferred claims. These improved conditions were, however, only temporary. In 1852, the financial status of the company necessitated the readjustment of affairs which permitted the company to fund the arrears and accruing interest upon the deferred debt up to January, 1854, into capital stock and to issue new bonds for the principal of the debt.[97]

---

[92] Susquehanna and Tidewater Canal Company, *Annual Report,* 1848.

[93] Harlow, *Old Towpaths,* 171.

[94] MSS. Petition from Franklin County to the Legislature in 1844. Many of the citizens had worked on the canal and during the panic had received scrip. They memorialized the Legislature to force the canal company to meet its obligations even if it were necessary to use forceful methods. Petition in the Archives Division of the Pennsylvania Historical and Museum Commission.

[95] *Statement of the Susquehanna and Tidewater Canal Company to the Governor of Maryland, 1842;* Hazard, *The United States Register,* VI, 393-5.

[96] Susquehanna and Tidewater Canal Company, *Annual Report,* 1844.

[97] Susquehanna and Tidewater Canal Company, *Annual Report,* 1852 and 1853. The debt to be exchanged amounted to $1,170,000.

Floods in 1857 caused damage along the waterway to the amount of $50,000. To pay for repairs the officials were forced to suspend payment of interest to the State of Maryland, and two years later were forced again to make a general suspension.[98] As the country drifted into war, the condition of the Susquehanna and Tidewater Canal Company's finances became much worse. Finally, in 1872, it was found necessary to lease the canal to the Philadelphia and Reading Railroad Company.[99]

Obstacles impeding the descending navigation of the Susquehanna River were removed by the cooperative action of Pennsylvania and Maryland by 1826. But no important amount of traffic was able to ascend the stream. Not until the completion of the Susquehanna and Tidewater Canal in 1840 was return trade to the Conewago Falls practicable. However, the construction of the canal across the isthmus which gave Philadelphia a waterway to Chesapeake Bay made impossible Baltimore's hope of a monopoly of the trade which passed through the canal and down the river. The point of rivalry in the lower Susquehanna had merely been moved south to Havre de Grace where canal and river business centered. In the competition for this trade Philadelphia gained a good half of the business, but Baltimore, too, profited by the steady arrival at her wharves of anthracite coal vessels which also carried return goods into central Pennsylvania.

APPENDIX V

The Number of Boats Towed from Havre de Grace, the Southern Terminal of the Susquehanna and Tidewater Canal, to Philadelphia and Baltimore, 1849-1857

Year	Philadelphia	Baltimore
1849	2626	1560
1850	2576	1640
1851	2933	2047
1852	2899	2412
1853	2842	2521
1854	2817	2556
1855	3137	2642
1856	3024	2648
1857	2292	2317

(Taken from *Hunt's Merchants' Magazine*, XXXVIII, 383.)

---

[98] Susquehanna and Tidewater Canal Company, *Annual Report*, 1859.

[99] Susquehanna Canal Company to the Philadelphia and Reading Railroad Company—lease, found in Pamphlets, Vol. 2021 in the Pennsylvania State Library.

APPENDIX VI

Table of the Tolls Taken by the Susquehanna and Tidewater Canal Company, 1840-1860

Year	Amount in Dollars
1840	41,558
1841	70,852
1842	66,855*
1843	72,052
1844	86,906
1845	99,684
1846	110,470
1847	131,940
1848	138,491
1849	156,272
1850	156,965**
1851	164,446
1852	174,740
1853	178,284
1854	180,350
1855	211,141
1856	209,906
1857	149,234***
1858	147,608
1859	145,226
1860	146,152

*General condition of poor business.

**Forty-four-day suspension of trade on the Pennsylvania Canals.

***Flood and general depression. Union Canal enlarged.

(Compiled from *Annual Reports* of the Susquehanna and Tidewater Canal Company and Poor, *History of the Railroads and Canals of the United States,* I, 533.)

APPENDIX VII

Analysis of Tolls of the Susquehanna and Tidewater Canal Company

Year	Tolls Northward	Tolls Southward
1842		44,942
1843		50,153
1844		59,561
1845	25,822	72,502
1846	28,301	80,433
1847	33,380	96,517
1848	38,451	96,242
1849	43,172	108,085
1850	41,814	108,929
1851	36,834	119,329
1852	37,549	128,250
1853	41,581	127,199
1854	36,526	135,599

(Compiled from the *Annual Reports* of the Susquehanna and Tidewater Canal Company.)

APPENDIX VIII

Traffic on the Susquehanna and Tidewater Canal

Year	Grain bu.	Flour bbl.	Lumber sq. ft.	Timber cu. ft.
1845	983,260	90,127	41,949,162	72,889
1850	1,241,458	108,227	63,081,641	24,076
1855	633,230	20,981	108,369,045	587,196
1860	550,577	8,775	111,780,400	9,978

	Coal (tons)	Iron (tons)	Boats Cleared
1845	70,124	28,124	4461
1850	127,290	45,718	6169
1855	232,865	37,114	7859
1860	229,292	92,023	6157

(Meyer, ed., *History of Transportation before 1860,* Table 34, page 226, compiled from the *Annual Reports* of the Canal Company.)

APPENDIX IX

Merchandise Sent into the Interior via the Susquehanna and Tidewater Canal

Year	Lbs.
1845	17,623,816
1847	25,058,719
1849	29,701,790
1851	31,944,140
1853	31,735,494

(Compiled from the *Annual Reports* of the Company.)

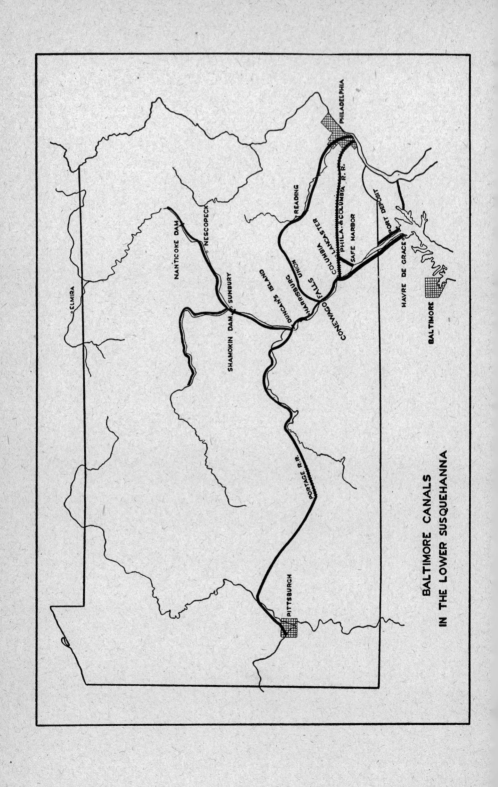

BALTIMORE CANALS
IN THE LOWER SUSQUEHANNA

CHAPTER IV

THE CANAL ACROSS THE ISTHMUS

Across the narrow isthmus about fourteen miles wide which separates the waters of the Delaware and Chesapeake Bays ran an important thoroughfare from early colonial days. Across this neck of land wagons and stages plied; from each shore, water craft carried passengers and cargoes to Philadelphia or to the towns of the Chesapeake Bay. This was the main route between the North and the South, but the road was unendurably rough. Transshipment charges and wagon-carriage rates were prohibitively high. In order to reduce this cost and remove the hazards of land transportation, early colonial surveyors talked about the possibility of constructing a canal across the isthmus. Before 1800 some work was done, but nothing of an extensive character was undertaken. The states through which the route passed found it difficult to agree on plans and costs. Baltimore and Philadelphia engaged in a brisk preliminary round in their continuous commercial struggle. Not until the "canal rage" spread the spirit of enterprise abroad did activity to promote this much needed waterway reawaken. By 1829 the canal was completed. Men and freight now passed across the isthmus in canal boats; a thirteen-mile canal brought Philadelphia into close contact with the Chesapeake Region. Trade from the Susquehanna River, which had formerly centered in Baltimore, now found its way in part to the Pennsylvania metropolis. Trade on the Chesapeake and Delaware Canal was brisk; the rivalry between Baltimore and Philadelphia became more intense. Each year the traffic which passed through the canal increased until about 1870, when railroad competition became too strong for the Chesapeake and Delaware Canal.[1]

As early as 1679-80 men who had their eyes on the future began to talk about the advantages of a waterway across the narrow strip of land which separates the waters of Delaware Bay and Chesapeake Bay. Near the heads of these two estuaries, the distance which separates them is very short. Two travellers in their *Journal of a Tour of Maryland*[2]

---

[1] In 1871, it was proposed that the Chesapeake and Delaware Canal should be made into a National Ship Canal. For years the Canal Company agitated for this improvement. In 1906, a special commission was appointed by Congress to go into the matter. Finally, in 1919, the old waterway was purchased by the Government for $2,500,000 and improved.

[2] Danker and Sluyter, *Journal of a Tour of Maryland*, quoted by Scharf, *History of Delaware*, I, 423; Scharf, *History of Maryland*, II, 523.

noted the short portage distance between the waters of the two bays and
suggested the value of a canal at such an important site:

"Upon this road the goods which go from the South (Delaware)
River to Maryland by land are carried, and also those which pass inland
from Maryland to the South River, because these two creeks,—namely
the Apoquemene and the Bohemia—one running up from Maryland and
the other from the Delaware River, as the English call the South River,
come to an end close to each other, although they are not navigable so
far; but are navigable for eight miles,—that is, two Dutch miles, of fifteen
to a degree. When the Dutch governed the country the distance was
less,—namely, six miles. The digging of a canal through was then talked
of, the land being so low, which would have afforded great convenience
for trade on the South River, seeing that they would have come from
Maryland to buy all they had need of, and would have been able to transport their tobacco more easily to that river than to the great Bay of
Virginia, as they would now have to do for a large part of Maryland.
Besides, the cheap market of the Hollanders in the South River would
have drawn more trade; and if the people of Maryland had goods to ship
on their own account they would do it sooner and more readily—as well
as more conveniently—in the South River than in the great bay, and
therefore would have chosen this route, the more so because so many of
their goods, perhaps, would, for various reasons, be shipped to Holland
as to England. But as this is a subject of greater importance than it
seems upon the first view, it is well to consider whether it should not be
brought to the attention of higher authorities than particular Governors.
What is now done by land, in carts, might then be done by water for a
distance of more than six hundred miles."

The country was not prepared to dig canals at this early date; the idea
had to slumber almost one hundred years before the merits of a water
communication were again called to the attention of the people.

About 1765, or a few years later, the subject was taken up by Thomas
Gilpin, who had lived in the vicinity of the proposed canal and knew its
potential importance. On moving to Philadelphia, he devoted his time
to inducing merchants and citizens of the commercial center of the
province of Pennsylvania to support a canal project. Assisted by a few
friends, this sanguine enthusiast made careful surveys, explorations, and
estimates of different routes for a canal between the Chesapeake and
Delaware Bays.[3] In 1769 Gilpin laid his findings before a meeting of
merchants and traders of Philadelphia, who were interested in improving the trade of the Province, and also before the American Philosophical

---

[3] Simpson, *Eminent Philadelphians*, 391-3, gives a brief sketch of Thomas Gilpin;
Joshua Gilpin, *A Memoir of the Rise, Progress and Present State of the Chesa-
peake and Delaware Canal, Accompanied with Original Documents and Maps*, 3;
Scharf, *History of Delaware*, I, 423; Scharf, *History of Maryland*, II, 523.

Society, which was the natural repository of all scientific ideas of the day.[4]

The Society was interested; it appointed a committee "to View the ground and consider in what manner a water communication might be best opened between the provinces of Maryland and Pennsylvania, and particularly by what means the large and increasing number of frontier settlers, especially those of the Susquehanna and its branches, might be enabled to bring their produce to market at the cheapest rate, whether by land or water."[5] To enable surveys to be made, the merchants of Philadelphia took up a subscription of £200. When the results of the committee were made known, they were rejected by the Society partly because of the great expense involved and partly because the proposed route was too far south to be of importance to Philadelphia.[6]

A second committee was then appointed with more specific instructions. The committeemen surveyed routes for a canal and reported the feasibility of constructing a waterway large enough for barge navigation between the two bays. They then surveyed the lower Susquehanna River and the country contiguous to it and reported that the river could easily be made navigable with only a small expense. They informed their fellow-citizens of Philadelphia, "that the river Susquehanna is the natural channel through which the produce of three-fourths of the province must in time be conveyed to market for export, and through which a great part of the back inhabitants will be supplied with foreign goods."[7] So important did they deem the trade of the Susquehanna Valley that they suggested a road be constructed from Peach Bottom, Pennsylvania, on the river to tidewater at Christiana Creek, which flows into the Delaware River, to serve Philadelphia and the interior until the water route could be constructed. This report of the importance of the Susquehanna Valley met with enthusiasm in Philadelphia, but the commencement of war with Great Britain was absorbing the attention of the people, and no constructive action was taken.

Immediately after Yorktown, the Chesapeake and Delaware Canal scheme was revived; the country was aware, as a result of the war, of pressing needs for better communication and transportation. Pennsyl-

---

[4] Gilpin, *op. cit.*, 3; Armroyd, *A Connected View of the Whole Internal Navigation of the United States*, 80.

[5] American Philosophical Society, *Transactions*, I, 357.

[6] *Ibid.*, 357-9.

[7] *Ibid.*, 362; Gilpin, *op. cit.*, 4-6, Appendix, 11-13.

vania took the lead in agitating for a canal,[8] but could not interest Maryland or Delaware in the subject. However, the importance of the canal was enough to keep the idea before the people for a number of years. In 1793, Philadelphia's Society for Promoting the Improvements of Roads and Inland Navigation appointed a committee to investigate conditions along the Susquehanna River and the possibility of constructing a canal across the isthmus between the Delaware and Chesapeake Bays.[9] Failing to get any cooperation from her neighbors, Pennsylvania decided to act alone and organized a company to make a route to the Susquehanna River wholly within her own borders.[10] But this organization failed to accomplish its purpose and passed into bankruptcy by 1795.

Four years later, Pennsylvania again endeavored to interest Delaware and Maryland in chartering a corporation to construct a canal. Favorable resolutions were finally passed by the Legislatures of these two states,[11] although citizens of Baltimore strenuously objected to Maryland's support of a project which would draw the trade of the Chesapeake Bay and the Susquehanna River from their city to Philadelphia. One well-wisher of this vigorous, young Maryland commercial center wrote strongly against the canal and, in so doing, aired the opinion of many Baltimore citizens. He maintained:

". . . In sound policy the state should rather adopt some wholesome provisions to retain the exportation of these important articles (wheat and flour) from her own seaports, than assist in forming a highway for

---

[8] *Pennsylvania Archives,* Fourth Series, IV, 36; Post-Revolutionary Papers, XXII, 55, 56. Two letters are included in this volume of papers; one from the Governor of Pennsylvania to the Governor of Maryland dated November 25, 1785, asking his attention to the canal, and the second, dated the same year, to the Governor of Delaware asking his support for the project.

[9] William Irvine Papers, XI, 71. The entry for February 11, 1793, includes extracts from the minutes of the society. Other mention is found on pages 72 and 90; Letter Book of the Secretary of the Commonwealth, December 24, 1790; March 3, 1794, III, Letter from Thomas Mifflin to Nathaniel Rambsey, January 31, 1793.

[10] Gilpin, *op. cit.,* 4-L.

[11] *A Collection of Laws relative to the Chesapeake and Delaware Canal,* 1-15, 19-33.

1st. Laws of Maryland. Act passed 7 December 1799, Recorded Lib. I. G. No. 3. fol. 254. Maryland agreed to the canal providing that Pennsylvania declared "the river Susquehanna to be a highway and authorizing individuals or bodies corporate to remove obstructions therein at a period not exceeding three years from the first day of March eighteen hundred."

2nd. Laws of Delaware. Act passed 29 January 1801, chapter Seventy-eight, State Laws, Vol. III, 170.

their safe passage into Delaware. From the great superiority of situation and expense of portage across the isthmus between the Chesapeake and Delaware Bays, Baltimore, though much inferior to Philadelphia in wealth and population, hath of late commenced a degree of rivalship with that city. Remove the barrier, all competition is immediately terminated. She at once sinks into the station of an inferior or secondary market, and her decline will be followed by the loss of those advantages which Maryland at present enjoys from the influence of an extensive, lucrative, and improving commerce."

*   *   *   *   *   *

". . . I consider that Philadelphia and Baltimore alone are deeply interested in the issue of this business, and that, if effected, it will, by the address and superior management of an enterprising and politic state, conduct the Chesapeake trade into Delaware Bay, and consequently terminate in the destruction of Baltimore as an independent and valuable market. What then must be the determination of a Marylander, if this position be made equally apparent to his mind? He will, without hesitation, condemn the project that so materially threatens the welfare of the community in which he lives."[12]

Philadelphia was old; Baltimore was inexperienced and young. Philadelphia had a large supply of wealth; Baltimore lacked capital. The friend of the Maryland metropolis in his pamphlet ascertained that the difference in banking capital was more than ten to one in favor of Philadelphia. The superiority of her individuals' wealth was almost as great. Since this was the case, the author claimed, no better system could be devised by Philadelphia for giving activity to her capital than the canal proposal. The Chesapeake and Delaware Canal would be a subscription project; Philadelphia would buy most of the shares. The canal organization would be dependent on the city and the policy followed by the canal would be always favorable to the Pennsylvania metropolis. Emphatically the friend of Baltimore continued:

"The constitution of such a body . . . is a most formidable enemy to every commercial town on Chesapeake Bay. No scheme which can possibly be suggested . . . will escape their inquisitive minds; that spirit which for ever inclines one town to swallow up others, will more decidedly be brought into action by the address and management of such a body."

The author claimed that the canal would not only be a threat to Baltimore's present trade, but it "will entirely suppress every expectation of advantage from opening the Susquehanna." This river, the pamphleteer prophesied, bore, in the future, untold wealth for Baltimore. The time would soon arrive when all obstructions to navigation would be removed. Therefore, it was essential for the Maryland metropolis to keep this

---

[12] *Reflections on the Proposition to communicate by a Navigable Canal the waters of Chesapeake with those of Delaware Bay, addressed to the Citizens of Maryland,* 14.

trade for herself. If a Chesapeake and Delaware Canal were built, the writer insisted, Philadelphia or the canal authorities would pay bounties on produce from the Susquehanna Valley and reduce tolls on these goods in order to thwart Baltimore. Baltimore grew because she was protected behind the isthmus; ability and wealth must be acquired before she could rival Philadelphia on equal ground. Until the Susquehanna trade was firmly fixed, he claimed that a canal toward Philadelphia should not be tolerated. Furthermore, he maintained that Baltimore could not afford to allow a canal to be dug until the Susquehanna River had been opened to trade for a period of at least forty years.[13]

Notwithstanding the plea of the ardent friend of Baltimore, Maryland gave her support for a canal. Pennsylvania, Delaware, and Maryland finally agreed to terms and a company was incorporated to build the the canal.[14] Subscription books were opened in 1802 and a year later sufficient funds had been subscribed to permit the organization of the company.[15] Engineers were employed, surveys were made, and work was begun in May 1804. Digging was confined to a large feeder and was pursued rather vigorously until 1805 when a lack of funds compelled the company to discontinue work. The stockholders became alarmed; many refused to pay their subscriptions.[16] One hundred thousand dollars had been spent, yet no work had been done on the main channel. One-half of the shares were forfeited after the first payment of five dollars. The Philadelphia stock holders were, on the whole, the most faithful of the subscribers. Although less than half of the stock was held in Pennsylvania, chiefly in Philadelphia, more than three-quarters of the amount

---

[13] *Ibid.*, 40.

[14] *A Collection of Laws relative to the Chesapeake and Delaware Canal:*
Pa. Session Laws, 1799, April 11, chap. ccxxii, 478-9.
Md. Laws (ed. Kilty), 1799, Dec. 7, chap. xvi.
Del. Session Laws, 1801, Jan. 29, chap. xxxviii, 170-88.

[15] *Pennsylvania Archives,* Fourth Series, IV, 513. Governor Thomas McKean's address to the Assembly, February 16, 1803, mentioned that subscriptions to the stock of the Chesapeake and Delaware Canal Company were not taken as fast as expected. He requested the legislature to allow the company to keep their books open for a longer time. When the company was finally organized in May, 1803, only $400,000 of the authorized $520,000 capital stock had been taken. This impression differs somewhat from the one given by McMaster, *op. cit.,* III, 471, who says, "The scheme seemed so likely to be profitable that no difficulty was found in getting subscribers, and four hundred thousand dollars of capital stock were quickly taken."

[16] Gilpin, *op. cit.,* 33-4; McMaster, *op. cit.,* III, 471; Melish, *Travels in the United States,* 180. The traveller Melish seemed to believe that it was a good thing that the canal had failed. Although he had "never observed a finer situation for a canal," he believed the canal planned was too small and wished for the revival of work on a sloop navigation canal and not on a small ditch.

paid to the company for stock was paid by the holders from that state.[17]
Baltimore was not guilty of failure to meet its obligations, for its citizens
had not purchased a single share of the canal stock.

Under these circumstances there remained no source of financial aid,
except the states which had shown some interest in the project. Petitions
of the most explanatory nature, accompanied by statements, estimates,
calculations, maps, and everything that could throw light on the subject,
were constantly forwarded to Delaware, Pennsylvania, and Maryland
officials. Pennsylvania was made the special center of this propaganda.
A commission from the canal board visited the capital to point out the
benefits of their project to the State; they especially stressed the importance of this improvement in relation to the Susquehanna Valley trade.
A memorial to the State Legislature further stressed the importance of
the canal as an outlet for the resources of all central Pennsylvania. It
claimed that all the natural advantages Pennsylvania had enjoyed were
lost "for want of communications by means of which the produce of the
back country can be brought to market."[18]

The state governments were not interested. Unable to get anything
more than well-wishing resolutions from them, the directors of the canal
company turned in distress to the Federal Government. In a memorial
to Congress, they excused their request on the plea that this canal was a
matter of national, not merely local, importance. The Chesapeake and
Delaware Canal was to be the beginning of a great system of internal
improvements which would be a great benefit to coastal shipping. The
economic value of the canal was set forth with the aid of many statistics.
Each bay region, it was shown, produced something that the other
needed, but the enormous cost of land transportation and the great distance by water prevented the development of these commodities. The
memorial then stated that from the head of Chesapeake Bay to Philadelphia was estimated to be a 500-mile sea journey which took at least one

---

[17] Gilpin, *op. cit.,* 44-45.
  The original subscriptions were held:
  In Pennsylvania (chiefly Philadelphia) 824
  Delaware (chiefly Wilmington) 712
  Maryland (none in Baltimore) 256
                                                        _____
                                                         1,792
Although Philadelphia held less than half of the stock, the payment of sub-
scriptions is different. The sums received:
  Pennsylvania paid about $73,400
  Maryland paid about 18,300
  Delaware paid about 11,300
[18] *Memorial of the Directors of the Chesapeake and Delaware Canal Company to
the Legislature of Pennsylvania,* 1805.

week's time. The consequence was that coal from Liverpool was cheaper than Richmond coal on the Philadelphia market. The amount paid to freight a ton of goods from Europe was estimated to be about the same charged to haul a ton of goods nine miles over the inland roads of the United States. Since a canal across the isthmus would cause insurance rates to fall, eliminate the dangers of the land trip, reduce freight rates, and cause interstate commerce to become of paramount importance, the directors claimed all aid possible should be given their project.[19]

The petition found friends in Congress, but it was reported that the treasury did not "admit of any pecuniary assistance being granted."[20] After dealing with the Chesapeake and Delaware proposition periodically during the next few years, Congress finally asked the Secretary of the Treasury to investigate thoroughly the question of internal improvements as a whole. In his famous report, Secretary Gallatin recommended that aid be given to the Chesapeake and Delaware Company since it was revealed that the annual carriage across the peninsula amounted to 42,000 tons and a great number of passengers.[21] Bills for this purpose were lost in both the House of Representatives and the Senate in 1810; two years later a committee on canals lamented that foreign affairs made contribution toward the construction of the Chesapeake and Delaware Canal impossible.

Governor Snyder of Pennsylvania kept the movement awake in his State when, in 1813, he called on the Legislature to act on the Chesapeake and Delaware petitions. The lawmakers replied immediately with the law of March 25, 1813, authorizing the Governor to subscribe 375 shares of stock in the canal company if the United States Government would take 750 shares, Maryland 250 shares, and Delaware 100 shares.[22] A new memorial was almost immediately presented to the National Government. The committee to which the memorial was referred noticed the coastwise importance of the canal, the value of opening the coal and plaster of the Susquehanna Valley for market, and the need for a shorter, safer, and cheaper communication between the Delaware and Chesapeake Bays. They further reported:

"Your committee are informed that at this time the government is compelled to convey by land in the winter season, over the portage from the Chesapeake to the Delaware (a road rendered almost impassable for

---

[19] *Ibid.* This memorial may be found in *American State Papers,* Miscellaneous, I, 455.

[20] *Ibid.,* I, 452. Report communicated to the House on March 5, 1806, 1st session; I, 454, Report communicated to the Senate, March 21, 1806.

[21] Gallatin, *Report on Public Roads and Canals,* 15.

[22] *A Collection of Laws relative to the Chesapeake and Delaware Canal Company,* 47-8.

land carriage) the most bulky pieces of timber for the ship of the line building at Philadelphia, and that the expense of the conveyance over this short distance is enormous. . . ."[23]

Despite recommendations, the bill was tabled and forgotten.

Immediately after the close of the War of 1812, friends of the canal project again called on Congress for financial assistance. The petitioners maintained that neither their canal nor any similar work would succeed in the United States "unless the Government would patronize and assist the efforts of individuals until at least one work was carried into successful operation."[24] This plea, like all former ones, fell on deaf ears; the project slumbered on. Only true devotion to the plan enabled the directors of the canal company to keep alive their constitutional existence through these years when the country was too young to support large incorporate schemes and when the Federal Government was unwilling to befriend any internal improvement project.

After the panic of 1819 withdrew its dark clouds from the financial centers of the East, canal enthusiasts again turned to the Chesapeake and Delaware connection. New York was going ahead with her improvements; the Schuylkill River was being improved with the hope of an increased trade; Baltimore was casting anxious eyes up the Susquehanna River. Eminent Philadelphians took up the Chesapeake and Delaware project with renewed vigor. The Irish editor, Mathew Carey, and the earnest friend of internal improvements, Joshua Gilpin, became outstanding enthusiasts for the canal. In September 1821, it was publicly announced that the American Philosophical Society had determined to sponsor construction.[25] Leading Philadelphia newspapers vigorously indorsed the canal, stressing the fact that "Philadelphia must use her means of mind and money, to restore her prosperity, and to prevent its further decline."[26]

"An Old Observer", writing for a Philadelphia newspaper saw the true situation of Philadelphia's declining commerce and tried to awaken the commercial interests of the Pennsylvania metropolis. He claimed that their State rated only on a par with states of one-third the natural resources. Vigorously he protested against Pennsylvania's lethargy:

"Pennsylvania resembles a huge giant reclining on her ponderous limbs in besotted security. She seems as if her former prosperity and eminence, had satiated her; and that in the sullenness of satiety, she had

---

[23] *Niles' Weekly Register*, V, 206-8; *American State Papers, Miscellaneous*, II, 286. It was estimated that the cost of "wagonage" across the isthmus during one year of the War of 1812 amounted to not less than $414,000.

[24] *American State Papers, Miscellaneous*, II, 438.

[25] *Niles' Weekly Register*, XXVII, 64; *The Aurora*, September 13, 1821.

[26] *The Aurora*, September 15, 1821.

grown tired of her good fortune, and anticipated the miserable and destructive policy which has become the infatuation of her statesmen, and determined to be *let alone."*

The correspondent saw a growing competitor of his city in Baltimore. The Maryland commercial center was pursuing a course which was authorized by wisdom and planning; he believed that her people were interested in promoting prosperity. In good Philadelphia style, the writer suggested that his fellow citizens emulate the policy of the Marylanders. He advocated that the Susquehanna River should be opened at once "to the highest possible capacity of both its branches" so that produce could be sent southward to Chesapeake Bay. He then further suggested that *"the OPENING OF A SPACIOUS CANAL from the BAY of CHESAPEAKE, to the river DELAWARE,* be pursued to completion —and let the rival cities enter into competition for their share in the profits of our country."[27]

Public zeal was finally aroused in the revived Chesapeake and Delaware Canal project. In order to acquaint the people with the facts of the canal, Joshua Gilpin published a pamphlet in 1821, in which he included the past history of the project and some interesting material which was the result of his father's (Thomas Gilpin's) work.[28] The interest displayed by Philadelphia at this time Gilpin observed as the first "favorable circumstance that has occurred since the operations on the canal began." He insisted that this plan be nourished because Philadelphia needed the canal as soon as possible.

In the early part of 1822, the company was officially revived and a new board of directors elected. Realizing that another failure would definitely kill any hope for a canal, the promoters planned to advance with caution. New York canal experts were interviewed; the books of the company were moved to Philadelphia; new surveys were made; a permanent engineer, Benjamin Wright, was employed. The cost was now estimated at $1,339,159, which was more than twice the amount of the former guesses.[29]

Again an appeal was sent out to the three states through which the canal was to pass; Pennsylvania, as usual, was the chief hope the company had for gaining financial aid. The importance of the Susquehanna Valley trade, which the proposed canal hoped to tap, was again revealed to men who might have forgotten earlier memorials. Although Pennsylvania was planning her long system of State Works, the State officials felt that another avenue to the interior would be welcomed. Therefore,

---

[27] *Ibid.,* September 20, 1821.

[28] Gilpin, *A Memoir of the Rise, Progress, and Present State of the Chesapeake and Delaware Canal . . .*

[29] The Chesapeake and Delaware Canal Company, *Annual Report,* 1824.

the Legislature subscribed $100,000 to the Chesapeake and Delaware project while Maryland soon took $50,000 worth of stock, Delaware $25,000, and the Federal Government $300,000. Leading Philadelphians conducted vigorous campaigns in order to get support from that city. Their efforts, however, did not stimulate the public until 1823, when a great drive was conducted to complete the subscription list.[30] In April of that year, it was reported that citizens of Philadelphia had taken $230,000 worth of stock in the canal company.[31] The next year, the Chesapeake and Delaware Canal Company claimed that they had $1,000,-000 with which to begin work.

Philadelphia realized, at this time, that the most important object of the canal was to secure the trade of the Susquehanna Valley. In 1822, it was maintained that the river had forced into the lap of Baltimore goods worth $1,168,944, which was nearly all from Pennsylvania.[32] The Union Canal, which was being constructed between the Schuylkill and Susquehanna Rivers, it was claimed, would not be capable of handling all the growing business of the interior of Pennsylvania. The lumber and wood business alone required a canal from the Chesapeake to the Delaware, said the dealers in these commodities. The demand for wood became very important with the advent of the steamboat. The price on the Delaware was from $3.75 to $4.00 a cord, while on the Chesapeake it sold for about $2.12.[33]

Philadelphia also was agreeable to the construction of a canal along the lower Susquehanna River, although no one believed that the river trade would follow a toll canal. However, the Pennsylvania city was not enthusiastic about Baltimore's proposed canal to the Conewago Falls. Philadelphia dreaded the possible consequences of a continuous canal

---

[30] Some of the leading Philadelphians interested in the canal were Samuel Breck, Mathew Carey, Thomas P. Cope, J. C. Fisher, Paul Breck, Jr., Stephen Girard, William Meredith, Samuel Archer, William Lehman, Simon Gratz, and Joshua Gilpin. Carey, in a letter published for a few friends and not intended for the newspapers, gives an account of the work he did in the campaign for subscriptions. Not the least bit reticent, he writes that he devoted all his time to the movement and was its true leader. Carey was slated to be one of the directors of the company, but at the last minute someone removed his name from the ballot. This, of course, irritated the fiery Irishman, and the letter was written to express his ire. Carey, Letter on the Chesapeake and Delaware Canal.

[31] The York Recorder, April 29, 1823; "A Citizen of Philadelphia," Views Respecting the Chesapeake and Delaware Canal, 1. "The Citizen" claimed that the citizens of Philadelphia were almost the exclusive owners of the canal and had confided their interests in a board of commissioners chosen, with but one exception, from among themselves.

[32] The Aurora, October 12, 1822.

[33] Niles' Weekly Register, XXXV, 149.

from the mouth of the Susquehanna River to Baltimore. These facts made the merchant princes of the Delaware River port work for the rapid completion of their canal; they were extremely anxious that their route should be the best possible so that Baltimore could be conquered and the golden flow of trade from the Susquehanna Valley diverted to the Delaware.

Chief Engineer Wright did not complete his duties on the Erie Canal in time to accept the offer of the Chesapeake and Delaware Canal Company, and John Randel, Jr. was appointed in his place. The new engineer recommended a change in the route of the canal which was adopted; this called for the use of a southern route across the isthmus and was disliked by many friends of the project because it moved the Delaware terminal far from Philadelphia.[34] Engineer Randel soon got into other arguments with the canal officials and work was held up by the various disputes.

Great construction difficulties were also encountered. The first section of the channel was excavated through soft mud and loam which would fill up the ditch almost as fast as it was dug away. Then the route passed through a peat bog, material which could not be used for banks; earth transported to this section sank into the peat great distances before a solid foundation was reached. In another part of the line, clay and quicksand were found. However, the main obstacle encountered in the construction was the high ground and not the low marshlands. Down the center of the peninsula ran a low ridge, through which the company was forced to dig. The cut was more than a mile long, mostly through solid rock. It was ninety feet deep at its deepest point. The cut was regarded in its day as "one of the greatest works of human skill and ingenuity in the world." Not only was excavation tedious but also very expensive; landslides made construction hazardous and costly. With each landslide and every added expense, a cry went up from the enemies of the canal who were not satisfied with its location.[35]

The eastern section of the canal was finished in 1828. In the report for that year the President and Directors announced that even with only part of the canal open such was the preference given to Philadelphia's market "that large quantities (of produce) are shipped from Port Deposit to our metropolis, by the tedious and hazardous route of the Chesapeake and Delaware Bays, a distance of not less than six hundred

---

[34] "A Citizen of Philadelphia," *op. cit.,* 17.

[35] Harlow, *op. cit.,* 226, quotes the *Wilmington Gazette* which wrote in 1826, ". . . the canal will never be completed over the present route. . . ." However, public confidence was expressed in the fact that lots in Delaware City, a town laid out at the eastern terminal of the canal, brought $4,356 per acre in 1826. Scharf, *History of Delaware,* I, 423-4.

miles including a sea voyage."[36] Gun salutes, celebrating, and speech-making on October 17, 1829, marked the formal opening of the canal for which Philadelphia had waited so many years.[37]

The 13⅝-mile canal extended from Delaware City, forty-six miles below Philadelphia on Delaware Bay, to Chesapeake City on Back Creek, a navigable branch of the Elk River, in Maryland. The channel was 66 feet wide on the surface and ten feet deep; its locks were capable of passing the class of vessels generally used in bay and coasting trade. Construction costs were much more than had been estimated, amounting to $2,201,864 or 62% more than expected.[38]

From the time the canal opened in 1829 until ice closed the channel late in January 1830, 798 vessels had passed through the canal paying $8,500 toll. By February 23, 1830, the canal was again navigable and from that date until the first day of June, 1834, boats paid $18,613 toll.[39] Philadelphia newspapers and commercial journals kept a keen eye on the canal and reported weekly on the number of vessels and the amount of produce which passed through its locks. It was maintained that quite a considerable portion of the Susquehanna Valley trade was finding its way "to its legitimate market." From the accounts of the early activity of the canal, it can be seen that many of the boats cleared westward without cargo and that most of the produce carried was eastbound.[40] Lumber, timber, flour, wheat, whiskey, iron, oysters, fish, and merchandise were the important items on the bills of lading which Philadelphia business men received and gave out.[41] Cargoes arrived in Philadelphia from all parts of central Pennsylvania. Lycoming on the West Branch, Wilkes-Barre on the North Branch, and Mifflintown on the Juniata

---

[36] The Chesapeake and Delaware Canal Company, *Annual Report*, 1828.

[37] *Niles' Weekly Register*, XXXVII, 131; Hazard, *The Pennsylvania Register*, V, 396; Scharf, *History of Delaware*, I, 424. Many visitors witnessed the opening. Two military companies were present from Philadelphia; a United States schooner fired the salute; President Jackson was invited but was forced to send regrets; banker Biddle gave another of his appropriate internal improvement addresses.

[38] Chesapeake and Delaware Canal Company, *Annual Report*, 1830. The officials reported that the expenses were not a matter of surprise, but the fact that the canal was completed amid all the difficulties of public opinion, town rivalries, retarding mandates and injunctions, and natural obstacles was more surprising.

[39] *Ibid.*

[40] *Poulson's Daily Advertiser*, April 9 and March 25, 1830. On April 7, 1830, it was reported that twenty-two boats passed the Maryland bridge on the canal of which number nineteen were eastbound. It was asserted that there was a great deal of produce at Port Deposit, but that there were comparatively few boats to transport these goods and crops to Philadelphia.

[41] A noticeable amount of the wheat sent through the canal went to the famous Brandywine flour mills.

River traded with the Pennsylvania metropolis by way of the Susquehanna River, Chesapeake Bay, the Chesapeake and Delaware Canal, Delaware Bay and the Delaware River. Lancaster, via her Conestoga Navigation, sent much of her Philadelphia trade by the all-water route rather than by the turnpike.[42] Business between Port Deposit, at the mouth of the Susquehanna River, and Philadelphia was deemed brisk enough to warrant the establishment of a packet line early in 1830.[43]

In that same year, friends of the railroad which was being projected from Baltimore to York, Pennsylvania, sent a questionnaire to several of the large Baltimore commercial houses engaged in the Susquehanna trade to learn the effect of the Chesapeake and Delaware Canal on this business. The railroad men were interested in getting figures and statistics which they could use as arguments to support the need of their project to the Baltimore commercial people.[44] Replies revealed that some of the houses were seriously beginning to feel the result of the diverting influence of the Chesapeake and Delaware Canal although it had been open only a short time. Finley and Mosher, a Baltimore firm, reported that they feared the operation of the canal on the Susquehanna trade "will be disastrous to the interests of the city." Baltimore, they asserted, had been the leading flour center on the Atlantic seaboard but Philadelphia would soon usurp all the advantages that the Maryland city had so long enjoyed.[45] John Boggs & Company agreed with their fellow merchants that the canal would tend to divert possibly one-half of the wheat and flour business from Baltimore although they believed that the whiskey trade of Baltimore was secure.[46] A third firm, Wilmer and Palmer, lamented that the canal had ruined the Baltimore wheat trade with the flour mills of the Brandywine region. Prior to the opening of the Chesapeake and Delaware Canal, Baltimore had done a gainful business with the Brandywine millers by the sea route. However, each mill now owned its own sloops in which they collected wheat at Port Deposit and sold their flour to the Philadelphia market.[47]

The importance of the Susquehanna River trade to the canal across the Delaware peninsula can also be seen from the reports of the officials of the canal company. Three times within the first fifteen years of the canal's existence, it was reported that revenues on the Chesapeake and Delaware Canal had fallen because of navigation conditions on the river.

---

[42] *Niles' Weekly Register*, XXXVIII, 140; *Poulson's Daily Advertiser*, March 29, April 16, 19, 23, May 6 and 26, 1830.

[43] Hazard, *The Pennsylvania Register*, V, 240.

[44] *Address to the Mayor and City Council of Baltimore on the Trade of the Susquehanna and the Railroad to the River*, 20-23.

[45] *Ibid.*, 20-21.

[46] *Ibid.*, 23.

[47] *Ibid.*, 22.

In 1832, the river freshet occurred earlier than usual and was followed by a very dry summer. Rivermen, who were not prepared to descend on the early flood, were unable to take their produce to market at a later date. The following year, the river was not in good navigable condition and the canal officials regretted a slump in the Susquehanna Valley business. Again, ten years later, revenues of the canal company fell off because the Susquehanna season was late.[48]

The history of the first ten years of the canal company was very erratic. Tolls rose from about $25,000 to some $60,000 during the second year; the Chesapeake and Delaware Canal envisaged a future almost as sanguine as its early promoters had painted. But after 1830 no increase of any noticeable amount was reported until 1844.[49] Moreover, the financial condition of the company was unsound. A quarter-million-dollar law suit was lost by the canal company which disrupted all the financial plans and budgets of the organization. Engineer Randel had sued the company for relieving him of his contract to build the canal and secured the court's verdict. A controversy arising between the two factions caused each to attempt to collect tolls on the canal. Business was disrupted; revenues collected by the company fell to $35,572 in 1836. Only after a ten-year struggle which went through the Supreme Court was a reconciliation possible. Then, too, in 1832, a railroad, The New Castle and Frenchtown, was built parallel to the canal and robbed it of most of its passengers and a small portion of the light freight.[50]

The prospect of the completion of the Susquehanna and Tidewater Canal, however, kept alive the spirit of the Chesapeake and Delaware company during the years of general depression and local troubles. Formerly, Philadelphia did not want a canal along the lower Susquehanna which would assist Baltimore to reach the Pennsylvania hinterland. But now, the Pennsylvania metropolis also wanted a water connection with the Susquehanna Valley. Philadelphia wished to convey bulky country goods from this area to her wharves; she wanted a returning trade with central Pennsylvania, since the Chesapeake and Delaware company reported that as many as 1,478 canal boats were dispatched westward without cargoes in one year.[51]

In 1840, the Susquehanna and Tidewater was completed and Philadelphia citizens and business men almost immediately began a campaign

---

[48] The Chesapeake and Delaware Canal Company, *Annual Report*, 1832, 1833, and 1843.

[49] See Appendix, XI, 98.

[50] The Chesapeake and Delaware Canal Company, *Annual Report*, 1832. This line was later consolidated into the Baltimore, Wilmington, and Philadelphia Railroad. On the whole, the latter railroad did little freight service in its early years and has not been included in this study.

[51] Chesapeake and Delaware Canal Company, *Annual Report*, 1837.

to try to bring the bulk of the produce forwarded by this route to Havre de Grace directly to their city. It was proposed that a Steam Tow Boat Company be organized to tow canal boats through the bay to the canal so as to avoid transshipment. Committees were appointed at once; the Chesapeake and Delaware Canal Company was asked to cooperate in the undertaking.[52] A plea was sent out for all citizens of Philadelphia to examine the importance of this proposed company; it was considered absolutely necessary to make the cost of transportation from Havre de Grace to Philadelphia cheaper, or at least just as cheap, as from the former canal and river center to Baltimore.

In March, 1841, a towing company, composed mostly of members of the Philadelphia Board of Trade, was incorporated.[53] The new organization was successful from the beginning; it was claimed that much trade which formerly went to Baltimore was now towed to Philadelphia. In order to encourage this trade, the Chesapeake and Delaware Canal Company reduced tolls on most articles which passed through their channel to and from Havre de Grace.[54] The canal company was well pleased with the newly-organized towing company and reported that, despite their reductions, the tolls of the company had increased. The Philadelphia towing service was reported to be economical, safe, and convenient; the officials of the organization reported in 1841 that 459 boats were towed from Havre de Grace to Philadelphia and 502 from the latter city to the town at the mouth of the Susquehanna River.[55]

Between 1830 and 1860 the Susquehanna traffic furnished between one-quarter and one-half of the revenue of the Chesapeake and Delaware Canal Company. This was equal to the trade with the Chesapeake Bay centers. In 1850 timber from the Susquehanna River alone netted $19,443 in tolls while other produce forwarded from the river paid $7,197.[56]

[52] Hazard, *The United States Register*, IV, 16.

[53] *Ibid.*, VI, 59; *Niles' Weekly Register*, LXI, 352.

[54] Chesapeake and Delaware Canal Company, *Annual Report*, 1841.

[55] Hazard, *The United States Register*, VI, 75-6, reprints the report of the President and Directors of the Philadelphia and Havre-de-Grace Steam Tow Boat Company.

[56] Meyer, ed., *op. cit.*, 211:

TOLLS ON THE CHESAPEAKE AND DELAWARE CANAL

Year	To and from Susq. Tide. Canal	Susquehanna River To and from Port Deposit	Timber from the river
1840	858.81	10,769.72	7,138.83
1845	29,499.04	6,561.12	11,240.75
1850	63,041.04	7,196.63	19,443.34
1855	61,740.41	4,558.93	28,834.02
1860	38,519.15	2,048.77	32,523.97

In spite of these favorable reports, the amount of goods shipped over the Chesapeake and Delaware Canal was not enough to pay large receipts. Even after the opening of the Susquehanna and Tidewater Canal, revenues did not rise over the $100,000 mark until 1846. Not until fifteen years after its opening did the canal earn the interest on its debts; in 1847 the amount overdue reached the sum of $796,592.[57] In that year the bondholders agreed to convert all arrears into certificates due in twenty years. One issue of bonds matured in 1856, and for the purpose of funding these and consolidating all the debts of the company, the canal and property of the company was mortgaged as security for a new issue of bonds amounting to $2,800,000.[58] From 1847, when the tolls collected rose to more than $167,000, to 1860, the accrued interests were regularly paid and the financial status of the canal company became more secure.

After many defeats, a canal had been completed connecting the waters of the Chesapeake and Delaware Bays in 1829. The isthmus behind which Baltimore had been able to govern the descending trade of the Susquehanna River had been broken through. Philadelphia immediately had begun to divert trade from central Pennsylvania—especially wheat, flour, and lumber—from the Maryland port. The opening of a canal along the lower course of the Susquehanna River increased the amount of trade which the two cities had hoped to win. The revenues of the Chesapeake and Delaware Canal Company rose steadily after this date; at times almost one-half of the tolls received were paid for the passage of goods from the Susquehanna Region. Thus the Pennsylvania metropolis was able to regain much of the trade of the Pennsylvania hinterland after it had floated southward into Maryland and the vicinity of Baltimore.

---

[57] Poor, *History of Railroads and Canals of the United States,* I, 569.

[58] *Ibid.,* I, 569. All the different classes of indebtedness were converted into the new issue with the exception of $72,056.

APPENDIX X

Table of the Tolls and Tonnage of the Chesapeake and Delaware Canal, 1830-1860

Year ending June 1	Tolls received	Total tonnage
1830	24,658	......
1831	61,223	......
1832	63,073	......
1833*	61,160	......
1834**	54,092	......
1835***	47,511	......
1836****	35,572	.....
1837	56,482	......
1838	67,495	131,760
1839	67,518	120,260
1840	54,113	112,430
1841	69,415	125,980
1842	78,008	139,520
1843*****	66,018	127,200
1844	98,014	188,410
1845	97,559	195,040
1846	101,208	291,380
1847	167,510	341,580
1848	186,285	338,800
1849	173,030	351,550
1850	198,364	361,640
1851	215,889	389,440
1852******	190,141	411,340
1853	246,283	477,630
1854	246,695	534,080
1855	225,224	536,970
1856	225,483	568,680
1857	229,081	616,170
1858	207,006	563,510
1859	202,350	496,100
1860	216,256	623,150

* Poor Susquehanna River navigation.
** Interrupted river navigation and law suit.
*** Lack of water and court trouble.
**** The Randel trouble.
***** Susquehanna season late.
****** Baltimore and Ohio Railroad.

(Poor, *op. cit.*, I, 570, checked with *Annual Reports* of the Chesapeake and Delaware Canal Company.)

APPENDIX XI

Analysis of the Chesapeake and Delaware Canal Trade
(in thousands)

Yr. End'g June 1	Coal tons	Lumber sq.ft.	Timber cu.ft.	Grain bushels	Flour barrels	Groceries lbs.	Dry G'ds lbs.
1830	...	....	....	....	..	.....	.....
1831	...	7,119	....	289	101	.....	.....
1832	...	6,058	....	316	48	.....	.....
1833	...	11,237	....	299	20	.....	.....
1834	...	8,594	....	223	13	.....	.....
1835	...	18,143	....	131	13	.....	.....
1836	...	9,143	....	60	3	.....	.....
1837	20	24,424	1,200	40	11	.....	.....
1838	21	9,189	1,066	468	21	1,412	.....
1839	21	13,921	928	416	15	1,094	.....
1840	13	11,336	1,454	316	22	624	.....
1841	14	9,381	1,012	482	41	6,193	1,022
1842	13	13,128	1,226	463	54	10,904	2,861
1843	11	11,448	773	597	62	9,917	3,541
1844	13	25,926	1,012	889	78	15,456	13,298
1845	18	21,886	1,125	958	62	16,578	15,569
1846	18	25,097	571	1,536	84	19,587	20,037
1847	29	38,617	2,026	1,982	155	25,440	21,322
1848	36	49,374	1,641	1,141	116	28,518	24,489
1849	39	42,548	1,944	1,667	92	27,919	21,521
1850	54	44,795	2,145	1,826	144	32,103	23,645
1851	60	46,454	2,231	1,831	134	36,451	22,342
1852	60	49,294	1,528	2,044	120	37,939	16,735
1853	87	58,968	3,882	2,018	128	40,169	17,682
1854	123	56,548	3,414	2,113	110	39,130	15,243
1855	178	62,262	2,930	1,470	116	37,847	14,277
1856	161	64,534	4,014	1,760	156	37,579	13,108
1857	203	65,144	2,900	1,908	201	36,642	14,755
1858	178	52,544	2,904	1,896	155	34,193	16,979
1859	175	35,648	2,152	1,065	101	34,358	26,812
1860	193	58,833	3,143	1,646	148	43,072	31,303

(From Poor, *op. cit.,* I, 570.)

CHAPTER V

A GOLDEN LINK TO THE WEST

Improvements on the Schuylkill River from Philadelphia's own back door into the interior were contemplated at a very early date by the more progressive citizens of the Pennsylvania metropolis. The improved river channel was not merely to lead the trade of this river valley to the port of Philadelphia, but also to extend the economic hinterland of their city to the Susquehanna Valley and the great West. From Reading on the Schuylkill, these men planned an artificial waterway to the Susquehanna River near Middletown, a distance of some seventy miles. In 1762, 1770, 1791, and 1811 vigorous efforts were made to effect this construction, but the limitations of these days frustrated their desires. Finally, in the great canal building era, the Union Canal was constructed, linking Philadelphia with the Susquehanna Valley. The canal was built to carry trade from central Pennsylvania to the markets of the commercial metropolis of the state and to serve as a golden link in a proposed system of internal improvements to the West. The Union Canal was conceived with the blessing of Philadelphia; it was to divert the Susquehanna trade from Baltimore; it was to rival New York's Erie Canal for western business. But these large dreams were visionary. The canal was built on a small scale, and its locks could not pass the larger boats of the Pennsylvania State Canals or the Schuylkill Navigation from Reading to Philadelphia, which works it was to connect. It did not become a link to the West because of its physical limitations. Improvements, extensions, and enlargement kept the canal company alive until 1884 when the officials grimly reported, "The Union Canal is *non est;* it having been sold out, property and franchise, by the sheriff of Philadelphia."[1] From the Philadelphia point of view, the Union Canal was not a success; in the eyes of Baltimore, it never appeared a very pretentious rival.

The value of the development of a Susquehanna connection was sensed by men long before commercial rivalry between Philadelphia and Baltimore existed. William Penn, after he had located his favorite city on the Delaware, dreamed of a sister city which he proposed to establish on the Susquehanna River. Penn planned to connect the city with the East "by water, by the benefit of the river Schoulkill; for a *Branch* of that river lies near a *Branch* that runs into the Susquehannagh River, and is the

---

[1] The Union Canal Company, *Annual Report*, 1884.

100

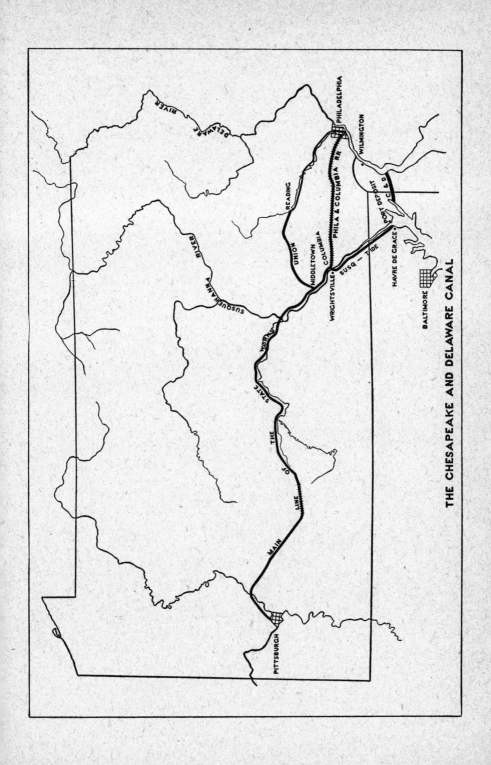

THE CHESAPEAKE AND DELAWARE CANAL

Common Course of the *Indians* with *Skins* and *Furrs* into our Parts."[2] This chimerical idea was beyond the power of the early settler and was soon forgotten by the busy pioneers.

After the town of Middletown was chartered in 1755 at the lowest port of entry on the broad, limpid Susquehanna River, progressive minds again turned to a canal project to link Philadelphia with that river, which was rapidly becoming a highway for the settlers in the northern portion of Pennsylvania. Plans were made for an all-water route from Reading to Myerstown by way of the Tulpehocken Creek, from that point to Lebanon by a lock canal, and from Lebanon to Middletown by way of the Quittapahilla and Swatara Creeks.[3] Two surveys of this route were made prior to the Revolution by David Rittenhouse and by William Smith, Provost of the University of Pennsylvania, about 1762 and 1770.[4] Although the American Philosophical Society sponsored one survey and Mayor Rhoads of Philadelphia corresponded with Franklin in London on the subject,[5] construction was not undertaken. The country was too young for such an undertaking, the West was still a wooded unknown, "engineering" was equally unknown in the vocabulary of that day.

Although America emerged from the Revolution, "crowned with laurels but distressed by want," friends of internal improvements banded together in 1789 to encourage and promote better communications. This organization, The Society for Promoting the Improvement of Roads and Inland Navigation, believed that the time was favorable to the execution of definite plans for improvements. One of their first interests was the canal from the headwaters of the Tulpehocken Creek to the westward flowing Quittapahilla. Other prominent Pennsylvanians also saw the

---

[2] Hazard, *The Pennsylvania Register,* I, 400. Reprints Penn's proposal "printed and sold by Andrew Sowle, at the crooked Billet in Halloway Lane, Shore Ditch 1690" which was entitled, "Some Proposals for a Second Settlement in the province of Pennsylvania."

[3] Some authorities believe that this was the route which Penn had suggested. However, Mr. Eshelman, a Lancaster County historian, believes Penn had reference to a route farther south.

[4] The exact date of the surveys seems to be a matter of question. Most likely the survey first made was in 1762, while the second one, sponsored by the Philosophical Society, was made in 1770 when that organization was interested in the Chesapeake and Delaware project. See *The Union Canal Company of Pennsylvania,* 3; Hazard, *The Pennsylvania Register,* I, 409-10; *An Historical Account of the Rise, Progress, and State of the Canal Navigation of Pennsylvania . . .,* 67; Davis, *Essays in the Early History of Corporations,* II, 109-110; Carter, *When Railroads Were New,* 5.

[5] Ringwalt, *op. cit.,* 41, quotes letter from Franklin to S. Rhoads, Mayor of Philadelphia, August 22, 1772. Franklin wrote that "rivers are ungovernable things," and favored the construction of a canal the entire distance from Philadelphia.

importance of this canal route. In answer to arguments that the location
of the Federal Capital at a proposed location along the Susquehanna
River would injure the trade of Philadelphia, Pennsylvania's Represent-
ative to the first Congress wrote:

"People are mistaken in supposing the permanent seat on the Susquehannah would injure the trade of Philadelphia, for whatever Improvements might be made, in consequence thereof, in the navigation of that
River, it can never be rendered equal to the communication with Philadelphia by a Junction of the Susquehannah to the Schuylkill, thro' the
Swatara & the Tulpehocken."[6]

The Philadelphia society was not satisfied to limit their activities to
agitation for a canal. Taking the matter in their own hands, the society
employed a surveying corps to examine the "middle ground" between the
two creeks to determine the practicability of the route. Their favorable
report soon interested the Pennsylvania Assembly in the project. When
the latter body advertised for a contractor to construct a canal, none
appeared. The society again offered suggestions to the lawmakers;
in a memorial they stated that they believed "the Most probable mode of
executing a work of such Magnitude will be to establish an incorporated
company who will risk a large capital to be raised by subscription."[7]
The Legislature took this advice and on September 29, 1791, passed an
act "to enable the Governor of this Commonwealth to incorporate a
Company for opening a Canal and Lock Navigation between the Rivers
Schuylkill and Susquehanna, by the waters of Tulpehoccon, Quittaphilla,
and Swatara, in the Counties of Berks and Dauphin."[8]

Robert Morris, David Rittenhouse, William Smith, Tench Francis,
and other prominent Philadelphians were named in the bill as commissioners. The capital of the new company was to be $400,000. Public
interest was aroused; Philadelphia published accounts of southern and
western New York state since it was maintained that the canal would
"lay open the market of Philadelphia for the reception of the produce of
all the Genesee country."[9] In 1791 it was estimated that it cost one
shilling sterling to ship a bushel of wheat from this region to Philadelphia; friends of the canal claimed that the waterway would reduce this
cost to four pence.[10]

---

[6] Judge Henry Wynkoop to Dr. Reading Beattie, September 18, 1789, reprinted
in The Pennsylvania Magazine of History and Biography, XXXVIII, 184-5.

[7] Journal of the Society for Improvement of Roads and Inland Navigation.

[8] Acts of the Legislature relating to the Union Canal, 1-13.

[9] Bird, "Early Transportation," in Publications of the Buffalo Historical Society,
I, 19, quoted by Whitford, History of the Canal System of the State of New
York, I, 826.

[10] O'Callaghan, ed., op. cit., II, 1113-1116.

A speculation craze gripped the country in 1791; investors were eager to support the canal company. When the books were opened for the sale of Schuylkill and Susquehanna Canal stock, the number of shares to be sold was greatly over-subscribed and the managers had to resort to a lottery to determine who should be given the privilege of owning stock.[11] Officials and investors desired to make their canal very complete. It was planned and authorized by law that the improvement should not only reach out to the fertile valley of the Susquehanna, but also become part of a navigation to the Ohio and Lake regions, which at this time were still wild and undeveloped. In order to complete the waterway's connection with Philadelphia, it was considered necessary to construct a short canal from the Delaware to the Schuylkill River north of that city.[12] The Legislature agreed with this proposal and on April 10, 1792, chartered the Delaware and Schuylkill Canal Company.

The Schuylkill and Susquehanna Company and the Delaware and Schuylkill Company were separate organizations, but they were controlled by practically the same people. Robert Morris served as president of both companies. Their purpose in common was to construct two short canals and improve the natural waterways between the artificial channels, so that Philadelphia would have a water route to the Susquehanna River over which produce could be carried at an estimated 2.5s per ton.[13] An eminent engineer, William Watson, was employed by the two organizations. But in their eagerness to commence digging, the managers began work late in 1792 under the superintendence of local, self-styled engineers before the Englishman could arrive in America.

After Watson's arrival, work progressed nicely. In 1794, President Washington viewed the work near Myerstown and found the locks in "admirable condition."[14] The Dutch traveller, Cazenove, visited the "great Canal" the same year. He claimed that seven miles of the ditch were completed and that, "The 5 adjoining locks to have the boats go down and up a 30 foot fall; the arched bridges, plain and well proportioned everywhere is done well. . . ."[15]

---

[11] McMaster, *op. cit.*, 75; Ringwalt, *op. cit.*, 44; Egle, *History of Pennsylvania*, 214. These accounts all give the same picture of the situation, but the amounts subscribed by the speculators vary.

[12] *Journal* of the Society for Improvement of Roads and Inland Navigation. On December 19, 1791, this group appointed a committee to view this proposed route.

[13] *An Historical Account of the Rise, Progress, and Present State of the Canal Navigation in Pennsylvania . . .*, 1, 62.

[14] *The Diaries of George Washington, 1784-1799*, IV, 210-11, entry, October 2, 1794.

[15] *Cazenove Journal*, Kelsey, ed., 46.

One year later, the reports were not so favorable. Funds were exhausted; work was discontinued. The two projects were defeated partly because they were born in a speculative boom and partly because public support was wanting. Although some Philadelphians worked strenuously for the canals, the improvements did not receive the wholehearted support of the city, which was interested in many schemes at this time. The German farmers along the route were bitter enemies of the project. They protested against the "unwarrantable Purpose of Compelling a Sacrifice of their property to the Selfish View of the Canal-Company."[16] Capitalists who subscribed to the stock, after they realized that this project was not going to be an immediate money maker, forfeited their shares after the payment of the first installment. Thus the canals were left without supporters or resources.

After the collapse of the companies' finances, the Legislature of Pennsylvania tried to save the floundering enterprises. Bills were passed granting the two companies the right to conduct semi-public lotteries to raise $400,000.[17] From the proceeds of the lotteries the Schuylkill and Susquehanna Canal Company was to receive two-thirds, and the Delaware and Schuylkill Company one-third of the earnings. However, after fifteen years, the entire earnings amounted to no more than $60,000. In the meantime, a stock subscription of 400 shares was taken by the State of Pennsylvania, but the incorporators could not procure enough additional funds to renew faith in the project.

Interest in the canal between the Schuylkill and the Susquehanna died temporarily with the suspension of work, although commercially-minded men continued to notice the importance of the route in diverting the Susquehanna River trade from Baltimore.[18] Gallatin's report on internal improvements in 1808 revived general interest in the canal. But the main spring was still missing; the necessary amount of capital to recommence work was lacking.

---

[16] State Roads MSS, S, No. 23. Petition signed by 89 people most of whom used only their mark. Letter Book of the Secretary of the Commonwealth, December 24, 1790-March 3, 1794, III, 530-31; *Cazenove Journal*, Kelsey, ed., 46-47. Cazenove was disgusted with the Germans' "stinginess and lack of conscience in money matters"; Davis, *op. cit.*, II, 154-6.

[17] *Acts of the Legislature relative to the Union Canal*, 27-28; Martin, "Lotteries in Pennsylvania Prior to 1833," in *Pennsylvania Magazine of History and Biography*, XLVII, 321.

[18] Cuming, "Sketches of a Tour to the Western Country," in Thwaites, *Early Western Travels*, IV, 36. In 1807 Fortescue Cuming passed through Middletown where he heard of the contemplated canal. The traveller wrote, "If this is carried into effect, it will draw to Philadelphia a vast quantity of produce, which now goes to Baltimore."

Renewed efforts were made to illustrate the pressing need for a connection between Reading and Middletown. Charles Paleske, one of the sponsors of the early attempt to construct a canal, writing in 1808, noticed that "rivalships" had been created between New York, Maryland, and Pennsylvania; Paleske asserted that the canal from the Susquehanna to the Schuylkill River would give Philadelphia the victory in this contest for trade. A short canal, he said, would prove to be the panacea for all the worries of the Pennsylvania metropolis.[19] Paleske's views were supported by Governor Snyder; the popular Democratic Governor advocated a canal to connect Philadelphia with the central part of the State, especially since New York was so "assiduously employed in the project of opening a water communication between Lake Erie and the Hudson River."[20]

William J. Duane, editor of *The Aurora* and a Democratic partisan of the most extreme type, joined the agitators for improvements in 1811 when he pictured the "shameful state of stagnation" into which Pennsylvania had allowed herself to slip.[21] Duane claimed that, although New York had surpassed Philadelphia and Baltimore was a keen rival, the laws of the Pennsylvania Legislature "resemble the petty acts of a borough corporation." He appealed to the citizens of the State to elect men to the Legislature who would stand for broad and liberal internal improvement programs.

After listening to Gallatin, Paleske, Governor Snyder, and Philadelphia's editor Duane, the Legislature of Pennsylvania, on April 2, 1811, enacted a law "to incorporate the Union Canal Company of Pennsylvania."[22] By this act the Schuylkill and Susquehanna Canal Company and the Delaware and Schuylkill Canal Company were to be merged into a new organization. Permission was granted to extend the right of the company to Lake Erie or other waters in the West by canal, lock navigation, or turnpike. Lottery privileges of the former canal companies were extended to the Union Company.

But consolidation of the old companies did not assure progress for the new company. Some old stockholders opposed the merger; new stock could not be sold. Congress was finally asked for aid, but its purse strings were closed.[23] Then the War of 1812 descended on the new

[19] Paleske, *Observations on the Application for a Law to incorporate "The Union Canal Company"* . . .

[20] *Pennsylvania Archives,* Fourth Series, IV, 752. Governor Snyder's annual message, 1811.

[21] Duane, *Letters addressed to the People of Pennsylvania.*

[22] *Acts of the Legislature relating to the Union Canal,* 38-51.

[23] *American State Papers, Miscellaneous,* II, 161. Memorial communicated to the Senate, December 6, 1811.

Union Canal Company and the project suffered a short period of comparative inactivity.

The gradual crystallization of the Erie Canal scheme finally began to stir Philadelphia into action. The Schuylkill Navigation Company was incorporated and began construction on a waterway from the port of the Delaware River to Pottsville, near the headwaters of the Schuylkill River. This route was intended to provide Philadelphia with a dependable communication throughout the Schuylkill Valley; its construction ignited the spark of action for an extension into the Susquehanna Valley. In 1818 Samuel Breck, a man of wealth and culture, wrote that if Philadelphia did not become the seat of the trade of central Pennsylvania, it would "dwindle into a small town." The Schuylkill Navigation, he asserted, is now taken for granted:

"This is an important link in the great western and northern chain; but the *golden* link—the essential and high connecting part of that series of water-routes, which is to convey so much wealth to Philadelphia, lies between Reading and Middletown. If we make a good channel by means of the waters of the Tulpehocken, . . . and those of the Swatara . . . and thus reach the great river, we are forever safe as a town. When we are once able to attract to our wharves the produce of the Susquehanna, we command the trade of waters, which meander through more than half the state; of waters which interlock on the north with lakes and rivers running into Ontario, and through the richest counties of the state of New York; waters which have their sources and navigable tributary streams within fourteen miles of those that run west; and by whose junction we open to ourselves a vast and ever-increasing trade, not only with all the fair, full-grown, and numerous daughters of the Mississippi, but with the 'mother of rivers' herself. . . ."[24]

The hopes and fears announced by Breck together with the general spread of the canal contagion reawoke public interest in the Union Canal Company. In order that the company might be reconstructed financially, the Legislature authorized the sale of more stock in 1819.[25] To give added confidence to investors, the Legislature further enacted, on March 26, 1821, a bill which stipulated a State guarantee of interest amounting to six per cent on new subscriptions.[26] A general appeal was made to the public. Samuel Mifflin, president of the canal company, and the directors, who were almost all prominent Philadelphians, disseminated pamphlets and used the Philadelphia press to herald their plans. A powerful crusade was undertaken to dispel all fear of future defeat. "Penn" writing for *The Aurora* forecast:

"The day star of prosperity is about rising; but as yet only glimmers feebly in the horizon of our long depressed and neglected state. The

---

[24] Breck, *Sketches of Internal Improvements*, 40-41.
[25] *Acts of the Legislature relating to the Union Canal*, 52-56.
[26] *Ibid.*, 57-59.

gloom of more than Egyptian darkness is about flitting from our borders, and I feel sanguine in saying that an epoch is approaching, when, under the auspices of general *Joseph* Hiester's administration, Pennsylvania will be restored to her former reputation. . . .

". . . Our present Governor will do his *duty,* and *if our* legislature is not blinded or infatuated by the artifices of men of base motives our state will rise to the proud eminence which she had heretofore held in the union and the opinion of mankind.

"Philadelphia, when the canal is cut, will become the queen of cities. On its borders, from the Susquehanna to the Schuylkill, will be seen towns, and villages, and hamlets. . . ."[27]

Friends of the canal found that crusading was no easy task; there were many enemies of the Union Canal in various parts of Pennsylvania. Conservative citizens were disturbed by the State's pledge to meet interest payments for the company. Individuals living in parts of the Commonwealth not traversed by the canal—especially those living in the physio-geographic area which faced Baltimore—complained about supporting improvements which led toward Philadelphia. The *York Gazette* cried:

". . . the people of York county will have to contribute the payment of interest for a project which is to wrest the Susquehanna trade from their shores and carry it through Reading to Philadelphia. There is one consolation left to the people of this county, that the project will be a fruitless one, and that the attempt to monopolize the Susquehanna trade, and turn it out of its natural channel, will result in an abortion, and consequently the only injury that can result to them, will be the loss of their money they will have to pay towards an experiment engendered by the avaricious spirit, and blind and grasping zeal of the Philadelphians."[28]

Despite opposition, the managers of the Union Canal Company began construction in 1821. Since work along the Schuylkill River had been undertaken by the Schuylkill Navigation Company, the Union Company gave all its attention to the construction of a canal from Schuylkill River to the Susquehanna. A new route was surveyed and the old construction of 1794 abandoned. Loammi Baldwin, who is considered by some to be the "Father of Civil Engineering in America," was hired as chief engineer, but he soon fell into disagreement with the canal officials over the size of the locks. He was then replaced by Canvass White,[29] who had been with the Erie Canal for some nine years.

Work progressed slowly. Philadelphia was very anxious that the canal be finished as soon as possible; her merchants began to fear that Balti-

---

[27] *The Aurora,* January 31, 1821.

[28] *The York Gazette,* April 17, 1821.

[29] *Letters on the Union Canal Company of Pennsylvania,* 1-18. Baldwin favored wide locks and not many years after he had been dismissed by the company they were extremely sorry that the canal had not been constructed according to his plans.

more's new project of canalizing the lower Susquehanna Valley as far
north as Middletown might ruin the Union Canal and Philadelphia's
hope of tapping the trade of the Valley. After considering the possibilities of the Baltimore project, the officials of the Union Canal conducted
examinations to learn whether the Baltimore canal would be constructed.
Happily, they reported in 1823 that "the result of late examinations
shows that no rival work leading from the Susquehanna to a neighbouring State, is likely to be ever undertaken; and the impracticability of
an ascending navigation from the tide, by the bed of the river, is now
conceded by all."[30] It appeared that the Union Canal was safe from
intruding rivals from the South.

Until the canal was completed, Philadelphia ardently supported the
project, sang its praises, described its hopeful future, and complimented
its engineers. But its supporters had to be patient; construction was a
slow process. The topography of the country through which the route
passed presented a difficult problem to the engineers. In the vicinity of
the summit level, the channel passed through a limestone belt which,
with its many fissures, allowed the water of the canal easy escape.
Finally, this problem was solved by planking the worst places so that
the ditch would hold water.[31] In the autumn of 1827 the managers reported that their 77-mile canal was completed. The summit level was
almost 500 feet above tidewater; the total lockage of the four-foot-deep
channel was 519 feet. This lockage was overcome by 93 lift locks which
were 75 feet long and 8½ feet wide. In order to pass the watershed with
ease, a 729-foot tunnel, one of the first constructed in America, was dug.[32]

The canal which David Rittenhouse and Robert Morris had failed to
build was now in navigable order. The merchant princes of Philadelphia
were happy; the canal-builders heralded their accomplishment as:
"the most important step towards developing the riches of Pennsylvania,
and giving to Philadelphia the advantages of her geographical position
in relation to the interior of her own state . . . The Union Canal is the
hope of Philadelphia, and so far as the commercial greatness and the
ample revenues of Philadelphia affords the state, is a matter of concern,
it is the hope of Pennsylvania."[33]
The canal was claimed, in official reports, to have effected a "new and
efficient impulse" on the port of Philadelphia.[34] A writer for *The Penn-*

---

[30] *Niles' Weekly Register*, XXVIII, 293; The Union Canal Company, *Annual
Report,* 1823.

[31] The Union Canal Company, *Annual Report,* 1827; Klein, *The Union Canal,* 11.

[32] Tanner, *Canals and Railroads of Pennsylvania and New Jersey,* 16; Hazard,
The Pennsylvania Register, I, 411; Harlow, *op. cit.,* 89-91.

[33] The Union Canal Company, *Annual Report,* 1827.

[34] Hazard, *The Pennsylvania Register,* I, 116. Report of the Commerce Committee in the House on the Philadelphia Breakwater.

sylvania Gazette said that on visiting the western terminal of the Union Canal he found a "commercial bustle," which was highly gratifying to a Philadelphian. He continued, "I say, again, let Philadelphia be true to herself, and at Middletown and Portsmouth, she may undividedly arrest the whole of the immense trade of the Susquehanna."[35]

Although the water route was circuitous, the annual report of the Union Canal Company for 1828 showed that 18,124 tons of freight paying $26,000 tolls passed through the canal. The connecting Schuylkill Navigation, which carried the Union traffic on to Philadelphia, reported that over $12,000 in tolls had been received from boats which had navigated the Union Canal.[36] Lumber, wheat, flour, country produce, fish, salt, gypsum, iron, coal, and merchandise were the chief articles on the bills of lading of the Union Canal boats. The small number of boats available and the unfinished outlet lock at the Susquehanna River limited business the first year.[37] But in consequence of the large amount of trade which sought the canal that season, about 150 boats were constructed for use in 1829.

The first report of the canal company was very encouraging to all its friends. Moreover, since construction had begun in 1821, the State of Pennsylvania had started her great system of internal improvements. Work on the Main Line of the State Works began in 1826 on the western sections and the Union Canal appeared destined to be the eastern link in this great route to the West. When this project was completed, Philadelphia thought that she would be able to reassert supremacy over New York. Before that time, the Pennsylvania metropolis planned to drive Baltimore from the Susquehanna Valley. The officials of the canal claimed that their organization could and would carry all of the produce sent to and from that contested hinterland.

Baltimore, however, did not appear to worry over the Union Canal. She had turned her full attention to the building of railroads; the construction of the Baltimore and Ohio system and the charter fight for the Baltimore and Susquehanna Railroad[38] kept the Chesapeake metropolis busy. Pennsylvania friends of the Maryland city stoutly claimed that the first year of the Union Canal had been a failure and that in a few years, with the construction of a railroad from Baltimore to the Conewago Falls, the canal to Philadelphia would cease to exist.[39]

---

[35] *The Pennsylvania Gazette,* April 1, 1828.

[36] *Niles' Weekly Register,* XXXV, 331; Hazard, *The Pennsylvania Register,* III, 26.

[37] The Union Canal Company, *Annual Report,* 1828. There were only seventeen boats in service the first year.

[38] See pages 118-130.

[39] *The York Gazette,* July 22, 1828, September 16, 1828.

The canal authorities themselves soon began to see the limitations of their project. It was evident that more water was needed to supply the canal during the dry seasons. Continual leakage was a heavy drain on the feeble supply. Therefore, as soon as the main line was completed, work was begun on a navigable feeder to Pine Grove. A dam which covered some 700 acres was built across the upper Swatara Creek to serve as a reservoir. The feeder, which was completed in 1832, was to supply water for the main canal and also serve as an avenue into the coal fields of that section of Pennsylvania. As a feeder this alteration was successful, but as an avenue for traffic, it never prospered. Baltimore, as well as Philadelphia, hoped for the success of this venture to tap the anthracite field near Pine Grove since both felt that the Union Canal would ship fuel to their markets.[40]

The officials of the Union Canal also soon began to see their hope of becoming the eastern section of the Pennsylvania State Works shattered. Ardent internal improvement sponsors believed that the Union Canal would "be wholly inadequate to the transportation of all the produce which may solicit an entrance into it."[41] One line of communication, it was believed, could not carry all the western and Susquehanna Valley produce which would demand a passage to Philadelphia. Therefore, in 1828, it was decided that a railroad should be constructed from Columbia to Philadelphia to serve as the official eastern link in the mongrel State Works. The railroad was not feared as a competitor of the Union Canal by canal-believers who had no faith in railroads. However, after its opening in 1834, the railroad carried much of the through western trade while the proximity of the State Works to the Chesapeake Bay caused large quantities to leave the State system at Columbia. The business and prestige of the canal towards Philadelphia suffered severely by the decision to construct an official link of the State Works from the Susquehanna River to Philadelphia.

Although the tonnage of 1830 was double that of the preceding year, the directors of the Union Canal Company confessed that up to that time the Pennsylvania Canal had not yielded much trade to the Union

---

[40] *Hunt's Merchants' Magazine,* XVIII, 99, gives a table of the Pine Grove Coal Business:

1833— 3,500 tons	1838—15,000	1843—22,000
1834— 6,911	1839—20,885	1844—29,000
1835—14,000	1840—20,500	1845—35,000
1836—12,000	1841—19,500	1846—55,500
1837—17,000	1842—32,500	1847—60,499

[41] MS. Petitions from Philadelphia and Mifflin Counties, Archives Division of the Pennsylvania Historical and Museum Commission.

Canal.[42] In 1831, tolls amounted to almost $60,000, an increase of upwards of 70% over 1830,[43] but business was still mostly of a local character. Through traffic figures were almost stationary.

The reason for this lack of through business was obvious. The canal was too small. Boats suitable for navigation on the Schuylkill Navigation, which joined the Union Canal at Reading, and on the Pennsylvania Canals, which met the Union at Middletown, were too large to pass the locks of the smaller canal. When the Union Canal was constructed, officials believed that a narrow canal which would pass narrow twenty-five-ton boats was more practicable than a larger canal. They claimed that Europe was using this type of boat which could carry an adequate load with greater ease and economy than wider boats.[44] The officials of the two navigations which connected with the Union Canal, however, disagreed with this theory and constructed their canals and locks to pass boats at least twice as large as the Union Canal boat. Under these conditions, through traffic meant transshipment and added expense.

The only solution was enlargement of the canal. The completion of the Philadelphia and Columbia Railroad made this work imperative. The chartering of the Susquehanna and Tidewater Canal in 1835 threw the canal officials and Philadelphia business men into a panic. The Philadelphia City Council met to try to discover some means to compete with this new Baltimore threat which would not only carry off the business of the diminutive Union Canal but also divert this trade to Baltimore. Mr. Aycrigg, a former engineer for the Union Company, announced that the one possible and practicable solution of Philadelphia's dilemma was the enlargement of the canal between Middletown and Reading.[45]

In 1837, the canal officially finally admitted that through traffic on the canal was hampered because the Union Canal could not pass large boats.[46] They were very reluctant to make this acknowledgment, since their treasury did not contain the necessary funds to make an extensive improvement. The State Legislature was asked to assist the company financially, so that their channel could be enlarged. After one failure to grant this request, the Legislature, in 1838, passed resolutions appropriating $400,000 for this work.

While the appropriation measure was in the hands of the Governor, public attention was focused on its importance. A public convention was held in Harrisburg in December, 1838, to arouse sympathy. Unanimous resolutions proclaimed this measure sound policy and deserving of State

[42] The Union Canal Company, *Annual Report*, 1830.
[43] *Ibid.*, 1831.
[44] *Ibid.*, 1827.
[45] *Mr. Aycrigg's Letter on the Supply of Water of the Union Canal.*
[46] The Union Canal Company, *Annual Report*, 1837.

patronage.[47] When the canal officials heard of the proposed convention, they appealed to the Pennsylvania Canal Commissioners for the service of an engineer to view the canal and determine if a supply of water were available to warrant enlargement. Engineer James D. Harris, who was assigned to this task sent in an early report:

"After a careful examination of the subject . . . he has arrived at the conclusion that the enlargement of the Union Canal is imperiously called for by the wants of the public, and by a proper regard for the interests of the commonwealth, and especially of the city of Philadelphia, and having settled in his own mind that a full supply of water for the increased trade can be commanded, as it may be required, he has no hesitation in recommending the work to be undertaken."[48]

At the same time, a committee reporting on the Swatara Mining District to the State Legislature supported the plea for enlargement. It claimed that under existing conditions coal from this region could not compete with Schuylkill Valley coal since the cost of transportation on the diminutive Union Canal amounted to twice the value of the coal.[49]

Despite these pleas, the straightforward Democratic Governor, David Rittenhouse Porter, vetoed the bill. The treasury was empty; a European loan had just been completed so that the debts of the State could be paid. Plainly and vigorously, he informed the public that expenses were to be curtailed and that the Union Canal appropriation would be impolitic and unwise.[50]

Governor Porter's veto unchained a bitter outcry by all the friends of the Union Canal. The Board of Trade of Philadelphia openly condemned the Governor for his action. They were horrified to believe that one man could snatch away their only solution to an all-important question.[51] The editor of a Harrisburg newspaper suggested:

"We therefore say to Schuylkill County, Lebanon, Berks, and to Montgomery counties, especially to the city and county of Philadelphia, that the present governor would suit Maryland better than them since he does, and will continue to forbid the opening of the Union canal. . . ."[52]
Everyone realized that the Baltimore and Susquehanna Railroad and the

---

[47] *Memorial of a Convention of Citizens of the Commonwealth for aid to enlarge the Union Canal;* The Union Canal Company, *Annual Report,* 1839.

[48] *Ibid.; Communication from the President of the Union Canal Company accompanied with a report of James D. Harris, principal Engineer relative to Enlarging the Union Canal,* read in the House of Representatives, February 9, 1839.

[49] *Report to the Legislature of Pennsylvania containing a description of the Swatara Mining District,* 51-2.

[50] *Pennsylvania Archives,* Fourth Series, VI, 664-666.

[51] Hazard, *The United States Register,* II, 78-9. Reprints the Annual Report of the Philadelphia Board of Trade, January 13, 1840.

[52] *Niles' Weekly Register,* LVII, 96, quotes from the *Harrisburg Chronicle.*

Susquehanna and Tidewater Canal would both be completed to Wrights-ville in 1840, and that the trade of the tiny Union Canal would be further diverted.

These fears were well grounded, for in 1841 the canal officials re-ported, "The navigation was opened on the 29th of March but it was soon perceived that without the most vigorous measures the trade would be drawn away by the Tidewater Canal."[53] Although the disastrous effects of this new competition were foreseen, the Union Canal Company could only await the inevitable. Revenues and tonnage accounts imme-diately fell. The year before the completion of the two Baltimore pro-jects, the Union Canal tonnage amounted to 138,000 tons, which was a record high. In 1841, when the Susquehanna and Tidewater canal was in full operation, the amount of tonnage that passed through the canal fell to about 83,000 tons, and continued to fall even lower.[54]

Finally, in 1849, the Legislature authorized the Canal Company to enlarge the western section of the canal from Pine Forge to the Susque-hanna River.[55] Work was begun two years later and upon its completion the company was authorized to enlarge the eastern division of the canal from Reading to Lebanon. By 1856 the entire route was improved, but the expense of the enlargement ruined the company financially.[56]

Business on the canal immediately responded to the improvement; tonnage figures climbed to a new high. Boats of 75 to 80 tons carried more than 270,000 tons in 1857 which paid some $130,000 in tolls. Then suddenly a new competitor appeared. In 1856 the Lebanon Valley Rail-road celebrated its completion from Reading to Harrisburg;[57] immedi-ately it began to rob the canal of its trade. Canal revenues fell annually; it was destined that the Union Canal was doomed. The last hope of the "golden link" to the West disappeared when the canal passed into the hands of trustees for the bondholders in 1860.[58]

The decision of the officers of the Union Canal Company to construct their canal for narrow twenty-five-ton boats was a costly decision for the canal company and for the city of Philadelphia. Unable to pass the boats of its connecting waterways, the Union Canal failed to gain the trade of the Susquehanna Valley or the West. Since Philadelphia had no canal of larger size north of the Chesapeake and Delaware Canal, much of this produce was shipped to Baltimore. Philadelphia tried desperately to

[53] The Union Canal Company, *Annual Report*, 1841.
[54] See Appendix, XII, 114.
[55] The Union Canal Company, *Annual Report*, 1849.
[56] The total costs of construction now amounted to almost six millions of dollars.
[57] Poor, *op. cit.*, I, 453.
[58] *Reports of the Committee of Bondholders of the Union Canal Company of Pennsylvania.*

assist the Union Company complete enlargement plans, but it was not until too late—when railroads had been definitely established—that the Union Canal was physically able to compete with other canals of the Susquehanna Valley.

APPENDIX XII

Union Canal

Comparative Statement of Its Business

Year	Tons transported	Tolls received
1828	18,124	$15,512
1829	20,522	16,676
1830	41,094	35,133
1831	59,970	59,137
1832	47,645	59,061
1833	85,876	103,462
1834	84,536	119,870
1835	118,978	135,354
1836	117,136	133,025
1837	110,032	107,590
1838	126,870	123,575
1839	138,568	135,163
1840	115,292	110,855
1841*	83,624	66,601
1842	83,106	57,477
1843	76,595	53,538
1844	79,871	56,580
1845	102,593	60,036
1846	114,920	62,682
1847	139,256	91,356
1848†	153,222	95,953
1849	148,332	86,800
1850	128,438	76,269
1851‡	45,768	17,319
1852	152,143	84,056
1853	195,011	105,871
1854	172,696	98,787
1855§	151,571	72,915
1856§	247,307	107,844
1857	271,387	131,022
1858	205,517	104,101
1859	263,040	110,613
1860	246,871	108,080

* Susquehanna and Tidewater Canal in full operation.
† From November 1, 1847, to January 1, 1849, fourteen months.
‡ Open only from Lebanon to Reading during enlargement of western division.
§ Open only from Lebanon to Middletown during enlargement of eastern division.

APPENDIX XIII

Comparative Statement of Land and Water Carriage from Middletown to Philadelphia, 1794

Water Carriage

Schuylkill and Susquehanna Canal	70 miles
Schuylkill, from Reading to Norristown	46 "
Schuylkill and Delaware Canal	16 "
	132 "

Toll on 20 tons of produce for 86 miles of canal navigation
    at 10 cents per mile is £40-6-3

Hauling 20 tons 132 miles

One man 5 days	1-05-0
One boy 5 days	1-00-0
One horse 5 days	1-10-0
Freight or hire of a boat	18-9
	£45-0-0

Or £2 5s. per ton
Or 3s. 1¼d. per barrel of flour
Or 1s. 2¼d. per bushel of wheat
The above produce is conveyed to market by 2 men and 1 horse.

Land Carriage

From Middletown to Philadelphia ....100 miles
The present price of carriage from Middletown to Philadelphia
    is 5s. 6d. per hundredweight or for 20 tons £100-0-0
Or £5 10s. per ton
Or 9s. 7½d. per barrel of flour
Or 2s. 1¼d. per bushel of wheat
The same by land required 20 men and 80 horses.

(*American State Papers, Miscellaneous,* I, 858.)

CHAPTER VI

BALTIMORE REACHES NORTHWARD

At the beginning of the second quarter of the nineteenth century Baltimore was temporarily disheartened and crippled. Wagon days were passing; the plan for a canal along the lower Susquehanna River had not matured. Philadelphia, constructing her Union and her Chesapeake and Delaware Canals, was about to gain an advantage in the competition for the trade of the Susquehanna Valley. In order to revive prosperity and gain the western trade, Baltimore projected the Baltimore and Ohio Railroad to the West. This revealed a new method of accomplishing the purpose of canal construction, and it was only natural that the Maryland city should sponsor a plan to build a railroad northward where canal projects had failed. In 1827, this scheme took the form of a serious project—a project which was more alarming to Philadelphia than any previously suggested. In the Pennsylvania Legislature, Philadelphia's friends and representatives continually refused to charter such a railroad company; for four years the State metropolis waged a successful battle. Then Baltimore won. The railroad marched northward; section after section was constructed until finally, in 1858, the railroad reached Sunbury. At every turn Philadelphia tried to hinder the progress of the road, while Baltimore and Maryland gave it generous assistance. In this contest the crux of the great commercial rivalry between the two cities was uncovered. The Baltimore and Susquehanna Railroad sponsored constructions which were not only to draw the trade of the Susquehanna River to Baltimore but to tap all the important east-west improvements of Pennsylvania. In grasping all, the Baltimore-sponsored railroad ruined itself financially and, ironically, was purchased by the Pennsylvania Railroad Company.

As early as August, 1827, Baltimore began to consider the possibility of building a railroad northward through the Susquehanna Valley. It was maintained by her merchants that "the period for systematic and powerful exertion" had arrived. Baltimore's rivals were forging ahead at a rapid pace; it was deemed essential to the future of Baltimore to wage an immediate counter-attack. A meeting of the delegates of four turnpike companies whose roads led into the Susquehanna Valley convened in the Maryland metropolis in 1827. These men discussed the needs for a western and northern connection with the interior, and appointed a committee to survey the country between Baltimore and York

116

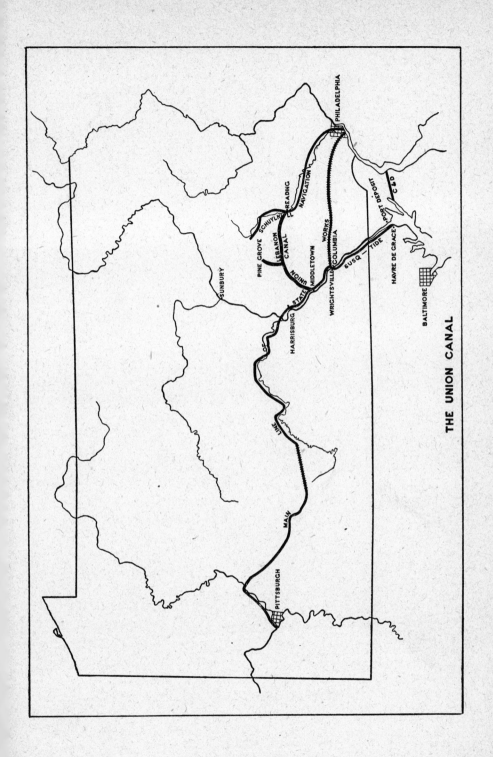

THE UNION CANAL

Haven to determine if a railroad could be constructed between these two points.

In bold, unrestrained, outspoken language these friends of Baltimore published their opinions concerning the situation that confronted them. Viewing the region contested for by the ports of New York, Philadelphia, and themselves, they said:

". . . the great plans which are going on and in a great measure maturing in New York, and those which are projected and will be completed in Pennsylvania, show a determination on the part of our rival cities, to push as far as unlimited capital, seconded by liberal views and great enterprise, a competition, which can only be dangerous, if we permit their schemes to be matured, and the current of trade to take a settled direction in the channels provided for it by our rivals—for commerce, like water, will seek its level, depending on natural or artificial causes, and if we once permit it to be diverted from its natural channel, it will be found most difficult to bring it back. If on the other hand we enter early into the field of competition, and improve our natural advantages, we make the efforts of our rivals tributary to our views, and they cannot make a foot of canal or rail-way, erect a bridge, or pave a turnpike road which does not necessarily lead the trade, or commerce embarked upon it directly to our own door. We have nothing in fact to do but to take up the work where they leave it, and to finish at a trifling expense a great line of natural communication, which the exertions of our spirited and enterprising neighbors have conducted within our reach."

*   *   *   *   *

"The New-York canal connecting the waters of lake Erie with the Hudson river, is a violent effort to drag by artificial means, the trade of that country out of its natural channel down the different branches of the Susquehanna, which stretch almost to the foot of the lakes, and skirt the borders of the canal itself. Even in their present natural condition, they attract an immense trade, and when improved by the efforts of Pennsylvania, they will exhaust the Erie canal at every pore of its unnatural burdens, and conduct them to the borders of our own state; so in like manner will the canal up the Juniata, and the western branch conduct to the same point, the trade of the fine country east of the Allegheny ridge, and that which the same exertions may have transported over the ridges. The whole trade then of the country referred to, seeks its outlet in the valley of the Susquehanna, and pursuing the artificial channel provided for it, terminates at the end of the eastern section of the Pennsylvania canal at Middletown, at which point the competition for its possession between Baltimore and Philadelphia must commence."[1]

Since Baltimore was known to be closer to Middletown than its rival, Philadelphia, it was felt that an improved communication between the Maryland city and the little river town would win all the Susquehanna trade for the Marylanders. In bold conclusion the turnpike delegates asserted:

---

[1] *Report and proceedings in Relation to a Rail Road from Baltimore to the Susquehanna*, 4-6.

"Baltimore Must and will be the Great Central City of the Union—
No Rival Can Impede Her Progress—No Competition disaffect Her
Destined Elevation, If Her Citizens are but True to Themselves, and
Unite with Their Characteristic Enterprise, to Improve the Advantages
and Cultivate the Resources, which Providence Has Placed At their
Disposal."[2]

After numerous surveys it was decided that a route from Baltimore to
York Haven (the milling center on the western bank of the Susquehanna
River near Middletown) by way of York would be the most practical
route. The citizens of southern Pennsylvania, especially those about the
town of York, showed an immediate interest in the proposed railroad
and pledged their full support to the project.[3] With this guarantee, the
Legislature of Maryland, on February 13, 1828, incorporated the Baltimore and Susquehanna Railroad to extend from Baltimore to the Pennsylvania State Line in the direction of York. Enthusiasm for the road
caused the stock to be over-subscribed in a few days.[4] Work of a constructive nature was commenced during Baltimore's centennial anniver-
sary on August 8, 1829, amid elaborate ceremony.[5]

Friends of the railroad expected Pennsylvania immediately to charter
the road through that State. As early as December, 1827, petitions were
presented to the Legislature praying for the incorporation of a company
to construct a railroad from the State line below York to the Conewago
Falls and Carlisle in the Cumberland Valley. It was asserted that this
improvement would avoid all the dangers of river navigation, that it
would be open for business for the greater part of the year, and that it
would supply the interior of Pennsylvania with return merchandise and
necessary commodities from the neighboring seaboard. A Maryland
delegation was sent to Harrisburg during the session of the Legislature
that year, but action was not pressed since the friends of the railroad
realized that preliminary plans could be made before a charter was obtained. The Baltimore sponsors of the railroad felt certain that the
Pennsylvania Legislature realized that:

"The prosperity of Baltimore is tributary to the prosperity of the
interior of Pennsylvania, and would be attributing to an intelligent

---

[2] *Ibid.*, 22.

[3] *The York Gazette,* August 21, November 6, December 25, 1827.

[4] Scharf, *Chronicles of Baltimore,* 425; *The York Recorder,* April 1, 1828. Baltimore took 38,500 shares; York only 180. The small amount subscribed by York
was in marked contrast to her interest in the project. It was said that the lack
of a general incorporating act enabling the road to pass through Pennsylvania,
and the "1st of April" pressure, when obligations had to be met, were the reasons
for this low subscription.

[5] *Maryland Magazine of History and Biography,* XXIV, 237-45 quotes *The
American,* August 8, 1828, and August 10, 1828.

people, a most short sighted and illiberal policy, to suppose they would deny to themselves the benefit of a safe, cheap, and certain communication to a market for their produce because it happened to be beyond the imaginary line which separates the two States."[6]

Philadelphia became alarmed as soon as she heard of the proposed railroad; her editors marshalled their forces in full strength to combat their rival's latest move.[7] Philadelphia was fully convinced that no measure had ever been proposed "so immediately and expressly designed" to injure their city. The Philadelphians knew enough geography to realize that Baltimore was closer to the river port of Middletown, the western terminal of the Union Canal, and the State Works at Columbia than their city. They envisioned the Baltimore railroad as a project to divert the trade of the expensive State Canals and Railroads; their petitions claimed, "it would be a paltry return to our State for her immense expenditures, to become the mere thoroughfare of wealth passing to Baltimore.[8] Friends and investors of the Union Canal claimed that the railroad would render their project useless and so deprive Philadelphia "of an important trade, to which she is in every point of view entitled." But most irritating of all to Philadelphians was the boldness of Baltimore's "barefaced, exorbitant, and unreasonable demands." One caustic editor, with the Baltimore turnpike men's report on his desk, answered the Baltimore request:

"It may seem churlish and unkind, not to give permission to make a road, but the point is, if we do, we may give with it the whole trade of the state. We have, and shall expend millions, to bring the trade of the west to our seaboard, and now when we are about to receive some return for our expenditures, Baltimore steps in, and says, let us take the profits; let our citizens make a road, that shall take away all your trade, and if you don't give us the privilege, without restriction or qualification, we will denounce you as illiberal, unneighbourly, &c, &c.

*   *   *   *   *

"To say that this would be illiberal is preposterous, and a violation of reason and common sense. We are, at a great expense, to form a channel of trade, and Baltimore must be permitted to take the benefit of it. We are to labour to fill the cask, and Baltimore is to tap the bottom of it. We are to fill up, and she draw off. This will, in truth, be the effect of the railroad. Can there then be a doubt as to the course our Legislature ought to take? She ought to say at once to these applicants, 'we cannot take the bread out of the mouths of our citizens to give it away. They have laboured to make these improvements, and it would be unjust to

[6] The Baltimore and Susquehanna Railroad Company, *Annual Report*, 1828.

[7] *The Pennsylvania Gazette*, January 12, 15; February 6, 7, 9, 11, 13, 14, 15, 16, 19, 23, 25, 1828; *Niles' Weekly Register*, XXXIII, 331.

[8] MS. Petition from Philadelphia County to the Senate and House, 1828, Archives Division of the Pennsylvania Historical and Museum Commission.

deprive them of the benefit of their industry. Our metropolis, too, has strong claims upon us, and you have yourselves stated, that the object of your work is to take from her a trade to which she is entitled by every principle of justice, equity, and property. It is also our duty and our interest to secure it to her.' "[9]

Philadelphia claimed that the State owed to her the trade of the entire Commonwealth because of the large amount of revenue she paid into the State treasury, because her institutions and benevolences spread influence in every section, because she was the traditional commercial metropolis of the State and the lender of large amounts for State improvements. They appealed to the Legislature to withhold a Baltimore charter. Nothing must be left to chance, Philadelphia claimed; the Baltimore project must be killed "at once, totally, and forever." Allow the railroad and Baltimore would be the greatest commercial emporium of the nation. Philadelphia incessantly asserted that she was not illiberal in her demands but that her citizens "did not have so much 'brotherly love' as to give to Baltimore all the profits of our canals." The commercial group of the Pennsylvania metropolis warned their representatives that they would have to brave public indignation if they bartered away the canals which Providence had placed in their keeping; the lawmakers were continually reminded of the results of political suicide. The granting of such principles as the citizens of Baltimore ask, Philadelphia maintained, are "not due to any principles of comity or justice" and are "repugnant to every principle of state pride and state policy."[10]

Philadelphians denounced the Maryland delegations which visited Harrisburg in the interest of chartering the railroad. She protested against a sister state using its press to "excite divisions and sectional feelings between the citizens of another state." Then some pedantic individual recalled a former struggle between the two cities in which case Baltimore had not been generous. After Pennsylvania had granted a charter for the Baltimore and Ohio Railroad to pass through her territory, Maryland had refused to allow Pennsylvania to tap the new line within her state. Baltimore had favored this refusal since she did not want any outside influence to tap her communication to the West.[11] Now, at this time, the case was reversed. Could it be possible that the same city that had been so selfish was now asking to tap Pennsylvania's Main Line to the West? Were the Baltimoreans really as liberal as they asserted? Why should Pennsylvania cater to such men who so easily

---

[9] *The Pennsylvania Gazette,* February 6, 1828.

[10] *The Pennsylvania Gazette,* March 14, 1828.

[11] *Ibid.,* March 1 and 20, 1828. There was much plausibility in this argument. Maryland had foolishly refused to allow the connection which would certainly have been beneficial to the Baltimore and Ohio.

forgot their own shortcomings? Such were the questions that were asked in the warehouses of the Philadelphia merchants in the spring of 1828.

The arguments and invective of Philadelphia were matched by the Baltimore supporters. The southern tier of counties of central Pennsylvania was very much interested in the railroad to Baltimore, and its representatives in the Pennsylvania Legislature became the mouthpieces for the Baltimore cause. Since much of this area was geographically closer to the Maryland city than to Philadelphia, its trading interests had always been in Baltimore. Furthermore, the construction of the Pennsylvania State Works embittered the citizens in this area, since some of their taxes were used to construct improvements which did not benefit them directly, as the State's projects did not touch this area and competed with the turnpike roads which passed through the southern part of the Pennsylvania Commonwealth for the business of the West. Old sectional rivalries between this section of the interior and the seaboard came to the fore again; the anti-masonic party, in opposition to the administration in power, gained many friends in Lancaster, York, Adams, and Cumberland counties.

When Baltimore planned an improvement to reach into this disturbed area, the people welcomed the idea. They were determined that Philadelphia should not prevent its construction. They attested that with the railroad to Baltimore, all the people of central Pennsylvania would have a choice of markets and that such choice was of great importance to the producers in giving them a constant demand and a fair price for their goods. The citizens of the southern counties were indignant that Philadelphia should oppose any improvement, especially one which was to be made at the expense of private individuals. They pointed out that Philadelphia would not be taxed to build this railroad as York and other citizens were taxed to construct the State Works.[12] These interior people claimed that they were the "poor step-child of the state," that they never got anything from the State and were now "denied the poor privilege of spending their own money." They were at a loss to conceive how the railroad to Baltimore would divert trade from the Pennsylvania metropolis, "a course which it *never* pursued." The aroused citizens of York claimed, "That among the important rights of a free people, is that of having unrestrained commercial intercourse with each other" and "that we owe it to ourselves as a paramount duty of self-preservation to protect ourselves against the consequences of a commercial tyranny by guarding against the establishment of a commercial monopoly."[13] In final determination the settlers of the southern counties announced, "The voice of

[12] *The York Gazette,* January 27, 1829.
[13] *Ibid.,* December 16, 1828. Prints the resolutions of a town meeting held in York on December 13, 1828.

two hundred thousand farmers of Pennsylvania must and will be heard in a state that has always boasted of her republicanism."[14]

Pleased with the support she was receiving from her rural friends of Pennsylvania, Baltimore was very hopeful over the future. She was unanimously in favor of the railroad into the Susquehanna Valley and believed that the charter would be granted by Pennsylvania without much protest.[15] The Baltimore promoters held that the important question before the legislators convened at Harrisburg was: Should Pennsylvania producers have the opportunity of disposing of their goods at the most convenient market or must they be forced to travel to an inconvenient one just because it happens to be within the borders of their State. The Marylanders claimed that they were not trying to interfere with the construction of an eastern link in the Pennsylvania improvement system but that they merely wished to have a road to compete with it.[16] The Marylanders liked to retell how their State, in a liberal mood, had authorized the construction of the Chesapeake and Delaware Canal. Although this charter had not been given without protest, they contrasted it with the policy of Pennsylvania in her opposition to the chartering of the railroad northward from Baltimore. Above all, the Baltimore railroad sponsors insisted that they asked no money or aid from their sister State but only requested "to be allowed at their own expense to disburse funds in Pennsylvania and furnish her with a market that must annually return to her, in the form of goods and money, *the full value* of any produce her citizens wish to dispose of."[17]

The bill to charter the Baltimore and Susquehanna Railroad in Pennsylvania was defeated in the Legislature early in 1828, but the sharpshooting between the two rival cities continued through the medium of the press. Shortly after the defeat of the bill, there appeared on the desk of each member of the House of Representatives a burlesque memorial signed "Tom, Dick, and Harry." It was an angry attack on Philadelphia, stating:

"That your memorialists reside in the city of Philadelphia, and *therefore* consider themselves entitled to a monopoly of the trade of the state for which your honourable bodies are appointed to legislate. This being *self-evident*, it follows that it is their proper province to insist that every legislative measure should have their *exclusive* good in view, and be cal-

---

[14] *Ibid.*, January 20, 1829.

[15] *Baltimore Chronicle,* February 3, 1828.

[16] Since the Baltimore and Susquehanna Railroad was first talked of, Pennsylvania had authorized the construction of the Philadelphia and Columbia Railroad which was to serve as the eastern link for the State Works. This meant that trade would pass through Columbia on its way to Philadelphia and that Columbia would, therefore, become a more important river town than Middletown.

[17] *Baltimore Chronicle,* February 15, 1828.

culated to secure and perpetuate their vested right to the sole enjoyment of the interior trade of this Commonwealth."[18]

The Philadelphia editors accused Baltimore of this slanderous memorial; they said it was a direct broadside from the shores of the Chesapeake. They declared that neighbors should be prevented from interfering with the affairs of the Pennsylvania Legislature. "Is our state so far degraded," asked the editor of *The Pennsylvania Gazette,* "so pliant, so abject, so obtuse, that her legislature is to be bearded and ridiculed into the sacrifice of the rights of her citizens?" Baltimore merely answered all the remarks and accusations with a smile, claiming no part in the entire affair, but undoubtedly was pleased with the commotion within Pennsylvania.

At the beginning of the next session of the Pennsylvania Legislature, friends of the railroad again planned to apply for a charter. Public meetings were held in York and Carlisle to consider the best approach.[19] A York meeting held December 13, 1828, spoke for the whole southern section of Pennsylvania when it resolved:

"That it is the interest of the interior to contribute its support, as it is the wish of this meeting to cherish friendly feelings towards the metropolis of our state, but that we cannot extend a servile friendship for an ungenerous return, and shall never carry along with it our own interests and those of the community at large."

On December 20, 1828, Emmett M. Doudel of York brought the question of the railroad charter before the House of Representatives of Pennsylvania. This year the petitioners abandoned their former request for the chartering of a company to extend the Baltimore and Susquehanna Railroad from the Mason and Dixon Line, and now asked Pennsylvania to confer the privileges and immunities of a Pennsylvania corporation on the Maryland-incorporated Baltimore and Susquehanna Railroad Company. This was immediately dubbed "An act to vest in the State of Maryland commercial jurisdiction over one-half the territory of Pennsylvania."[20] But Philadelphia was apparently expecting reappearance of this subject, and her delegates were prepared to remonstrate against it as soon as it came before the members. William Lehman, a loyal Philadelphian and an official of the Union Canal Company, insisted that the matter be referred to the Committee on Inland Navigation and Internal Improvements of which he was chairman. After a long

[18] *The Pennsylvania Gazette,* March 13, 1828. The petition is here printed in full.

[19] *The York Gazette,* December 2, 16, 1828; January 20 and 30, 1829. Other central Pennsylvania communities showed much interest and gave support to the proposed railroad.

[20] *The Pennsylvania Reporter,* January 30, 1829.

quarrel over this suggestion, it was voted down, and the bill was referred to the Committee on Corporations.[21]

In the Senate the bill was referred to the Committee on Roads, Bridges, and Internal Navigation of which Stephen Duncan of Philadelphia was chairman. In its report, this committee confined itself to the question of State interest, showing that an advance in the commerce of Philadelphia was of importance to the whole Commonwealth. It illustrated that Philadelphia contributed more than half of the State's revenue for that year and that with the increase of business, resulting from the completion of the State Works, it would become much more. Therefore, the committee presented a negative report maintaining that the incorporation of the Baltimore and Susquehanna Railroad would be an injustice to a large portion of the people of Pennsylvania.[22]

Philadelphia was pleased;[23] York was angry. *The York Gazette* said it was "altogether a one sided report, drawn up by Mr. Duncan, who represents the citizens of Philadelphia and made before a full examination of public opinion could be brought before the legislature."[24]

Senator Henry Logan of York immediately drew up a long preamble and resolutions containing the view of the friends of the proposed railroad, with a critical examination of the arguments used by Duncan which he proposed to the Senate as a substitute for the report presented by the Committee on Roads, Bridges, and Internal Navigation.[25] Logan maintained:

"Upon every view of the subject, which a candid and dispassionate examination presents, it is manifest that the construction of a rail road from the Maryland line to the Susquehanna River, and from thence to some eligible and practicable point in the Cumberland valley, would greatly advance the interest, improve the trade, increase the value of the

---

[21] *The York Gazette*, December 30, 1828. The York paper followed the bill through the Legislature very closely. The proceedings were reprinted in full and numerous editorial comments appended. Philadelphia was often referred to as the City-of-Want-all-Trade.

[22] Hazard, *The Pennsylvania Register*, III, 65-68. Report read in the Senate January 17, 1829.

[23] *Ibid.*, III, 64. Hazard, in a short editorial, favored the stand taken by Philadelphia.

[24] *The York Gazette*, January 20, 1829. Friends of the Baltimore and Susquehanna Railroad were naturally not friends of the Pennsylvania Canal System. When a bill authorizing a loan for the State Canals came up, they warmly denounced it. Since the loan was to be secured through the house of Baring, it was attacked as being unpatriotic and un-American.

[25] *The Preamble and Resolutions offered by Mr. Logan . . . on granting the Baltimore and Susquehanna Rail Road Company the privilege of extending their rail road into the State of Pennsylvania.* Read in the Senate January 24, 1829. *The York Gazette*, February 3, 1829, carried this speech in full.

soil and productions of people of the southern part of this state; whilst, at the same time, it would not conflict with any interest of the state at large, or any portion of the people thereof."[26]

Prospects for the passage of a bill favoring the railroad were very dim. Nevertheless, the editor of *The York Gazette,* with bitter pen, continued to battle for Baltimore and again roundly condemned Philadelphia. He wrote that the southern portion of Pennsylvania was in a less enviable position than the slaves of the deep south:

"The bondsman of the south has the privilege of cultivating a little spot of his own, and by the consent of the master, he carries it to that market where he can make the most of it. — He does not therefore forego his freedom, not employ his labour and pour out his sweat without some recompense. But what do we get from the masters who rule over us? What recompense is made to us for yielding a portion of our natural rights in obedience to our government, and paying millions to support it? Nothing! Our money is squandered to the exclusive accomodation of other sections of the state—and to us denied even the poor privilege of making our own roads with our own Money. — Too much, as Gen. Ogle would say, in a Christian country, and as we get absolutely nothing for the substance which is exacted from us directly and indirectly, in the shape of imposts, taxes, and duties upon licenses, so do we positively not stand in near so favorable a relation to our government as the slave of the south doth to his master."[27]

The Legislature disposed of the railroad issue early in February, 1829; it was defeated by a one-sided vote.[28] All the arguments of the previous session were used against the bill. One additional reason added to Philadelphia's support this year. The Legislature had adopted preliminary measures for the construction of a railroad through the Cumberland Valley which would project in the general direction of Philadelphia.[29] This road was designed to cover the same territory which the Baltimore and Susquehanna Railroad hoped to serve. It appeared as though Philadelphia was planning to use the Baltimore idea of tapping this region as a venture for herself.

But the faithful Baltimore supporters in York County were not seriously disturbed with the defeat of the railroad bill this year. They had devised another scheme which they hoped would be more beneficial for their own prosperity. On April 8, 1829, they managed to have an act passed which extended the life of an old company, which had been incor-

---

[26] *Ibid.,* 12.

[27] *The York Gazette,* January 27, 1829.

[28] *Ibid.,* February 10, 1829; *Poulson's Daily Advertiser,* February 7, 1829; *Niles' Weekly Register,* XXXV, 425-6. The vote in the Senate was 23 to 5. Niles claimed that it could not approve of the principle on which the decision was made. It claimed that the good of the country cannot be determined by State lines.

[29] See pages 144-146.

porated in 1825, whose purpose it was to make the Codorus Creek navigable from the town of York to its mouth near York Haven on the Susquehanna River. Since this navigation would be located along the route that the railroad had planned to follow, its promoters held the Codorus Navigation as part of a possible route to the Susquehanna River. It was maintained that the short distance between York and the Baltimore and Susquehanna terminal on the Mason and Dixon Line could be linked by a railroad built without a State charter.[30] York was greatly pleased with this plan, because it would make her community a point of transfer and not merely a station along the main line.

When the Legislature convened for the 1829-30 session, it found the railroad business again awaiting it. The southern counties claimed that if passage was withheld this year, it would place them "in a situation from which the subject of a tyrant might find an excuse for revolt."[31] The editorial war grew more deadly; debates in the Legislature grew more pointed and bitter. This year the railroad friends were petitioning only for the right to construct a line from York to the Maryland Line, which they felt certain Philadelphia would not deny them. But Philadelphia had not forgotten the Codorus Navigation bill of the previous year and immediately recognized the railroad bill as the same measure proposed in former years dressed in a new guise. Grant them this short railroad, Philadelphia protested, and you give them exactly what they wanted when they asked for a longer road.[32]

A split in the Philadelphia delegation made it possible for the bill to pass the House of Representatives in March 1830. Philadelphia was badly frightened. A contributor to *Poulson's Daily Advertiser* using the pen-name "Penn," wrote, "*Now* or *never* is the time to come forward and respectfully *to remonstrate* against the passage of the bill" for its enactment "will prove the FUNERAL KNELL of our city and county."[33] "A Native of Philadelphia" added that every ton of goods taken southward brought Philadelphia nearer to bankruptcy. He prayed that Pennsylvania should try to settle all her internal problems peacefully and that "our neighbours may not take so deep an interest in our *internal* improvements AND OH that B**********s may not go again to H********* to treat our *legislature* to hot suppes and Whiskey Punch."[34]

---

[30] *The York Gazette*, May 12, 1829, August 24, 1832. Baltimoreans were skeptical of the route and feared that their York friends were scheming against them for their own benefit. The Marylanders went so far as to look about for a different route to the river.

[31] *Ibid.*, December 1, 8, 1829.

[32] Hazard, *The Pennsylvania Register*, V, 200.

[33] *Poulson's Daily Advertiser*, March 25, 1830.

[34] *Ibid.*, April 3, 1830.

A large town meeting was held in Philadelphia with the mayor in the chair on March the twenty-fifth to remonstrate with her delegates in the House of Representatives. Plans were also made to devise plans to check the progress of the measure in the Senate. The Philadelphians insisted that the resources of the State should not be carried to "a foreign market" in a manner which would impoverish the metropolis of the Commonwealth and aggrandize the citizens in a rival commercial center. They said that the railroad would:

". . . rend assunder the bonds that now unite together the different parts of the commonwealth; that it will create a permanent discordance between the interests of the eastern and western parts of the state. That its energies will no longer remain united—but that the state will hereafter be consigned to the most interminable disputes; and that reciprocity of good feeling will be banished from its councils."[35]

York immediately called a town meeting to attack the "out-door influence" which Philadelphia was planning to exert in the Senate. The Yorkers, recalling past struggles, reflected:

". . . a similar contention arose when we asked for the incorporation of our turnpikes, the same jealousies were excited, the same arguments used and the same results foretold—still, the old course of trade is pursued, the produce is still sold in Baltimore and goods still bought in Philadelphia. The latter has still prospered, the state still remains uninjured. . . ."

Resolutions were passed by the York meeting commending the Representatives for passing the bill and condemning Philadelphia "for unwarranted interference." Committees were appointed to carry the objects of the meeting into effect.[36] The internal rivalry within Pennsylvania seemed to have reached a crisis.

However, when the railroad bill was brought before the Senate, Philadelphia interest predominated. The bill was immediately doomed. This decision caused much ill feeling in the southern counties; York called another town meeting to air its sentiments. A disposition was manifest to adopt strong measures. Philadelphia's acts were declared "illiberal, unjust, promotive of invidious hostility, contrary to the spirit of social compact, and calculated to aggrandize a part at the expense of the whole." The State metropolis was tagged the "spoiled child of the commonwealth"; her attempts to guide trade as "a blight upon the commerce and property of the state at large."[37]

[35] *Ibid.*, March 27, 1830; Hazard, *The Pennsylvania Register*, V, 212-13.

[36] *Niles' Weekly Register*, XXXVIII, 107; Hazard, *The Pennsylvania Register*, V, 245-6.

[37] *Niles' Weekly Register*, XXXVIII, 107, 125; Hazard, *The Pennsylvania Register*, V, 246; *The York Gazette*, April 13, 1830.

Despite the numerous defeats, the supporters of the railroad plan did not give up hope. Baltimore voted $100,000 as a subscription to the stock of the Maryland-incorporated Baltimore and Susquehanna Railroad, while York made plans to construct a railroad without a charter from the Maryland line to her city.[38] Voluntary grants of land were solicited so that a direct line could be had without the necessity of legal documents. The President of the Maryland-chartered road upheld this rash plan saying:

"A Rail Road company having once obtained the right of soil over which it passes, has no more occasion for a charter or the protection of law, than the proprietor of a steam boat would for a charter to navigate the free waters of Chesapeake Bay."

However, when the Legislature reconvened, the Philadelphia papers reported that the York folks were again at Harrisburg *"boring* for their favorite Baltimore project."[39] Public meetings were again held; old arguments were marched and countermarched before the crowds. Sound arguments often gave way to the noise of the sensitive trade centers which became active whenever their rival for commercial purposes attempted to encroach on what they considered closed territory. Committees were reappointed; pressure was again applied.[40] The battle in the Legislature was renewed; the delegates of York, Adams, and Cumberland counties fenced bitterly with Messrs. Simpson, Davis, Pettit, and Brown of the Philadelphia district. The latter group asked if it were prudent to drain Philadelphia of her life blood. They maintained that if the railroad bill passed their city would become "a second Palmyra." "If this system obtains," said Davis, "the state will soon be like the old Commodore who died in the West Indies and who was sent home in old Jamaica rum; the sailors tapped him (as Maryland wishes to tap this state), and on his arrival he was found lying on his beam ends, as dry as this tapping would leave us, if we do not put a stop to it."[41] In one debate the Philadelphia delegate referred to his city as the goose which lays the golden egg, since she paid so much into the State treasury. He was immediately answered by many taunts. One opponent retaliated by saying that in at least one sense this was true, "Philadelphia was a goose in one sense, for he saw a gander among her offspring." A York editor commented, "If mother goose did not get corn to feed on from the country, her eggs and ganders would soon cease to make such a proud array." Philadelphia's influence in the Legislature was still strong; the charter bill again suffered defeat.

---

[38] *Niles' Weekly Register,* XXXVIII, 125, 205; *Address to the Mayor and City Council,* 14-15.
[39] *Poulson's Daily Advertiser,* February 4, 1831.
[40] *The York Gazette,* January 11, 1831.
[41] *Ibid.,* January 25, 1831.

Success which was attending the Baltimore and Ohio Railroad helped rally support to the Baltimore and Susquehanna project as it entered its fourth year of the charter struggle in the Pennsylvania Legislature. Governor Wolf added to this movement when he announced in his annual message that he favored the incorporation of the railroad company.[42] But the opponents of the measure did not give in without protesting every inch of the way. Public meetings were held in Philadelphia in protest; the charter, they reasserted, should never be allowed. Their representatives were informed that they must continue to work against the incorporation.[43] Resolutions and the proceedings of the meeting were printed and widely disseminated. A committee was appointed from the Common Council of the city to journey to Harrisburg and exert all its influence to stop the measure.[44] Philadelphia enthusiasts again donned all the paraphernalia of war.

York fought back as hard as she could; she was supported by many delegates from the Susquehanna Valley. Baltimore was unusually disturbed; if the bill did not pass this session, it was proposed to hold a large public meeting to take into consideration the propriety of closing the navigation of Back Creek through which the Chesapeake and Delaware traffic passed.

At Harrisburg, the heat of battle became more intense than ever before. Debaters became so outspoken that some of their remarks could not be recorded as these gentlemen were "out of order." Various amendments were presented by those who feared that the bill would pass in order to take the teeth out of its immediate importance. One amendment suggested that the railroad company be prohibited from charging less tolls than those which the State was planning to charge on the Philadelphia and Columbia road. Another required a law to be passed by the Maryland Legislature granting Pennsylvania the privilege of tapping the Baltimore and Ohio Railroad. A third suggested amendment, and one which Philadelphia favored wholeheartedly, stated that the Baltimore Railroad should be built to Columbia and that it should not be put under contract until the completion of the Philadelphia and Columbia Railroad.[45] The Pennsylvania metropolis believed that it would have no trouble winning the trade gathered at Columbia and that Baltimore would not be able to divert business from this channel at a later date.

Regardless of committees, resolutions, and amendments, the bill to incorporate the York and Maryland Line Railroad became law on March

---

[42] *Pennsylvania Archives*, Fourth Series, V, 1000.

[43] *Niles' Weekly Register*, XLI, 377; Hazard, *The Pennsylvania Register*, IX, 46-48; *Poulson's Daily Advertiser*, January 19, 1832.

[44] Hazard, *The Pennsylvania Register*, IX, 64.

[45] *The Columbia Spy*, February 2 and 23, 1832.

14, 1832.[46] When news of the passage of the bill reached York, a big celebration was staged. In describing this event *The York Gazette* wrote:

"Men, women, and children seemed to have but one wish, the wish of testifying to one another how deep, sincere and heartfelt was their joy. Words were inadequate to the purpose. So, too, was the cordial shaking of hands. Another way was struck out. The national flag was unfurled over our heads. The bells rang merrily and long. The cannon growled in the distance. At night there was an illumination, not partial, but general. A procession was formed, composed of the people, and set in motion by our excellent band of music. In a word, the town was literally alive in spite of wind and weather—and it was cold enough to blunt the blade of a razor—till about nine o'clock, when the lights were extinguished, and the thousands separated."

The charter granted, however, was defective in many respects and was of doubtful value. However, at the next session of the Legislature a supplement was obtained so that it could be of practical use to the company.[47]

Work which had been begun on the Maryland-chartered Baltimore and Susquehanna Railroad while the charter fight was young progressed rather slowly. By July 4, 1831, the seven-mile first division was completed. Since the company could not build in Pennsylvania, it then turned to the construction of a branch road to Westminster, Maryland.[48] The following year, the English-built locomotive, Herald, was put into operation by the company. When this engine arrived, it had wheels four feet in diameter, which were much too large for the numerous, short curves of the first division. Smaller wheels had to be substituted on the Herald and the wooden track, which did not stand up under the weight of the locomotive, was relaid after a short period.[49]

Baltimore had grappled with a strong hand for the railroad she deemed so important; but a big task still confronted her. After Pennsylvania granted a charter for a railroad from York to connect with the Baltimore and Susquehanna, a road which was really an extension of the latter, the railroad company reported that nothing was wanted except a loan sufficient to carry on the work of construction.[50] The large internal improve-

---

[46] The Baltimore and Susquehanna Railroad Company, *Annual Report*, 1832; Poor, *op. cit.*, I, 517; *The York Gazette*, March 20, 1832.

[47] The Baltimore and Susquehanna Railroad Company, *Annual Report*, 1835.

[48] *Ibid.*, 1831; Scharf, *Chronicles of Baltimore*, 457.

[49] The Baltimore and Susquehanna Railroad Company, *Annual Report*, 1836; Varle, *View of Baltimore*, footnote, 107.

[50] The Baltimore and Susquehanna Railroad Company, *Annual Report*, 1835. Many subscribers forfeited their stock during the long struggle in the Pennsylvania Legislature for the charter.

ment meeting held in Baltimore in December, 1834, gave the company confidence when it passed resolutions concerning the practicability of the Baltimore and Susquehanna Railroad.[51] A memorial was thereupon drawn up and submitted to the Maryland Legislature soliciting aid on behalf of the railroad. In accurate terms, the importance of the road was pictured to the lawmakers:

"The great canal of New York is the outward line of demarcation for the circumscription of this trade (the commerce of the Chesapeake region) and, as the second parallel approaches nearer to a besieged city than the first confining and cramping its inhabitants to a still more limited range, until a sortie becomes necessary to relieve themselves from its pressure, so the Pennsylvania works, crossing from east to west, have narrowed still further the trade of the Chesapeake."[52]

The Maryland House of Representatives answered the plea for funds with the grant of a million dollar loan to the company. As soon as this news reached Baltimore, a huge town-meeting, with Jesse Hunt in the chair, convened. A committee was immediately appointed to hasten to Annapolis to use its pressure when the bill came before the Senate.[53] This action, on the part of Baltimore, was unnecessary; the spirit of internal improvement had taken hold in the Maryland Legislature and the bill was easily passed by the second chamber.

Besides the problem of raising funds, the company also had to face difficult construction and engineering problems and a bad labor situation. The topographical features of the country between York and Baltimore exhibit an irregularity of outline and variety of aspect which is extremely unusual for a district so near the seaboard. This region is broken with numerous high, steep hills scattered between narrow, rocky valleys. The surveyors found it necessary to wind the railroad through these narrow, unproductive vales which at places are barely wide enough to house the brisk little stream which races in and out under the railroad trestles. Near York it was impossible to avoid a hard grade so the engineers constructed a tunnel through the ridge.

While construction was slowly meeting the problems which nature forced her to solve, labor troubles caused added worries for the railroad authorities. The large number of public works under construction caused a scarcity of workmen. High wages were demanded. Early in 1836, a strike was called on the Baltimore and Susquehanna Railroad, "an imita-

---

[51] *Niles' Weekly Register*, XLVII, 233.

[52] *Memorial to the General Assembly of Maryland in behalf of the Baltimore and Susquehanna Rail Road Company; Memorial of the President and Directors of the Baltimore and Susquehanna Rail Road Company.*

[53] *Niles' Weekly Register*, XLVIII, 121. This bill also called for a loan of two million dollars to the Chesapeake and Ohio Canal Company.

tion of a fashion very prevalent."[54] Some stopped work and attacked those on duty. Jails soon housed the strikers who were deemed out of order although construction was retarded by the disturbance.

The original intention of the promoters of the Baltimore and Susquehanna Railroad had been to construct a through line to the Susquehanna River. Naturally, they were not satisfied with a mongrel system of railroad to York and slackwater navigation from that town to the mouth of the Codorus Creek. The railroad officials had, from an early date, shown their disapproval of the York plan which called for the incorporation of the York and Maryland Line Railroad and the use of the Codorus Navigation. They did not want a line like the Pennsylvania State Works; they certainly hoped to avoid transshipment costs. But during the charter struggle in the Pennsylvania Legislature the entire situation had changed. The eastern link of Pennsylvania's trans-Appalachian improvement changed the commercial center of the Susquehanna River from Middletown to Columbia. The Codorus Navigation, therefore, was not so effective a tap as its officials had hoped. The Philadelphia and Columbia Railroad defeated the York plan and left Baltimore free to construct a through railroad to the Susquehanna. Naturally, the Baltimore railroad men wished this new line to be constructed to the growing town of Columbia.

On April 15, 1835, the Pennsylvania Legislature created the York and Wrightsville Railroad Company as a private firm.[55] From its birth, the future of this road was bright. The old York and Wrightsville Turnpike Company had paid remarkable dividends. The railroad was to connect with the Pennsylvania State Works and would be a link in the through line from Philadelphia to Baltimore or from Pittsburgh to Baltimore. When the books were opened in June, 1835, for the taking of subscriptions, more than three times the capital stock was immediately taken.[56] With the consent of the authorities of Baltimore and Maryland, the financial supporters of the Baltimore and Susquehanna Railroad Company, the

[54] *The York Gazette,* March 29, 1836; The Baltimore and Susquehanna Railroad Company, *Annual Report,* 1836. The workers demanded a dollar a day and an increased number of "jiggers." (A "jigger" was a small measure of whiskey supplied at intervals during the day for the workers' refreshment.)

[55] Tanner, *Description of the Canals and Railroads in the United States,* 132; Poor, *op. cit.,* I, 517; Meyer, ed, *op. cit.,* 413. In 1835 Pennsylvania authorized the extension of the Philadelphia and Columbia to Wrightsville. By October tracks were laid across the Columbia bridge. Soon after this time, an application was made by certain citizens for a charter for a railroad from Wrightsville to York. The State had previously considered making this section of railroad as part of the State Works, but not desiring at this time to extend the State's obligations, these plans were surrendered and the private company chartered.

[56] *The York Gazette,* July 7, 1835.

officials of that organization assisted in the organization and construction of the new section to the river. Five of the seven officials of the York and Wrightsville Railroad were Baltimore citizens.[57]

When the railroad engineers began to cut a path through the farms of this section for the railroad, the residents petitioned the Legislature to withdraw the charter. These requests were hastily thrown out; instead of considering such action, the Anti-Masonic Legislature on March 21, 1836, passed an act incorporating a railroad from Wrightsville to Gettysburg. This meant that there would be two roads from Wrightsville to York. The enactment of this measure caused a veritable political war among the editors and politicians of this section. The "Extra-Railroad" was the subject of heated discussion.[58] Thaddeus Stevens, who planned this road and served as its President, was roundly denounced. After much wrangling, the two roads were incorporated into one company known as the Wrightsville, York, and Gettysburg Rail Road Company. This agreement stipulated that the Baltimore and Susquehanna Company was to subscribe to the capital stock of the new organization the amount of the loan formerly made to the Wrightsville and York Company, and to furnish additional funds for the completion of the section of the railroad from York to Wrightsville as loans to be repaid with interest secured by a mortgage of the property of the Pennsylvania company. On the other hand, the Baltimore and Susquehanna Railroad Company secured the right to use the railroad from York to Wrightsville with their own locomotives until the completion of the York to Gettysburg section. After that date, the Wrightsville, York, and Gettysburg road was required to transport the cars of the Baltimore and Susquehanna so that trade to and from Baltimore would be carried on without any delay at York.[59]

In August, 1838, the railroad from Baltimore to York was opened for business. With the opening of this great artery it was claimed that the town of York was "transferred into a vast hive, the receptacle of the wealth of the surrounding country." From the completion of the railroad on August 23, 1838, to October of the following year, its earnings amounted to $99,622. It carried during this period almost 20,000 tons of freight.

The thirteen-mile Wrightsville to York division was completed in May, 1840, and opened for traffic.[60] It practically belonged to the Balti-

[57] *Ibid.*, August 18, 1835.

[58] *Ibid.*, April 19, March 22, July 26, August 9, 16, September 6, 26, 27.

[59] The Baltimore and Susquehanna Railroad Company, *Annual Report*, 1839.

[60] *Hunt's Merchants' Magazine*, XX, 486; *Niles' Weekly Register*, LVIII, 144; Scharf, *Chronicles of Baltimore*, 503; The Baltimore and Susquehanna Railroad Company, *Annual Report*, 1840.

more and Susquehanna Company which at this date owned all its stock and held most of its mortgage. From the beginning it was operated as a part of the older company. The year this division opened, the earnings of the Baltimore and Susquehanna Company increased to $138,716, this increase occurring mostly in the freight department.[61] Three transport lines were organized to conduct business with Pittsburgh after the Baltimore railroad had a junction with the Pennsylvania State Works. Producers from Chambersburg and Carlisle began to ship goods to Baltimore via York. The Cumberland Valley folk shipped their produce to Harrisburg over the Cumberland Valley Railroad, then to Lancaster over the Harrisburg, Portsmouth, Mt. Joy and Lancaster Railroad, from which point it was transferred to the Philadelphia and Columbia line and carried to Columbia, from which center it was forwarded over the Wrightsville and York division to York. In 1840 this trade seemed "likely to become of an important magnitude."[62]

Although the total earnings had risen almost $40,000 over the 1839 totals, business in 1840 was not as brisk as had been anticipated. The same year the York and Wrightsville division was opened, the Susquehanna and Tidewater Canal was completed to Wrightsville.[63] With the construction of this canal, the point of competition between Philadelphia and Baltimore for the strictly river traffic and for much of the trade of the Pennsylvania Main Line moved south to Havre de Grace. There was scarcely enough trade between Wrightsville and Baltimore to give both the railroad and the canal prosperity. In 1843 the railroad deemed it necessary to wage a rate war against the canal which caused a great drop in the revenues for the next few years.[64] The effect of the canal on the receipts of the railroad can best be seen from the figures for 1846 when floods injured the canal. In that year the gross tonnage on the railroad

---

[61] See Appendix, XIV, 141.

[62] The Baltimore and Susquehanna Railroad Company, *Annual Report,* 1840. The trade between Baltimore and Pittsburgh over the Baltimore and Susquehanna Railroad in both directions was:

1839 (yr. ending September 30)	4,106 tons
1840	6,854
1841	7,734
1842	9,076
1843	12,777
1844	18,615
1845	21,813
1846	28,089

(compiled from the *Annual Reports*)

[63] See page 74.

[64] The Baltimore and Susquehanna Railroad Company, *Annual Report,* 1843, 1844.

jumped from 112,000 to 151,000 while the earnings amounted to the new high figure of more than $210,000.[65] Local freight made up little of this total because of the sparseness of population along the railroad.

Business on the railroad was also hampered by a lack of rolling stock and the need of roadbed repairs. In 1846 the company was forced to ask the Maryland Legislature for authority to borrow money for rolling stock.[66] Besides the lack of funds, the company was also handicapped by the stand taken by the Maryland Governor. For some time the company was forced to operate without the purchase of additional machinery and rolling stock because of the Governor's strict reading of the law.[67] By 1850 the Baltimore and Susquehanna Railroad Company owned only fourteen locomotives, eighteen passenger cars, and 377 freight cars although they boasted of a $50,000 station in Baltimore, the most "spacious and commodious" south of New England.[68]

Despite the fact that the railroad was not as profitable as had been dreamed, Baltimore felt that she commanded a geographic advantage over Philadelphia because of her road. But, in 1846, this advantage was challenged. On the 13th of April of that year, the Legislature of Pennsylvania chartered the Pennsylvania Railroad Company with authority to construct a line from Harrisburg to Pittsburgh. From the eastern terminal of this new route, produce would be carried to Philadelphia by way of the Harrisburg, Portsmouth, Mt. Joy, and Lancaster Railroad and the Philadelphia and Columbia Railroad.[69] This new railroad gave the Pennsylvania metropolis a through rail connection with the West; Baltimore's chances of diverting business under these conditions certainly would be slight.

The Maryland city, however, found a solution to this new turn of events in a railroad chartered just eight days later. On April 21, 1846, the Pennsylvania Legislature chartered a company to construct a railroad from York to Bridgeport, a small town on the west bank of the Susquehanna River opposite Harrisburg.[70] This company immediately became affiliated with the Baltimore and Susquehanna Company, although the latter was financially embarrassed and could help very little. In order to pay for completing the various lines of the railroad and their fixtures, to

---

[65] *Ibid.*, 1846.

[66] *Ibid.*, 1846; *Report of the Directors on the Part of the State in the Baltimore and Susquehanna Rail Road Company to the Legislature of Maryland, 1846.*

[67] *Report of the Directors on the Part of the City in the Baltimore and Susquehanna Rail Road Company, 1847.*

[68] *Hunt's Merchants' Magazine*, XXIII, 46.

[69] See page 151.

[70] Poor, *op. cit.*, I, 518; Wilson, *History of the Pennsylvania Railroad*, I, 238; Hall, ed., *Baltimore, Its History and Its People*, I, 485.

discharge the debt which had been allowed to accumulate, and to redeem notes and scrip which had been issued, most of the company's funds were needed. No dividends had ever been paid.

The financial standing of the Baltimore and Susquehanna Company made the public reluctant to subscribe stock in a project which it was backing. But Baltimore saw the importance of the extension and gave its support. Writing in 1847, some of the Baltimore railroad supporters insisted:

"Now is the time to move,—if the opportunity is permitted to pass, years may elapse before the same advantage may be presented; in the meantime Philadelphia will be reaping the fruits of the immense trade which Baltimore should have, and which she is now entitled to."[71]

It was maintained that the extension of the Baltimore railroad to Bridgeport would secure for the Chesapeake metropolis a more favorable position to compete for the trade of the Susquehanna Valley and the West than she had at Columbia before the new situation arose. At Bridgeport the railroad could tap the proposed new railroad to Pittsburgh and would be able to control much of the trade of the river. From this point it was about 106 miles to Philadelphia, while Baltimore was almost twenty miles closer.

After liberal offers by Maryland and Baltimore for funding the Baltimore and Susquehanna Railroad Company's debt,[72] the citizens of Baltimore came forward and subscribed $530,000 in capital stock and $200,000 in bonds.[73] The merchants of the city of Baltimore had benefited from the railroad into the Susquehanna Valley and were willing to give it further support. They saw, in 1847, a substantial jump in the gross freight and earnings of the railroad, while net earnings had soared to $77,000. The British consul, writing at a little later date, reflected the importance of the road to the Maryland city in which he lived:

"The Baltimore and Susquehanna Rail Road contributes largely to the commerce of this port. The terminus being at York, Penn., it is in immediate contact with the 'Key Stone State,' and Baltimore thus is enabled to divert to her warehouses a vast portion of the western traffic, which would otherwise be attracted to Philadelphia."[74]

---

[71] *Report of the Directors on the Part of the City in the Baltimore and Susquehanna Rail Road Company,* 1847.

[72] In a Maryland statute which passed during the December session, 1847, the Maryland Legislature stated that as soon as connections with the Pennsylvania Railroad were secured, the arrearages of interest due the state by the Baltimore and Susquehanna Railroad Company upon loans made to the company should be funded for fifteen years and its payment postponed provided such connection be made before March 1, 1851.

[73] Wilson, *History of the Pennsylvania Railroad,* I, 238.

[74] British Consular Reports, F. O. 5/517, McTavish to Palmerton, September 10, 1850.

With Baltimore's support the Baltimore and Susquehanna Railroad Company was able to reorganize, financially, in 1848. Work on the proposed new section, which was called the York and Cumberland Railroad, was begun the next year. By February, 1851, this division was completed and open for business.[75] A permanent contract was thereupon drawn up between the Baltimore and Susquehanna Company and the York and Cumberland Company for operating the road. The Baltimore and Susquehanna Railroad obligated itself to furnish the locomotives, and passenger, baggage, and mail cars necessary for operation of the road for which they were to get one-third of the passenger and one-half of the freight earnings of the new division.[76] From the fifth of February until October 1, 1851, the earnings of the York and Cumberland Railroad were $20,214, of which the older company received $7,931. The Baltimore and Susquehanna Company thereupon reported:

"Strong in the natural advantage of her geographical position, sustained by the operation of liberal and enlightened legislation on the part of sister states, our city has it now within the limits of her own will, to solve the problem of her future prosperity."[77]

The Maryland city decided that her "future prosperity" was in more railroads. When the line to Bridgeport was completed, Baltimore wished to push farther north, cross the Pennsylvania Railroad, tap the anthracite coal fields, and reach into New York state to connect with the great New York system of improvements.[78] The Pennsylvania Legislature granted this desire by incorporating a company to construct a railroad from Bridgeport northward along the Susquehanna River to Sunbury.[79] This legislation became law on April 14, 1851, after a bitter struggle. Philadelphia opposed the charter since she did not wish the Baltimore route to cross the Pennsylvania Railroad. Again the Pennsylvania metropolis denounced the intrusion of an outsider. Again she feared the loss of the trade of central Pennsylvania and the great western hinterland. In addition, she argued that no one from another state should be given access to the anthracite region.

In the act that passed the Legislature, more than 140 prominent men of the business and political worlds of Baltimore and the Susquehanna Valley were empowered to solicit subscriptions for stock in the company

---

[75] Poor, *op. cit.*, I, 518; The Baltimore and Susquehanna Railroad Company, *Annual Report*, 1851. This section was finished less than one month before the date stipulated by the Maryland Legislature in its funding agreement of 1847.

[76] Poor, *op. cit.*, I, 518.

[77] The Baltimore and Susquehanna Railroad Company, *Annual Report*, 1851.

[78] Andrews, *Trade and Commerce of the British North American Colonies and upon the Trade of the Great Lakes and Rivers*, 321.

[79] Susquehanna Railroad Company, *Annual Report*, 1854; Wilson, *op. cit.*, I, 238.

which was officially called the Susquehanna Railroad Company. The company was required to begin construction within three years and complete the route within eight. In addition to the main line, authority was also granted to extend the road to Williamsport and Wilkes-Barre.[80]

Baltimore was pleased with the situation. One of her delegates to the Susquehanna Railroad Convention which met at Sunbury in the spring of 1851 declared:

"It will be found upon an examination of the facts to which we invite attention that Baltimore has been very suddenly, within the short space of the last year or two, almost unconsciously to herself, placed in a position of singularly advantageous relationship to this valley of the Susquehanna; that circumstances over which she has exerted no control and towards which she has not even contributed, in any manner whatever, are now in a progress of full development, which will with her assistance hereafter, *must render her the nearest and most convenient depot to the trade of the largest commercial circle that is connected with any city in the Union.*"[81]

Philadelphia did not overlook Baltimore's latest gain. Opposition to the new extension was very keen. Finally a change was enacted in the law which chartered the Susquehanna Railroad Company. As a supplement to an act incorporating the Sunbury and Erie Railroad Company passed March 27, 1852, stipulations limiting the privileges of the Susquehanna Company were appended. This company was now required to put the construction of the portion of the road between Bridgeport and Sunbury under contract for construction within one year from the passage of the act and to complete the same within two years. If the Susquehanna Company failed to meet these requirements, the Sunbury and Erie Railroad was to be awarded the privilege of constructing a railroad from Sunbury to the Pennsylvania Railroad.[82] Philadelphia worked hard to gain this change of legislation. The commercial citizens of the Pennsylvania metropolis saw a definite enemy in the Baltimore-owned road; they were anxious for the construction of a railroad in the Susquehanna Valley which would reach Sunbury, since it would be a valuable feeder for the Pennsylvania Railroad.

But the change merely stimulated the friends of the Susquehanna Railroad to hasten organization and construction. By June 10, 1852, officials were elected; work was put under contract in November.[83] The Baltimore Board of Trade gave the company a hearty blessing;[84] the city

---

[80] The Susquehanna Railroad Company, *Annual Report,* 1854.

[81] The Baltimore and Susquehanna Railroad Company, *Annual Report,* 1853; *Hunt's Merchants' Magazine,* XXXVI, 173-7.

[82] The Susquehanna Railroad Company, *Annual Report,* 1854.

[83] *Ibid.,* 1854.

[84] *Hunt's Merchants' Magazine,* XXVII, 627.

guaranteed the payment of the principal and interest of a $500,000 loan of bonds of the York and Cumberland Railroad Company to the Susquehanna Company. Baltimore interest was especially keen in this new division because of the wonderful direct connections it would provide for the Maryland city. At Bridgeport, Baltimore had a junction with the Cumberland Valley Railroad; eight miles distant from this point, the Susquehanna Railroad would cross the main line of the Pennsylvania Railroad. At Dauphin the new road was to cross the Susquehanna River and connect with the Dauphin and Susquehanna Railroad, a coal road of potential importance. Farther north the Lykens Valley Railroad, another coal line, was to be crossed; and about fifteen miles north of this point, the Susquehanna Railroad would meet the Treverton Railroad. Sunbury, the northern terminal of the road, was becoming a very important junction for railroads planned in northern Pennsylvania.

The Susquehanna Railroad Company began work with great earnestness in February, 1853, but financial troubles caused construction to be suspended in March, 1854. The 54-mile section from Bridgeport to Sunbury was never to be completed by the company which began construction. The various divisions of the railroad which was threading the Susquehanna Valley were consolidated into the Northern Central Railway Company on December 4, 1854, after having been granted legal permission by the Legislatures of Maryland and Pennsylvania.[85] Under the guidance of the old Baltimore and Susquehanna Railroad Company a great system was constructed which reached far into the Susquehanna Valley and crossed the important works leading westward from Philadelphia.[86]

Baltimore continued to give its support to the railroad of the Susquehanna Valley. Her activity in the Northern Central was especially stimulated by the possibility of gaining a large anthracite coal trade which the railroad officials held out to them. In the first annual report of the consolidated company, the authorities stated:

"Our citizens may, if they choose to devote themselves to this acquisition, establish a coal export on the Patapsco equal to that of the Delaware, which has constituted the most conspicuous element in the growth of the wealth of the City of Philadelphia. . . . What, therefore, the Schuylkill region was in the beginning to Philadelphia, the Susquehanna now is to Baltimore. What the former is, this day, to our neighbor city, the latter may be to our own, if Baltimore be true to that renown for

---

[85] *Ibid.*, LIV, 366; The Baltimore and Susquehanna Railroad Company, *Annual Report*, 1854. Maryland approved of the consolidation on March 10, 1854, and Pennsylvania on May 3, 1854.

[86] The first undertakings of this new organization were to complete the work commenced by the Susquehanna Railroad and to extend their lines from Baltimore to Canton to connect with the Philadelphia, Wilmington, and Baltimore Railroad.

liberal enterprise which she has won in past times, and which alone will conduct her to great prosperity."[87]

The growing importance of the Northern Central soon caused its downfall. The Baltimore and Ohio Company soon began to fear it as a rival and set about blocking its success. Personal and political pressure was applied to the Maryland Legislature which soon pressed the Northern Central to settle its debts to the state. This the railroad company confessed it was unable to do. Stocks fell; the earnings of the Northern Central failed to equal the expense of operation. The Baltimore and Ohio, in order to control the Northern Central, bought much of its stock. This, however, the former was forced to sell in the monetary panic which followed Lincoln's election. These shares were taken by the Pennsylvania Railroad Company and, together with later purchases on the London market, the control of the Baltimore road was transferred to the railroad of its rival city.

After bitter years of quarrels and blows, Baltimore had gained permission in 1832 to construct a railroad northward into the Susquehanna Valley of Pennsylvania. Annually the road crept northward until Sunbury was reached. The anticipation of future wealth and prestige was ever in the minds of its sponsors; the desire to tap Philadelphia's western routes of transportation and to dominate the coal trade caused the Baltimore and Susquehanna to grasp beyond its fading financial means. This suicidal policy made its passing inevitable.

---

[87] The Northern Central Railway Company, *Annual Report*, 1855.

APPENDIX XIV

Earnings of the Baltimore and Susquehanna Railroad Company and Its Affiliated Lines, 1839-1854

Year	Miles of road operated	Gross earnings freight	Gross earnings total	Net earnings
1839	67.5	$49,773	$99,622	$31,530
1840	80.5	78,501	138,716	47,952
1841	80.5	97,067	152,949	62,012
1842*	80.5	89,374	137,667	50,526
1843†	80.5	77,385	119,397	33,159
1844	80.5	99,376	148,017	33,768
1845	80.5	111,533	164,661	32,422
1846‡	80.5	150,683	210,635	48,149
1847	80.5	185,407	256,914	77,012
1848§	80.5	160,379	240,866	71,572
1849¶	80.5	187,777	274,893	89,313
1850	80.5	187,773	284,597	97,929
1851	107.5	244,455	362,157	133,256
1852	120.5	269,247	413,674	118,504
1853	120.5	325,789	508,229	206,232
1854	120.5	357,992	554,526	113,025

* Falling off of gross revenue for merchandise and increase in quality transported due to increase of short haul business.

† Reduction in receipts, not in tonnage, due to reduction of rates to meet competition of Susquehanna and Tidewater Canal.

‡Increase: 1846 floods injured Susquehanna and Tidewater Canal.

§ Falling off of freight transportation. The principal cause was due to a break in the Pennsylvania State Works. Also high prices of bread stuffs in 1847 brought larger quantities of wheat and flour to market in 1847 than usual.

¶ Water low in Pennsylvania Canal. Milk transportation began to assume considerable importance.

No dividends were paid between 1839 and 1854.

(Poor, *op. cit.*, I, 587)

CHAPTER VII

EARLY SYMPTOMS OF THE "RAILROAD MANIA" IN PHILADELPHIA

Business men of 1820 turned to internal improvements as the panacea of their commercial and financial ailments. In Philadelphia, not only were old canal projects revived but signs of railroad interest developed. Before England's famous Stockton and Darlington line was completed in 1825, the Pennsylvania metropolis had chartered a railroad from that city to the Susquehanna River. Undaunted by the failure of this first venture, other routes were soon proposed, especially after Baltimore had revealed its intention to build a railway northward from the Chesapeake Bay. In the southern section of central Pennsylvania, two roads were chartered and constructed to lead the trade of that area to Philadelphia before the current of business flowed too swiftly in a southerly direction. Farther north, Philadelphia encouraged the construction of a railroad across the rugged anthracite region between Pottsville on the Schuylkill Navigation and Sunbury to guide the trade of the North and West Branches of the Susquehanna to their wharves and warehouses. Projected and constructed under the overwhelming influence of the Pennsylvania State Works, the Philadelphia railroads in the Susquehanna Valley failed to grow into carriers of an extensive character and served chiefly as feeder routes.

An air of languid apathy dominated the commercial houses of Philadelphia after the panic of 1819 had stricken the country as a whole. Help was needed; help was offered. The far-sighted and progressive John Stevens of Hoboken, New Jersey, believed that Philadelphia could be benefited by his plans for railroad construction. As early as 1812 this competitor of Fulton in the field of steam navigation publicly advocated the theory of carriage by rail and predicted the practicability of using steam.[1] The boldness of his aims had marked John Stevens as a dreamer on whom the practical politicians of the day would waste no time. After numerous failures, he wrote on January 5, 1821, to the mayor of Philadelphia on the subject of railroads. The mayor sent his letter to the City Council, which showed no interest in the matter. But the business men of the city were desperate. Their tills were fast being depleted; their trade was passing to rival neighbors. The Erie Canal was under construction; steamers were plying on the Mississippi and Ohio Rivers. If the western trade was to be retained, some means of transportation was necessary and Stevens' railroad seemed likely to furnish the solution. Late in 1822, John Stevens, supported by prominent men[2] of the city of Philadelphia,

---

[1] McMaster, *op. cit.,* V, 138.
[2] Stephen Girard, Horace Binney, John Cauley and others.

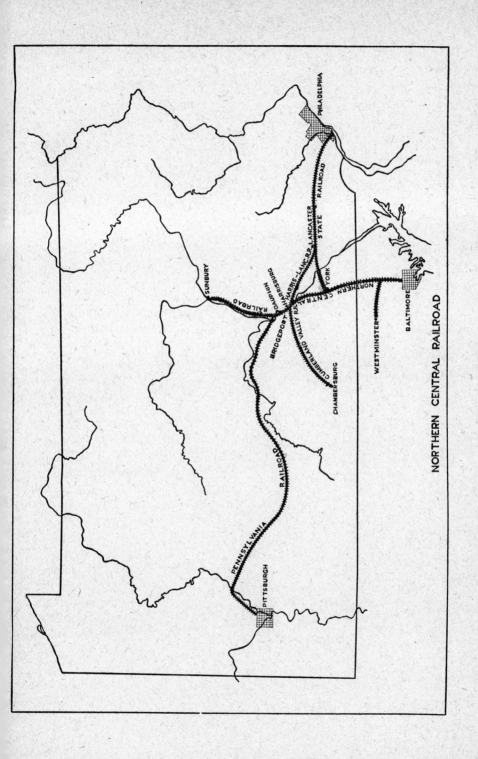

NORTHERN CENTRAL RAILROAD

applied to the Legislature of the State for a charter for a railroad company. It was their plan to construct a railroad from Harrisburg to Pittsburgh since canals then under construction were about to unite Philadelphia with the Susquehanna River.

But the Pennsylvania Legislature would not hear of this plan. The valuable trade of the Susquehanna Valley, despite Philadelphia's turnpikes, was flowing steadily into the lap of Baltimore. In the hope of diverting this trade to the state's commercial metropolis, the House of Representatives insisted that the railroad be constructed from Philadelphia to Columbia.[3] The Legislature carried its point and "The President, Directors, and Company of the Pennsylvania Railroad Company" was incorporated early in 1823 to construct a road along this route.[4]

No work of such magnitude had ever before been undertaken. *The United States Gazettte* said:

"This undertaking has for its object the opening and active communication between Philadelphia and the Susquehanna and its tributary streams, from whence flow millions of property annually. . . . This is one of the most important objects, or theories, if you please, ever presented to the city of Philadelphia. . . ."[5]

But the novelty of the plan was enough to spell its defeat. People could not believe that their old methods were obsolete.[6] What had science to do

---

[3] McMaster, *op. cit.*, V, 140.

[4] McClure, *Old Time Notes of Pennsylvania*, I, 122; Dunbar, *op. cit.*, III, 891; Scharf and Wescott, *History of Philadelphia, 1609-1884*, 2172.

[5] *The United States Gazette*, April 30, 1823.

[6] Plans for constructing a canal along this route were being made at this same time. Although it was believed that water would be scarce, hopes were high. See *Niles' Weekly Register*, XXV, 230; Hensel, "An Early Canal Project," in *The Lancaster County Historical Society Publications*, XVII, 101-5; MS. Charles Minor to Henry Welles, December 3, 1823, in the Society Collection of the Pennsylvania Historical Society, Manuscript Division. This letter not only shows the desire for a canal but illustrates the importance of the trade of this era. Minor wrote: "We are deeply engaged in getting forward a memorial to the assembly . . . to appoint Commissioners to explore the ground for a Canal through the Great Valley from Philadelphia to Columbia. There is a valley running through from river to river with only one intervening hill. At private expense we have ascertained that there may be brought an abundant supply of water to the Summit level. Our wish is, that a canal should be made that will permit arks and rafts to pass through, without unloading, or breaking the continuity of the voyage. There never was such elegant ground for a Canal in the world. Chester Co. alone, would furnish a market for a vast deal of up river produce. We now pay 6 dollars a cord for wood, 10 dolls. a hundred for rails; from 30 to 40 dollars a thousand for boards. Such a Canal as would insure to Philadelphia a good portion of the trade of the Susquehanna would yield, at the same price paid on the N. York Canal for transportation 20 per cent on the Capital We have been making enquires to find now—that 150 tons a day pass through the Valley in Waggons!. . ."

with hauling anything? Vocal obstructions greeted the new project on every side. The incorporators had little interest in the plan; their names seem to have been wholly used to influence the Legislature to incorporate the company. Aged John Stevens was defeated. He could not even raise $5,000 to construct a test mile, and the law granting him the charter was repealed in 1826. Philadelphia's great opportunity to gain the trade of the Susquehanna and to win the trade of the West was dissipated.

Although no financial aid was available, Stevens' railroad did attract attention in Philadelphia. Late in 1824 The Pennsylvania Society for the Promotion of Internal Improvements was organized in the city. Its members were determined to gather information on the new mode of transportation so that a comparison could be made between the merits of railroads and canals. Essays and treatises were collected; an engineer was sent abroad to study and inspect European railroads. He reported in favor of John Stevens' method of transportation and the society published and indorsed his report.[7] Thereafter, those who took any interest in commercial and economic problems were divided into two opposing factions —"the friends and advocates of canals and the friends and advocates of railroads."

Pennsylvania's decision to invest in a system of internal improvements seemed, at first, to be a decisive victory for the canal supporters. The State system was to be a water navigation. However, Baltimore's interest in railroads revived Philadelphia's enthusiasm. At a meeting of the Canal Commissioners on March 26, 1828, plans were proposed for the construction of a railroad from the Susquehanna River to Chambersburg as a branch of the State Works.

This decision to construct a railroad in the region west of the river was a very timely and direct blow at Baltimore. Chambersburg lay in the region which Baltimore turnpikes controlled. In 1827 the Maryland merchants proposed to construct a railroad from the Chesapeake into the Susquehanna and Cumberland Valleys. They were anxious to improve communication lanes with this rich region and continue to dominate its trade. Their action was a challenge to the port of Philadelphia. The Pennsylvania city again relied on her defensive plan of refusing a charter to the Baltimore project, but, furthermore, she now decided to construct a railroad herself. In 1829 a committee of the Legislature reported:

". . . the time has arrived when Pennsylvania has the means, without the aid of the people of other States, of making such improvements as will accommodate all parts of the Commonwealth; and the Committee believes that, as a sovereign State of the American Confederacy it is her

---

[7] Strickland, *Report on Canals, Roads and Other Subjects Made to the Pennsylvania Society for the Promotion of Internal Improvements.*

policy and her right, as far as possible, to adopt the principle that her highways are to be kept under her own control."[8]

While the Pennsylvania Legislature held up the Baltimore project, engineer William R. Hopkins reconnoitred the ground for the Philadelphia-sponsored railroad. Two routes had been proposed. One was from York through Gettysburg to Chambersburg; the other from Harrisburg through the Cumberland Valley to Chambersburg. Hopkins worked with great speed and the Canal Commissioners sent his report to the Legislature on January 17, 1829.[9] The report favored the Cumberland Valley route and illustrated the practical need for a railroad to Chambersburg.

Petitions immediately began to pour into the Legislature for the incorporation of a private company to construct the railroad. Citizens of the valley, of Harrisburg, and of Philadelphia earnestly took up the movement. The latter believed that they had discovered an offensive weapon to defeat Baltimore's demands for a charter. The Legislature concurred with their wishes; on April 2, 1831, the Cumberland Valley Railroad Company was incorporated to construct a road from Carlisle to the Susquehanna River at or near Harrisburg.[10] But the public did not respond to the call of the company for subscriptions. Enterprise began to lag and the franchise lapsed under the time limit of the act of incorporation.[11] In the meantime, Baltimore was successful in the Pennsylvania Legislature; the Baltimore and Susquehanna Railroad began its invasion of Pennsylvania soil. A Philadelphia victory seemed impossible.

But friends of the Cumberland Valley project were not willing to see it fail. Application was made to the government for further legislation which was granted on April 15, 1835, when the Governor approved a bill extending the time of the charter and authorizing the company to build a railroad from the Susquehanna River to Carlisle, Shippensburg, and Chambersburg. A fresh wave of enthusiasm met the officials. It was considered a certainty that the products of Cumberland, Franklin, and Perry Counties, which had hitherto gone to Baltimore, would be routed over the new railroad to Philadelphia.[12] *The American Volunteer* of Carlisle urging subscriptions to the new railroad said, "Surrounded as we are by a rich and fertile country, all that is now wanted to transform our place from a languid, inactive village to a splendid city is a safe, expeditious and cheap communication with Philadelphia. . . ."[13]

[8] *Report of the Committee on Inland Navigation and Internal Improvements,* 1829.

[9] Hazard, *The Pennsylvania Register,* III, 128-33.

[10] Poor, *op. cit.,* I, 433; Bates and Richards, *History of Franklin County,* 230.

[11] McClure, *op. cit.,* I, 125. The act chartering the company stipulated that the road be commenced within three years.

[12] Hazard, *The Pennsylvania Register,* XVI, 306.

[13] *The American Volunteer,* quoted by Wilson, *op. cit.,* I, 373.

Subscription for stock was taken in Harrisburg, Carlisle, and Philadelphia. Within two weeks enough had been taken to warrant the organization of the company on June 27, 1835.[14] Milnor Roberts was then appointed chief engineer. He immediately made a close survey of the route proposed and the country through which it passed. On October 23, 1835, Roberts reported:

"Philadelphia has a deeper interest than has generally been imagined, in the speedy completion of this improvement, as it will advantageously affect her interests to a very considerable extent. But few of her capitalists have turned their attention to the immense trade of Cumberland and Franklin counties. One obvious reason of this is, that it was in a measure *unknown* to the commercial community. Up to the present period nearly the whole of it has been taken to *Baltimore* upon the turnpikes leading from Chambersburg and Carlisle to that city. The fact that those turnpikes have yielded a handsome per centage on their cost is conclusive evidence of the extent of business they have engrossed.

"It is scarcely well known to Philadelphia that a large proportion of the justly celebrated *Howard street flour* is the product of the Cumberland Valley, in Pennsylvania, which has only been carried thither because it was evidently the most convenient seaport."[15]

The engineer claimed that the local tonnage over the approximately 50-mile railroad would amount to 50,000 tons—all of which would be forwarded to the Pennsylvania commercial metropolis.

As soon as construction was commenced, it was evident that further legislation was needed before the railroad could be a success. Fortunately the Legislature was favorably inclined towards the company, and in February, 1836, granted the privilege of constructing a bridge across the Susquehanna River and of extending the railroad to connect with the Pennsylvania Canal and the Harrisburg, Portsmouth, Mt. Joy, and Lancaster Railroad.[16] An uninterrupted communication for travel and trade between Chambersburg and Philadelphia was thereby made possible.

Construction on the railroad was very slow. Although the United States Bank, rechartered as a State institution, has subscribed $200,000,[17] funds were wanting. The depression of 1837 compelled the company to issue paper money. Work continued only because people were willing to accept the railroad "shin plasters" or any other semblance of money or

---

[14] Bates and Richards, *op. cit.*, 231. Thomas G. McCulloch of Chambersburg was elected President and Joseph Mitchell of Philadelphia, Treasurer.

[15] Hazard, *The Pennsylvania Register*, XVI, 306-8.

[16] Poor, *op. cit.*, I, 433; Bates and Richards, *op. cit.*, 231.

[17] In return for its charter the bank was forced to subscribe to certain internal improvements projected in Pennsylvania. Among others the Cumberland Valley Railroad was to profit by a $100,000 subscription. But through Nicholas Biddle, a keen supporter of the railroad, the bank subscribed an additional $100,000. See McClure, *op. cit.*, I, 125.

credit. In 1839 the officials of the company complained: "We start with half means, and are then forced to finish on credit at a ruinous cost, and our experience has been an example of the prevailing error."

On August 18, 1837, the section of the road from Carlisle to the Susquehanna River was opened. The locomotive, "Cumberland Valley," with its two drive wheels and wooden spokes, was hauled by canal-boat and hay wagon from Philadelphia for the occasion. By the end of the year the entire line was open for business. The track consisted of cross ties laid 4½ feet apart on the ground without ballast. Upon them were laid oak stringers, on which irons ⅝ of an inch thick and 2¼ inches wide were spiked. The ends of the iron bars were mitered. The irons often would become pressed away from their connections and curl up, piercing the bottom of the car. So dangerous were these "snake heads" that the bottom of the cars were covered with two-inch planks above which was a lining of boiler plate. In winter the engines had split hickory brooms fastened in front of the wheels to sweep away the snow. It was on this line, which carried many through passengers en route to Pittsburgh, that the first sleeper was used.[18]

The sanguine hopes of the company were soon dimmed by the appearance of a competitor. Thaddeus Stevens, an influential friend and political supporter of the Governor of Pennsylvania, owned valuable iron mines in Adams and Franklin counties. To facilitate the development of his mines, Stevens conceived the idea of constructing a branch of the State public works through his property and southward to connect with the Baltimore and Ohio Railroad. Early in 1838 he was made a member of the canal commission and before long was elected president of this body. In this position Stevens was able to secure legislation authorizing the desired railroad.[19] Since this branch would threaten the local trade of the Cumberland Valley Railroad, the officials of the latter company were very much disturbed over its construction and used all possible influence to combat the new line. Finally, the matter was referred to the Committee on Roads, Bridges, and Inland Navigation of the Senate for investigation. After a study of the merits of the two routes, this group reported:

". . . your committee have no hesitation in declaring their belief that the Chambersburg, or Cumberland Valley route, will be the easiest, cheapest, safest, pleasantest and shortest route to Philadelphia; and in consequence of those pre-eminent advantages, this road, which is being constructed and is now nearly completed, without any expense to the Commonwealth, will engross by far the greatest portion of the trade

[18] Poor, *op. cit.,* I, 416; *Niles' Weekly Register,* LIII, 192; McClure, *op. cit.,* I, 126.

[19] Bishop, *The State Works of Pennsylvania,* 230; Riddle, "Some Facts about the Cumberland Valley Railroad," in the *Publications of the Kittoching Historical Society,* IX, 251.

which can be diverted from the Baltimore and Ohio Railroad in the direction of Philadelphia."[20]

Stevens' railroad became a leading issue in the election of 1838. Its powerful backer used the political power of the State Works and all possible Machiavellian influences to re-elect Governor Ritner. But Stevens failed. The change of administration ended construction on the Tape Worm Railroad after almost $700,000 had been spent; Stevens' line had been vanquished and the Cumberland Valley was able to claim its first victory.[21]

In 1842 the earnings of the Cumberland Valley Railroad were over $70,000 but obstacles handicapped its future prosperity. The pioneer construction work of the road had to be replaced. Receipts scarcely paid expenses and interest on a debt of about $275,000 and a bridge debt of $472,000.[22] A hoped for southern road to connect the Cumberland Valley with the Baltimore and Ohio Railroad proved to be a failure.[23] The expensive Susquehanna River bridge connecting the Cumberland Valley with Philadelphia lines of communication served only five years when it became the victim of sparks from a passing locomotive. Furthermore, the railroad lost its hopes for serving as a link in a chain of western transportation when the Pennsylvania Railroad was chartered. Philadelphia had decided this latter act of fate; it felt that the Cumberland Valley Railroad would bring the east-west trunk line too close to Baltimore to be free from diverting influences.[24]

In 1849 the holders of the company's debt agreed to advance $400,000 for the reconstruction of the railroad with iron rails. The company was reorganized by a creation of preferred stock equal to the whole debt and

---

[20] *Report of the Committee on Roads, Bridges, and Inland Navigation,* quoted by Wilson, *op. cit.,* I, 338.

[21] Bishop, *op. cit.,* 230-1. A committee delving into the record of Stevens' road reported: "Of all the works of doubtful expediency constructed by the state, in the opinion of your committee, there is none so useless, so expensive, or of so little value as the Gettysburg railroad. It was commenced by fraud and intrigue, and will end in disgrace and loss to the commonwealth. The means of the commonwealth are inadequate to its completion, and if completed it could never be productive of general benefit. . . . The committee express their belief that a total abandonment of this work involves the least sacrifice of public funds the state can make upon it."

[22] Poor, *op. cit.,* I, 433.

[23] *Ibid.,* I, 442; Bates and Richards, *op. cit.,* 232. This link was chartered in 1838 as the Franklin Railroad Company. It never proved a success. Almost as soon as it was completed, its rolling stock was sold by the sheriff and the road placed in the hands of a sequestor who operated it with horsepower until 1852 when the whole road was sold for $18,000.

[24] *Niles' Weekly Register,* LXI, 352.

the new advancement.[25] Work was completed during the following year at which date the total cost of the line amounted to almost one and one-quarter million dollars.[26] About this time the railroad from York to Cumberland was completed giving the Cumberland Valley Railroad a direct connection with Baltimore. The construction of this road gave the Cumberland Valley a second seaboard outlet and centered the rivalry for the trade of the Cumberland Valley at Bridgeport.

By 1849 the earnings of the railroad from Chambersburg to Harrisburg had increased to over $100,000, about half of which was derived from freight charges. Thirty-seven thousand four hundred and thirty-nine tons of freight were carried, of which flour, ore, coal, grain, and lumber were the principal items.[27] East and west traffic was about equal. Tonnage figures, however, did not rise rapidly immediately after the Baltimore connection was completed in 1851, although much freight was carried from the Cumberland Valley Railroad to the Maryland city. For a short time traffic destined for the seaboard was about equally divided between the two rival cities while return goods were shipped chiefly from Philadelphia. However, after 1855, Philadelphia also began to dominate the eastward traffic;[28] the Baltimore connection declined as a competitor especially as the financial condition of the Baltimore road grew critical and the Baltimore and Ohio competition with it grew stronger.[29]

About the same time that the Cumberland Valley Railroad was first discussed, another railroad was conceived which was to divert the Susquehanna River trade from Baltimore. When engineers were surveying for the eastern link of the State Works, they reconnoitred the territory between Lancaster and Harrisburg but abandoned this route in favor of

---

[25] The Cumberland Valley Railroad Company, *Annual Report,* 1850.

[26] Poor, *op. cit.,* I, 433.

[27] The Cumberland Valley Railroad Company, *Annual Report,* 1849. This was the first year that tonnage figures were given.

[28] Table showing the places to and from which the Cumberland Valley Railroad delivered and received freight, 1853-57. (In thousands of tons.) Compiled from the *Annual Reports.*

Year		Eastbound	Westbound	
1853	to Harrisburg and Phila.	17.9	from	18.2
	to Bridgeport and Balt.	17.3	"	10.4
1854	to Harrisburg and Phila.	26.7	"	23.5
	to Bridgeport and Balt.	20.3	"	8.9
1855	to Harrisburg and Phila.	21.3	"	28.9
	to Bridgeport and Balt.	9.9	"	10.7
1856	to Harrisburg and Phila.	29.3	"	29.8
	to Bridgeport and Balt.	11.9	"	9.7
1857	to Harrisburg and Phila.	37.9	"	39.4
	to Bridgeport and Balt.	14.3	"	14.8

[29] See page 140.

the road to Columbia. But the announcement that Baltimore planned to construct a railroad to the Susquehanna River north of Columbia caused many people to believe that the Baltimore project would rob the State railroad of its anticipated business. With the first rumors of the Baltimore plan, Philadelphia petitioned for a railroad from Middletown to the Philadelphia and Columbia road in the vicinity of Lancaster. Appealing to State patriotism, it stated:

"The claim which the eastern counties, and especially the metropolis of the state, has upon the legislature for protection and favour, are more than sufficient to counter-balance all other considerations. It is the interest, as we trust it is also the pride, of every Pennsylvanian, to support and augment the trade of the metropolis of the state."[30]

Since the Pennsylvania Legislature refused all the pleas of Baltimore and her friends for a charter for the Baltimore and Susquehanna Railroad, little more was said about this proposed Philadelphia road. However, in 1832, when the Baltimore cause seemed strong enough to win in the Pennsylvania Legislature, the issue was again awakened. Public meetings were held at Portsmouth and Middletown to decide on the best method of arresting the trade of the river so that it would be secure for the merchants of their own State commercial metropolis.[31] They decided that a railroad to Middletown must be constructed since that point would be north of all avenues which could divert trade to the Maryland commercial city.

In the legislature the bill to incorporate this road met with opposition from the representatives of the southern counties of central Pennsylvania. They had just concluded the long struggle with Philadelphia for the charter of the Baltimore railroad. They were still in a fighting mood; they still disliked Philadelphia's attitude in commercial affairs. Spokesmen for the southern counties maintained that the proposed company would be a direct competitor of the State Works and would "render your canal from Middletown to Columbia, and your railroad from the latter place to Lancaster, perfectly valueless, after an expenditure of half a million dollars upon them. . . ." When the Philadelphia representatives brought memories of the Baltimore and Susquehanna struggle into the debate, the opponents of the Middletown and Lancaster route denied that they feared competition for the Maryland railroad. One speaker repeated that the only competitor that the new road would injure would be the State Works and sarcastically concluded:

---

[30] MS. Petition from Philadelphia County to the Senate and the House of Representatives, 1828, found in the Archives Division of the Pennsylvania Historical and Museum Commission.

[31] *Poulson's Daily Advertiser*, February 11, 1832.

"I am beginning to find their Pennsylvania feeling runs no further than their own interests dictate. Any contemplated improvements brought before the House, leading in the direction of Philadelphia will receive their support, no matter how ruinous it may prove to the public improvements, or how much it may interfere with the interests of the State."

A bill granting a charter to the Portsmouth and Lancaster Rail Road Company was passed on June 9, 1832, giving authority to a private company to construct a railroad from the junction of the Union and Pennsylvania Canals to Lancaster.[32] This legislation was a direct blow aimed at the newly chartered Baltimore railroad to York; Philadelphia hoped to frighten investors in that company and possibly prevent its construction.

For a time interest in the Portsmouth and Lancaster Railroad waned. But friends, fearing the death of the project, revived it in 1833 under the leadership of Simon Cameron and James Buchanan. Public meetings were held; the Philadelphia press urged support. Governor Wolf finally granted the necessary letters patent for the creation of the company on June 3, 1834, after which Buchanan was elected president of the organization.

A movement was immediately inaugurated for the extension of this proposed road to Harrisburg to meet the Cumberland Valley line. This link between Portsmouth and Harrisburg, it was claimed, would insure Philadelphia of the trade of the rich Cumberland Valley.[33] It was pointed out that this trade formerly was carried to Baltimore and therefore the proposed railroad would be of particular importance. The Harrisburg lawmakers were easily convinced and the route was officially chartered in 1835.

The thirty-six-mile Harrisburg, Portsmouth, Mt. Joy and Lancaster Railroad was completed three years later and did a $65,000 business in its inaugural year. Business continued to be good during the next few years but it was soon realized that this road could not operate satisfactorily without being affiliated with the new through railroad to the West built by the Pennsylvania Railroad Company. The Pennsylvania Company, on the other hand, saw the advantages of the Harrisburg, Portsmouth, Mt. Joy, and Lancaster Railroad and made arrangements to lease the latter's road early in 1849 rather than build their own route.[34] With this action the Harrisburg to Lancaster railroad became a link in the great western trunk line of Philadelphia's latest bid for supremacy. The trade of the Susquehanna thereafter was of only minor importance.

The rugged hills of northeastern Pennsylvania attracted little attention in the days before anthracite coal was important. Although the tongue of

---

[32] Poor, *op. cit.*, I, 445.
[33] *Poulson's Daily Advertiser*, March 30, 1835.
[34] Poor, *op. cit.*, I, 416, 445.

land which separates the Delaware and Susquehanna Rivers in this region is very narrow, the few transverse road communications attracted little of the trade of the Susquehanna Valley. But when a market appeared for the coal of this region, activity and enthusiasm for internal improvements appeared. Coal "raised up in our formerly barren and uninhabited districts an intelligent and permanent population and converted the mountains into theatres of busy life and our hitherto waste and valueless lands into sites for flourishing and populous villages."[35]

Just prior to the big coal boom, Philadelphia sponsored a canal, the Schuylkill Navigation, through the Schuylkill Valley to Pottsville which happened to be situated on the border of the southern coal field. This navigation was constructed with the double purpose of carrying local products to the Pennsylvania metropolis and of becoming a link in a western improvement.[36] When the canal was completed in 1825, coal immediately became its most important freight; other local trade was of only passing importance.

But the second purpose for the original construction of the Schuylkill Navigation Canal was not overlooked. Within a short time after the canal was officially opened, petitions were circulated through Columbia, Lycoming, Schuylkill, Northumberland, and Union Counties asking for an extension of the canal from Pottsville to the Susquehanna River. The citizens of these counties felt that they had been totally excluded from the State-sponsored improvements. They asserted, "that to them no means of transportation presented itself but the hazardous one of navigating the River Susquehanna at the risk of their lives and property."[37] Public opinion in this section held that a connection between these points was the most practical way Philadelphia could prevent the riches of Baltimore, gained from the Susquehanna trade, from piling higher.

By April, 1826, the petitioners were favored with legislation authorizing the incorporation of the Danville and Pottsville Railroad Company to connect the two towns named in the company's title. In pursuance of this act, explorations were conducted and some rough maps made; but the charter was found defective in many particulars. Two years of trial demonstrated that the stipulated capital, $300,000, was not sufficient to construct a railroad. Applications were therefore made to the legislature

---

[35] Parker, *Report to the Senate on Coal*, 1834.

[36] Jones, *Anthracite-Tidewater Canals*, 128; Hazard, *The Pennsylvania Register*, III, 302. The Schuylkill Navigation was begun in 1815. At that time it had no interest in the coal trade which "was not regarded as an object of much importance."

[37] MS. Petitions for the incorporation of the Pottsville and Danville Railroad, December, 1825. Found in the Archives Division of the Pennsylvania Historical and Museum Commission.

for supplementary legislation to correct this defect and to authorize the construction of the railroad from Sunbury and from Danville to the northern terminal of the Schuylkill Navigation Canal.

Philadelphia now began to back the movement. She saw in this railroad a route that would lead her to two convenient collecting centers of the Susquehanna Valley via the rich, developing coal lands of Schuylkill County. Public meetings were held endorsing the plan. The press gave its support.[38] The enthusiasm shown in favor of the railroad combined with a keen desire to thwart Baltimore led to the enactment of the desired supplementary legislation in March, 1828. When news of this act reached Philadelphia, *The Pennsylvania Gazette* noted:

"This work is a highly meritorious undertaking. . . . It will be a very great convenience to the farmers and traders upon the branches of the Susquehanna, will facilitate the transit of the trade of those streams to this metropolis; and will pass through, and enliven, a dreary and unproductive portion of the interior of our state."[39]

Monocure Robinson, a well-known engineer, surveyed the route of the proposed railroad and reported that it was very practicable. General interest, however, lagged when it came time for investment of capital. However, Philadelphia did not forget the Danville and Pottsville Railroad. Throughout 1829 Philadelphia newspapers carried notices and editorials concerning this road and the country through which it was to pass. The editor of *Poulson's Daily Advertiser* inquired:

"Is it not a truth, that every mile the produce of the North and West branches of the Susquehanna passes Sunbury, it falls in some degree into the fangs of Baltimore influence?" "See," he added, "the late insurrection in this particular in the camp where Philadelphians expected their interests safe—at Lancaster. The Conestoga navigation in now open, and Susquehanna coal arks are arriving with their cargoes at that city, and those arks re-loading with the flour and whiskey of Lancaster, and passing down to the Chesapeake markets,—and the strongest feelings are expressed by those interested in the Conestoga navigation, in favor of a sloop navigation from Columbia to tide. What do Philadelphians think of the Columbia and Philadelphia railway under these circumstances? It will just be occupied in conveying the wheat which the canal may convey to Columbia to the water power on the Conestoga, where it will be ground and the flour sent down to Baltimore and the Chesapeake markets."[40]

These startling facts demanded action. The "fangs of Baltimore" could not be allowed to penetrate too deeply into the Susquehanna Valley. Meetings were held in Philadelphia by friends of the internal improvements. A committee was appointed to gather facts concerning the proposed rail connection. These fact gatherers reported that they deemed it

---

[38] *The Pennsylvania Gazette*, February 19, 20, March 10, 1828.
[39] *Ibid.*, March 31, 1828.
[40] *Poulson's Daily Advertiser*, January 7, 1829.

unnecessary to present arguments to show that it was "to the interest and in fact the duty" of Philadelphians to lend support to all lines of communication with the Susquehanna. But they maintained that "in point of distance, geographical facilities, ease of construction, and convenience for trade, a railroad from Sunbury and Danville on the Susquehanna to Pottsville on the Schuylkill, promises advantages not enjoyed by any other route." From Sunbury to Philadelphia by the proposed road they estimated to be sixteen miles shorter than via the Columbia Railroad and fifty miles shorter than the Union Canal route.[41] Moreover, the committee held that the north river towns were closer to Philadelphia than to Baltimore, which was not true of Middletown or Columbia. From Sunbury to Philadelphia they reported to be 152 miles; from the same town to Baltimore was 155 miles. But from Middletown, the entrance of the Union Canal, to the Pennsylvania metropolis via the canal it is 146 miles but only 88 miles to Baltimore. Therefore, after descending the river from Sunbury to Middletown, one was 67 miles nearer the Maryland city but only 8 miles closer to Philadelphia.

In conclusion, a new and very serious angle was presented by the Philadelphia committee:

". . . we cannot refrain from adverting to the very liberal and flattering preference which our fellow citizens in the interior have shown for this their own metropolis, over that of a neighboring state, as indicated by the recent vote in the legislature of our state, upon the application of the citizens of Baltimore to make a rail road from the Susquehanna to that city. But it cannot be concealed that the vote of preference was given

---

[41] In support of the statement on distance the following facts were presented by the committee:

				Miles
"From Sunbury to	Philadelphia via Columbia Railroad	....		168
Do	Do	Pottsville	....	152
		Difference in favor of the latter	....	16
From do	by the Union Canal is	....		202
Do	via Pottsville	....		152
		Difference in favor of the latter	....	50
From Danville to	Philadelphia via Columbia Railroad	....		182
do	do	Pottsville	....	148
		Difference in favor of the latter	....	34
From do	via the Union Canal	....		214
do	via Pottsville	....		148
		Difference in favor of the latter	....	66"

Hazard, *The Pennsylvania Register*, III, 133.

under the belief that Philadelphia would exert herself to open every advantageous avenue to her market. Should this just expectation be disappointed, it may occasion a reaction, and cause those who relied upon it, to throw themselves into the arms of their second choice, which we know to be Baltimore. In addition, therefore, to the obvious dictates of their own interest Philadelphia is pledged to do all that in her lies, to meet favorable advances now made to her."[42]

The "obvious dictates" and the moral pledge which the committeemen spoke of met with little enthusiasm. A year passed; no action was taken. By autumn of 1830, it was manifest that a crisis was at hand. Philadelphia had been warned that if she folded her arms and "reposed in a state of lethargy, while the citizens of Baltimore are straining every nerve to grasp at 'one fell swoop' all the trade that flows the Susquehanna, the fault rests upon their heads. . . ."[43] But the Pennsylvania metropolis did not listen. The river folk became impatient. In a public meeting held at the Court House in Sunbury on November 22, 1830, the citizens asked Philadelphia, plainly, what steps she planned to take.[44] "If for such an object, Philadelphia will not move one muscle of her mighty arm," they announced that the trade of the Susquehanna "MUST AND WILL proceed to meet the Baltimore Railway." Those gathered at the meeting said they were anxiously expecting a decision "whether their future market shall be Baltimore or Philadelphia." A committee was then appointed to go to Philadelphia and confer with friends about the railroad while a second group was sent to Pottsville to arouse interest.

Meanwhile, a public meeting was held in the latter town in support of the Sunbury gathering. The citizens of this coal town of mushroom

---

[42] Hazard, *The Pennsylvania Register*, III, 133-4. The committee offered the following resolutions:

"*Resolved, 1st.* That this meeting feel highly gratified to find, by the report of an able and experienced engineer, that a rail road from Pottsville, on the Schuylkill, to Danville and Sunbury, on the Susquehanna, is practicable, and can be made at a small expense.

"*Resolved, 2ly.* That in so much as the citizens of Baltimore are using every exertion in their power to lead off the trade of the Susquehanna to that city, and thereby diminishing the trade and wealth of Philadelphia, and of the state generally, it is important, that this work should be immediately commenced, and prosecuted with energy until its final completion.

"*Resolved, 3dly.* That a committee of seven be appointed to request the commissioners of the rail road to open books for subscription to stock; and to cooperate with said commissioners in procuring subscriptions, and in corresponding with other committees interested in the prosecution of this undertaking."

[43] *Poulson's Daily Advertiser*, September 22, 1829.

[44] Hazard, *The Pennsylvania Register*, VI, 380. Hazard published the full proceedings of this meeting. General Daniel Montgomery, a staunch friend of the railroad, was in the chair.

growth were anxious for the immediate construction of the railroad since they saw local advantages in being located on a western trunk line.[45]

About this same time a Sunbury friend of the project who had collected all the possible facts, information, and arguments in favor of a Pottsville and Danville Railroad, which was also called the Central Railroad, published a number of essays over the name Amicus Veritatis.[46] Seriously, this "friend of truth" suggested:

"If a generous emulation, or an honourable ambition, can excite our metropolis, let her mark the strides of Baltimore. How magnificently she marches, with lesser means, by railway to the Ohio! An enterprise at once bold and honourable and sagacious, has expunged the word *impracticable* from her vocabulary. Already her 13 miles completed under prodigious obstacles and vast expense, yield an abundant reward, and the stock, still in its infancy, is at par. While she wends her way in triumph to the west, she stretches one arm 70 miles to York Haven for a part of trade, even after the refusal of a charter, and is about to reach the other, with another line of railway to Washington City. Yes!—and the wealth of the Susquehanna, Baltimore will more completely, and more deservedly command if Philadelphia pauses and deliberates for another season. Must our goodly city have 'a little more sleep—a little little more slumber'. Let her open her view to the wealth gathered from the twenty five thousand square miles by this great river into the Sunbury basin by the confluence of the two great branches. There, with all its accumulations, it offers itself to Philadelphia, if she will but smooth the way for it, less than 50 miles, to meet her on the Schuylkill navigation. Virtually, and commercially, Philadelphia may be deemed as placed at the head of that navigation—for so far it has cleared her way, and the commerce of half a million people is collected in the great reservoir, formed at Sunbury by the Shamokin Dam. Will Philadelphia cut across the obstructing isthmus, and let these immense products pass down to Pottsville, in effect into her own secure possession? — If she will not accept it upon these conditions, Baltimore will gladly meet us upon any terms. Our people prefer our own city for many reasons, but 'if our brethern the *Jews* will not hear us, we shall turn to the Gentiles.' "

Sunbury's Amicus Veritatis argued fervidly for his cause. The Union Canal and the Chesapeake and Delaware Canal, he contended, would not secure the trade of the Susquehanna Valley for Philadelphia but they would "prove mere practical *decoys,* to allure this great wealth into the port of the sagacious Marylanders." Philadelphia must have a railroad

---

[45] *Ibid.,* VI, 381. Burd Patterson who had been in the coal business for some time was chairman of the Pottsville meeting. Many coal men were interested in this railroad since it would open their mines to extensive and steady markets.

[46] *Ibid.,* VI, 378-9, 391-3, 401-2, 402-5, 405-6, 406-7. In a short editorial (*Ibid.,* VI, 416), Hazard said that these essays gave a most satisfactory account of the Susquehanna trade, the improvements of the river, and the country through which it flows.

in northeastern Pennsylvania to win the trade of the Susquehanna, said Amicus Veritatis, and it should be constructed with all possible speed.

The propaganda committees from Sunbury and Pottsville found Philadelphia awakening to the situation. Her citizens were interested in the country through which the proposed road was to pass; many of them owned coal lands which the Pottsville and Danville Railroad would open. John Sergeant, Stephen Girard, Nicholas Biddle, Mathew Carey, Cadwalader Evans, and many other prominent Philadelphians endorsed the plan. Newspapers carried articles in favor of the immediate construction of the road; editors commented favorably on the essays of Amicus Veritatis. A correspondent to *Poulson's Daily Advertiser* wrote:

"I cannot, however, force myself to believe that the capitalists of our city can be so ineffably stupid not to see their situation! It is true Philadelphia can exist without the Susquehanna trade! and she may occupy a respectable rank in the Union; but, ... the man, or set of men, who could produce to her the exclusive benefit of our river trade, would erect to himself a monument of fame which would endure until time and eternity formed a junction."[47]

Friends of the proposed project entered into correspondence with the Schuylkill Navigation Company to secure a statement from that company that they would improve their canal to meet the great trade of the proposed railroad. With an eye on their own tills, the Schuylkill Company eagerly promised this assurance.[48] From Sunbury to Philadelphia, interest in the proposed railroad across the barren hills of northeastern Pennsylvania was keen and active.

On December 23, 1830, a large public meeting in Philadelphia called for the subscription of stock. Books were soon opened at Danville, Sunbury, Pottsville, and Philadelphia. Stephen Girard alone subscribed for 4000 shares and his generous support attracted many other capitalists.[49] By April 26, 1831, the full amount of stock was taken and the company duly organized.

But this movement to thwart Baltimore lost its impetus shortly after the company was organized. The death of the two outstanding friends and patrons of the railroad left the project without any leaders. The passing of Philadelphia's merchant prince, Stephen Girard, was a heavy blow. Although he had been primarily interested in opening the extensive coal lands which he owned in Schuylkill County, Girard's interest in the Pottsville and Danville Railroad gave confidence to other investors. General Daniel Montgomery, Sunbury's railroad pioneer, died the same

---

[47] *Poulson's Daily Advertiser,* December 10, 1830.

[48] Hazard, *The Pennsylvania Register,* VI, 409.

[49] McMaster, *The Life and Times of Stephen Girard,* II, 439. Girard was elected a director of the company of which his nephew by marriage was president. At one time it was suggested that the road take the name of its great benefactor.

year. As a member of the Sunbury committee which had visited Philadelphia in the interest of the railroad, he had done much to make the
organization of the company possible.[50]

Nevertheless, partial construction was commenced; short sections at
each end of the proposed Pottsville and Danville Railroad were finally
begun. By 1834, the eastern section, about ten miles long, from Pottsville to Girardville was completed. It included "no less than six incline
planes, of an unusually bold construction, a tunnel of great beauty, and
a line of road surpassed by none in the world, for the wildness of the
country in which it was executed, and for the difficulties which have been
successfully overcome."[51] The powerful stationary engines reminded a
traveller of the quotation, 'Here's all hell in Harness.' The western line
was opened in 1835 to a village called Paxinos and was extended two
years later to Shamokin. Business on this line was very slight[52] and
horse power was used almost exclusively until 1852.

With the completion of the eastern division a special drive was
launched to complete the whole line. The company asked for State aid
to finance their work. This request was referred to the Committee of
Inland Navigation and Internal Improvements in the House of Representatives. This committee realized that since the State had assisted
other private improvements as the Union and Chesapeake and Delaware
Canals, the request of the Pottsville and Danville Railroad had strong
foundations. But the Commonwealth's own improvement system overshadowed all other ventures at this time and the legislature refused to
grant anything more than a pledge of the payment of interest upon the
stock of the company which was authorized to be sold. Thus the railroad
across the narrow isthmus between the Schuylkill and Susquehanna Valleys suffered a long period of inactivity as no one wished to invest in a
railroad lost in the wilderness.

The three railroads by which Philadelphia hoped to divert Susquehanna Valley trade from Baltimore were a direct result of Baltimore's
bid for a railroad charter authorizing the extension of the Baltimore and
Susquehanna Railroad into Pennsylvania. Although Philadelphia had
toyed with the railroad idea at an earlier date, the Baltimore plan caused
Philadelphia to seek an offensive weapon to be used against the Marylanders. As such, these lines were of limited success: one carried produce

---

[50] Day, *Historical Collections of the State of Pennsylvania,* 610.

[51] Hazard, *The Pennsylvania Register,* XIII, 108-10; XIV, 277, quotes the report
of the Committee on Inland Navigation and Internal Improvements, Relative to the
Danville and Pottsville Railroad, by Keating. Read in the House of Representatives, June 29, 1834.

[52] Poor, *op. cit.,* I, 503. For the year ending December 23, 1840, the western
division carried 352,010 pounds.

for both cities, a second was soon absorbed in the Pennsylvania Railroad and served as a link to the West, while the much talked of Pottsville and Danville route failed to pierce the rugged hills of the barren coal lands between Pottsville and Sunbury.

APPENDIX XV

Earnings of the Cumberland Valley Railroad Company, 1850-59

Year	Gross freight earnings	Gross total earnings	Net earnings
1850	$41,198	$92,756	$46,495
1851	51,905	108,887	64,340
1852	53,971	104,717	50,718
1853	77,913	141,207	68,145
1854	82,093	156,340	57,659
1855	77,005	147,411	46,472
1856	90,751	161,483	29,212
1857	114,321	189,426	51,435
1858	88,649	156,463	86,279
1859	96,040	170,509	95,695
Average	77,384	142,920	49,645

(Poor, *op. cit.*, 434.)

APPENDIX XVI

Abstract from a MS. Cumberland County petition, December 19, 1831, for aid for the Cumberland Valley Railroad found in the Archives Division of the Pennsylvania Historical and Museum Commission:

"The importance of this contemplated road has so forced itself upon public attention, that nothing but the absolute want of adequate means can prevent its execution — Its great direct utility to a most valuable section of your territory is too obvious to require a remark. It will furnish the only means by which that section of country can be made to participate in the general benefit of the great Improvements of the Commonwealth: — and in return of the great Improvements a most valuable auxiliary to those improvements, by conducting to them, and, through them, to our great commercial emporium, a large & valuable trade, which now finds its way to Baltimore at great expense and loss: — would be brought through them, from Philada instead of the places from which it now comes, under much disadvantage. When we consider the great facilities for constructing a rail road from Carlisle to the Susquehanna: the fertility of this valley; and its relations to other portions of our common country; it would seem impossible to doubt, that its stock must become very valuable. But the work is too great for individual enterprise; & we find it impracticable to obtain the necessary means of completing it by individual subscription. We, therefore, respectfully and earnestly pray, that the Governor may be authorized to subscribe on behalf of the State, for a portion of the stock. And we are persuaded, that we shall not be thought unreasonable, when we pray, that that portion be one thousand shares: — "

APPENDIX XVII

Analysis of the freight carried by the Cumberland Valley Railroad,
1853 (in thousands of pounds)

	Eastward to	
	Harrisburg & Philadelphia	Bridgeport & Baltimore
Seed	179	696
Hay	91	621
Agriculture products	723	2029
Iron	328	288
Leather	979	162
Paper	285	30
Bark and sumac	127	83
Blooms and castings	2986	147
Grain	4050	9969
Pig iron	409	583
Pork and bacon	183	175
Potatoes	51	144
Straw paper	888	40
Ore	5687	...
Whiskey (barrels)	.7	11
Flour (barrels)	54	72
Cattle and horses	5766	106
Hogs	3524	677
Sheep	468	...
Miscell.	69	7
	Westward to	
Dry Goods	5522	738
Hides	1162	233
Iron	1028	181
Marble	196	20
Mill Stones	60	55
Nails	213	92
Oysters	15	898
Rags	230	83
Salt	268	1503
Fish	358	1053
Whiskey	316	32
Sand and sandstone	357	1925
Pig iron	497	67
Tobacco	6	21
Furniture	373	122
Plaster	88	5363
Lumber	2715	5992
Coal	23022	2283

(From the *Annual Report* of the Company, for the year ending
September 1853.)

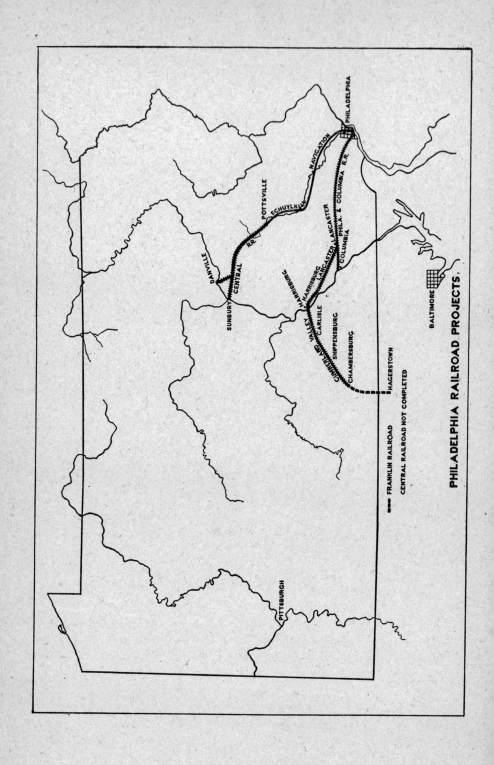

PHILADELPHIA RAILROAD PROJECTS.

FRANKLIN RAILROAD
CENTRAL RAILROAD NOT COMPLETED

CHAPTER VIII

SUMMARY

For eighty years the commercial tournament between Philadelphia and Baltimore for the trade of the rich hinterland of the Susquehanna Valley had continued. Before 1780 preliminary skirmishes had revealed "rivalships", but the economic spheres of the two cities had not overlapped in the Susquehanna Valley to any great extent. From 1780 to 1860, however, the contest between the two gladiators was extensive and hostile. As the jousting grounds developed and widened, frequent, strong, desperate blows were struck by both contestants. Baltimore, with a geographical advantage, usually assumed the offensive, but her task was difficult since she was always forced to carry the contest into Pennsylvania territory. Philadelphia, usually able to control the Pennsylvania Legislature, not only tried to defend herself from Baltimore's thrusts but also countered with offensive drives. Editors and correspondents, local politicians and State officials, merchant princes and intrepreneurs, bankers and capitalists, farmers and shippers—all cheered and supported their favorite entrepôt and passed bitter, outspoken, stinging, and, at times, unsportsmanlike remarks about the rival city. The crowds who watched the successive stages of the struggle were much alike in essentials—they were all optimistic, self-congratulatory, irrepressible in their enthusiasm, and undaunted in their outlook. Their one economic principle was that a town must create trade rather than have the trade come to the commercial seat of its own accord.

Until 1829, roads, pioneer wagon trails and improved turnpikes, and the river freshets were the important weapons at the disposal of the two combatants. East of the Susquehanna River, Philadelphia controlled trade both to and from that district while Baltimore dominated business in the fertile valleys west of the river although much return merchandise was forwarded into this section from Philadelphia. The flood currents of the tortuous Susquehanna River, although impeded by natural obstacles which Philadelphia strove to keep intact, carried produce to the Maryland city, and gave Baltimore a general advantage over the Pennsylvania metropolis. Rivermen in their home-made boats annually carried whiskey, flour, grain, agricultural products, some iron and lumber to the Chesapeake valued at more than one and one-half million dollars. Philadelphia, in boom times, tried desperately to divert this southern flow of trade to her own wharves by means of canals planned to tap the river trade at important points, but these efforts were always more or less "sudden, sporadic, forced, and exotic phenomena instead of a slow, natural, outgrowth of a broad necessity."[1]

The dawn of canal interest in America caused the rivals to take up this new means of winning trade. Philadelphia revived her former projects and constructed the Union and Chesapeake and Delaware Canals before 1830; Baltimore, after battering down Philadelphia's defense and securing a charter, completed her Susquehanna and Tidewater Canal by 1840. Philadelphia's canals not only tapped vital points but the Pennsylvania city also prospered as a result of the Susquehanna Tidewater which carried produce to Havre de Grace, from which point Philadelphia tow boats towed many cargoes through the Chesapeake and Delaware Canal and on to Philadelphia. The canals of the two cities projected to gain the Susquehanna trade suffered from the limitations of the day and were not as prosperous as had been anticipated. Furthermore, the influence of the Erie Canal pared down the size of the jousting grounds, while developing interest in the struggle for western trade caused the Susquehanna area to wane in importance. However, Philadelphia seems to have wrested much of the earlier river trade from Baltimore which caused the Maryland city to appreciate her earlier position and to seek new means of regaining supremacy.[2]

Baltimore's successful Baltimore and Ohio venture in railroading caused the enterprising Marylanders to project a railroad northward into the Susquehanna Valley with the hope of diverting Philadelphia's canal trade and of gaining a portion of the anthracite coal trade of Pennsylvania. Philadelphia's defense against granting a charter was more formidable than ever, but gradually her resistance weakened under the constant thrusts of the Baltimorians and the Pennsylvania friends of the Maryland project. Annually the Baltimore and Susquehanna Railroad loomed as a bigger threat to the wealth and prosperity of the Pennsylvania metropolis. Three railroads were planned by the Pennsylvanians to thwart the plans of their rival; Philadelphia believed that an offensive

---

[1] Dunbar, *History of Travel in America*, III, 770, quoted from an uncited source. This statement refers in general to all early canals, but is fitting to Philadelphia's early Susquehanna and Schuylkill and Chesapeake and Delaware Canals.

[2] Comparative table of the revenues of the canals. (In thousands of dollars.)

No. of years after construction	Union (finished 1827)	C. & D. (finished 1829)	S. & T. (finished 1840)
1	16	42	25
5	59	87	54
10	106	156	68
15	57	180	98
20	91	145	173

of this type would possibly win where a defensive stand had apparently lost. But Pennsylvania was too busy with her mongrel State Works to assist her metropolis to build these lines. Although two projects were finally completed, they were not successful diverting routes of the Susquehanna trade. The Baltimore railroad, on the other hand, gradually crept up the Valley to Sunbury, but in hoping to grasp all, this venture lost its financial balance and was finally sold to the Pennsylvania Railroad Company.

The struggle was not over in 1860, but improved methods of transportation widened the economic interests of the two cities and the bitterness of the Susquehanna struggle shifted to wider fields. Miles and distances no longer presented serious physical limitations, but struggles for wealth, prestige and supremacy continued to be an essential part of human existence.

APPENDIX XVIII

Baltimore Whiskey Inspections with an Analysis of that Received from the Susquehanna Valley

Dates by week	Inspections hhds.	bbls.	Received by river hhds.	bbls.	Received via B.&S.R.R. hhds.	bbls.	Received miscellaneous
1838							
Mar. 24			119				(All wagon before this date)
31	612	1572	560	154			
Apr. 21	447	1818	441	915			
28	346	1442	342	851			
May 5	91	1011	79	330			
12	636	2164	604	1200			315 bbls. fr. Phila.
June 2	302	1357	285	164			
30	208	416	201	76			
July 21	15	416					All by wagon.
28	18	539					" " "
Aug. 11	11	312					65 bbls. stored Susq.
18	11	158					All by wagon.
Sept. 1	43	734					80 bbls. fr. Phila.
Oct. 20	29	814					136 " " "
Nov. 3	257	502	219	544	20		
10	93	594	85	91		191	
17	205	992	58	240	12	154	
24	347	1207	340	200		353	
Dec. 22	8	825				68	
1839							
Jan. 5	33	687				150	55 bbls. fr. Phila.
15	49	906			49	321	
19	77	1121			64	492	
26	44	806			25	240	

Dates by week	Inspections hhds.	bbls.	Received by river hhds.	bbls.	Received via B.&S.R.R. hhds.	bbls.	Received miscellaneous
1839							
Feb. 2	57	939			24	227	
9	46	1177	34	459			
16	28	1051			14	363	
Mar. 2	37	816			3	366	
9	20	890				242	
16	278	1566	129	435	36	477	
23	216	1149	116	135	7	315	
30	259	1369	237	637		286	
Apr. 13*	371	5173	371	4499		140	
May 4	250	541	211		4	27	
24	269	939	265	45	4	289	
June 1	589	1155	539	734		118	
8	232	1152	217	654	15	45	
22	340	1063			324	424	
July 6	16	659	16	327		256	
13	65	784	59	466	6	87	
27*		672		373		17	
Aug. 3		121					50 from Phila.
17	8	424		269	8	47	
24	13	691			12	247	
31	18	317			15	169	
*Two weeks.							
Sept. 7	1	547			1	399	
28	43	680	30	36	18	241	
Oct. 19	5	685		20		191	
26	21	885			21	123	294 bbls. fr. Susq.
Nov. 9	20	583			9	146	via Phila.
16	4	655			3	248	
30	130	1796			36	1077	22 hhds. stored Susq.
Dec. 7	346	1374					* See below.
14	146	1668			74	1482	20 hhds., 100 bbls.
1840							
Jan. 4	84	414			59	257	28 hhds. fr. Phila.
11	119	1677			115	560	
18	51	1450			46	803	
Feb. 1	45	1097			19	236	
8	42	1482			12	767	
15	9	755			7	263	
22	102	2200			37	1643	
29	94	1231	72	20	18	439	
Mar. 21	119	2252	107	1103	2	252	
28	246	750	147	137	7	577	
Apr. 4	129	1284	121	149	3	479	
May 2*	125	2013	115	395	32	807	
9	281	1512	252	338	29	553	

*22 hhds., 112 bbls., stored Susquehanna and 235 hhds., 689 bbls. from Susquehanna via Philadelphia.

Dates by week	Inspections hhds.	bbls.	Received by river hhds.	bbls.	Received via B.&S.R.R. hhds.	bbls.	Received miscellaneous
1840							
June 6	265	761	261	290		287	
20	122	745	119	428	3	159	
July 11	88	968	75	396	2	233	
18	17	487	14	372	3	97	
25	6	645		23	2	224	hhds. bbls.
Dec. 5	99	1917			3	597	85 922 S. T. C.
12	21	499				233	21 152 " " "
19	145	1863			9	1016	100 287 " " "
1841							
Jan. 2	35	754			32	497	
9	173	1341			167	883	
16	112	775			163	578	
23	40	629			40	305	
30	48	814			32	384	
Mar. 6	92	852			92	599	
13	20	540			20	254	
27	149	1421			97	855	50 25 fr. Phil.
Apr. 3	39	1182			39	846	
17	42	1360	28	1117	14	179	
24	95	2062	95	1360		240	
May 1					20	885	20 494 S. T. C.
8	110	2828				143	110 2543 riv. & c.
22	12	1609			12	444	892 " " "
29	4	363			42	363	
June 5	225	1594				484	225 866 riv. & c.
19					1	2823	504 1971 " " "
July 10	46	1197			46	441	
17		390				85	
24	2	645			2	324	
31	56	599			56	149	
Aug. 7	19	594			19	175	
21*	113	996			113	584	
28	125	1097			125	611	
Sept. 4	22	962			22	828	
18*	63	1912			34	1113	495
Oct. 2*	16	1004			16	355	(fr. New Orleans)
9	296	1702			276	795	
23*	304	1095			303	510	
30	103	2296			103	1576	
Nov. 6		630				439	
20	27	1069			27	452	
27	80	899			80	407	
Dec. 4	132	354			132	360	
11	65	626			74		
17	59	653			59	109	

Compiled from the Baltimore trade news printed in the *Columbia Spy*.

BIBLIOGRAPHY

Bibliographical Aids.

Ames, H. V. and Shimmel, L. S., "Report on the Public Archives of Pennsylvania," in *Annual Report of the American Historical Association,* 1900, II, 267-93.

> Much time is saved by consulting this and the following two reports before beginning research.

Ames, H. V. and McKinley, A. E., "Report on the Public Archives of the City and County of Philadelphia," in *Annual Report of the American Historical Association,* 1901, II, 231-344.

Ames, H. V., "Public Archives of Pennsylvania," in *Annual Report of the American Historical Association,* 1904, 629-40.

Bausman, Lottie M., *A Bibliography of Lancaster County, Pa., 1745-1912.* A publication of the Pennsylvania Federation of Historical Societies, 1916.

Bining, A. C., *Pennsylvania History: A Selected Bibliography of Secondary Works on Pennsylvania History.* Printed by Pennsylvania State Library in October issue of 1933 *Pennsylvania Library Notes.*

> A very convenient list of the most important secondary volumes of Pennsylvania history.

Bradford, T. L., *The Bibliographer's Manual of American History,* edited and revised by S. V. Henkels, 4 vols. Philadelphia, 1907.

> This manual contains an account of all the state, territory, county, and town histories relating to the United States.

Buck, S. J., *Travels and Descriptions, 1765-1865.* The Illinois State Historical Library Collection, IX, 1914.

> Though compiled primarily for use of students of Illinois history, it is, nevertheless, of value to the student of the general field of American History.

Channing, Hart, and Turner, *Guide to the Study and Reading of American History.* Boston, 1914.

> A list of State and local histories of Pennsylvania may be found here.

Check List of Pennsylvania County, Town, and Township Histories, 1792-1892. Harrisburg, 1892.

    This aid is out of date.

Griffin, G. G., *Writings on American History.* Washington, 1908-31.

Griffin, A. P. C., *List of Books and Periodicals relating to Railroads.* Washington, D. C., Library of Congress, 1904.

Hasse, Adelaide R., *Index of Economic Material in Documents of the States of the United States: Pennsylvania, 1790-1904.* Published by the Carnegie Institute of Washington.

    This index contains all possible economic material; its value is unlimited.

Ludewig, H. E., *The Literature of American Local History: A Bibliographical Essay.* New York, 1846.

    This is an old and outworn guide.

The Commonwealth of Pennsylvania, Department of Public Instruction, pub., *Articles Published by Societies belonging to the Pennsylvania Federation of Historical Societies.* Bulletin No. 2 of the Pennsylvania Historical Commission, Harrisburg, 1933.

    Gives the titles of publications, papers read, etc., and the special work of the members of the Federation.

Winsor, Justin, *Narrative and Critical History of America.* 8 vols. Boston and New York, 1886-9.

    The bibliography is good for works published before 1850.

I. *Primary Source Material.*

A. Manuscript Material.

Baltimore's New Fall Road begun as an Indian Trail from the records of Joseph B. Legg, Enoch Pratt Public Library, Baltimore.

British Consular Reports, Public Record Office (London), (abstracts and excerpts bearing on economic material kindly lent by Professor R. G. Albion, Princeton University).

    These reports are of great importance because of the broad perspective with which the consuls viewed the economic situation of their respective posts.

Excerpts from the Original Minute Book of the Proprietors of the Susquehanna Canal started in 1783 (owned and kindly lent by J. Alexis Shriver, Corresponding Secretary of the Maryland Historical Society).

    As the original minutes of the company are now not available, the permission to use these Excerpts was greatly appreciated. From them a formerly untold story of the old Susquehanna Canal came to light.

Executive Minutes of Pennsylvania, 1790-1838. Archives Division of the Pennsylvania Historical and Museum Commission, Harrisburg, Pa.

William Irvine Papers, Pennsylvania Historical Society.

Journal of the Society for the Improvement of Roads and Inland Navigation. Photostatic copy in the Archives Division of the Pennsylvania Historical and Museum Commission, Harrisburg, Pa.

Letter Books of the Secretary of the Commonwealth, III-X (1790-1861). Archives Division of the Pennsylvania Historical and Museum Commission.

These books contain many official letters on internal improvements projects.

Petition in the Archives Division of the Pennsylvania Historical and Museum Commission, Harrisburg, Pa. (Filed by counties from which submitted.)

Petitions on every type of subject are included in this valuable collection. Most were submitted to the State Legislature.

"State Roads." Archives Division of the Pennsylvania Historical and Museum Commission, Harrisburg, Pa.

More than one hundred volumes of manuscripts have lately been put into excellent shape for the student of history.

B. Printed Collections.

American Philosophical Society, *Transactions,* 1768-.

American State Papers, Miscellaneous. 2 vols.

Kittochtinny Historical Society *Papers.* Vol. IX (Riddle, H. A., ".Some Facts about the Cumberland Valley Railroad.")

Lancaster County Historical Society *Publications.* 39 vols. These volumes contain several good articles on the Lancaster Turnpike and on the Conestoga Navigation.

The Maryland Magazine of History and Biography. 30 vols. Baltimore, 1906-35.

O'Callaghan, E. B., ed., *The Documentary History of the State of New York.* Albany, 1849-51.

Volume two contains very good material on the Genesee Country and its trading relations with Philadelphia and Baltimore.

Pennsylvania Archives, Fourth Series. Harrisburg, 1900-02.

The Fourth Series contains the Executive Messages and valuable communications from the Governors of Pennsylvania relating to internal improvements.

Pennsylvania, *Senate Journal,* particularly Vol. 1821-22 which contains a report of the Committee on Roads, Bridges, and Inland Navigation, made in the Senate, March 23, 1822. This report includes an alphabetical list of the turnpike companies and bridges of the State with all available facts concerning each.

Pennsylvania Magazine of History and Biography, 1877-35. 59 vols.

Washington, George, Writings of (W. C. Ford, ed.). 14 vols. New York, 1889-93.

Washington, George, The Diaries of, 1748-99 (J. C. Fitzpatrick, ed.). 4 vols. Boston and New York, 1925.

The Western Pennsylvania Historical Magazine. 17 vols. 1918-34.

C. Newspapers and Periodicals.

The Aurora.

The Baltimore American.

The Baltimore Gazette.

The Columbia Spy.

The Independent Gazetteer.

Poulson's Daily Advertiser.

The United States Gazette.

The York Gazette.

The York Recorder.

Hazard, *The Pennsylvania Register,* January 5, 1828-December 26, 1835. 16 vols. Philadelphia.

————, *United States Commercial and Statistical Register,* January, 1839-July, 1842. 6 vols. Philadelphia.

Hunt's Merchants' Magazine and Commercial Review, 1839-1870. 63 vols. New York.

Niles' Weekly Register, 1811-1849. 75 vols. Baltimore.

D. Travels.

Bailey, *Journal of a Tour in Unsettled Parts of North America in 1796 and 1797.*

Brissot de Warville, Jean Pierre, *New Travels in the United States of America; including the Commerce of America with Europe.* trans. from the French. 2 vols. London, 1792-4.

Cazenove Journal, Kelsey, ed., Haverford College Studies, No. 13, 1922.

A very important account of a Dutch commercial agent who travelled through the Susquehanna Valley seeking fields for financial investments.

Dickens, Charles, *American Notes for General Circulation.* London, 1842.

Faux, W., *Memorable Days in America, November 27, 1818-July 21, 1820.* London, 1823. Reprinted in Thwaites, *Early Western Travels, 1748-1846,* Vol. XI, pp. 17-305; XII, pp. 9-138.

This account contains some good material but this is embedded in lots of chaff.

Ferguson, William, *America by River and Rail.* London, 1856.

Contains but one reference to the Susquehanna trade.

Fearon, H. B., *Sketches of America, a Narrative of a Journal of Five Thousand Miles Through the Eastern and Western States of America.* London, 1818.

Fithian, Philip Vickers: Journal, 1775-76, ed., Albion and Dodson. Princeton University Press, 1934.

This itinerant minister travelled through the Susquehanna region and recorded notes on the soil, the river, and trade on the river.

Flint, J., *Letters from America, 1818-20,* in Thwaites, *Early Western Travels,* vol. IX.

A very fair observer who depicted conditions in America with candor and good will. His writings are especially good for an economic study.

La Rochefoucauld-Liancourt, Francois Alexandre Frederic, Duc de, *Travels through the United States of North America the Country of the Iroquois, and Upper Canada, Performed in the Years 1795, 1796, and 1797.* 4 vols. London, 1800. Trans. by Neuman.

La Rochefoucauld travelled through the Susquehanna Valley on his way to the West. He is not very cordial in his criticism of American conditions, roads, etc.

Melish, John, *Travels in the United States of America, in the Years 1806, & 1807, and 1809, 1810 & 1811. . . .* 2 vols. Philadelphia, 1812.

This is a very good source for information on the Susquehanna River.

Schoepf, J. D., *Travels in the Confederation, 1783-84.* 2 vols. Philadelphia, 1911.

> Dr. Schoepf was a very careful observer.

Thwaites, Reuben G., ed., *Early Western Travels, 1748-1846, a Series of Annotated Reprints of Some of the Best and Rarest Contemporary Volumes of Travel.* . . . 32 vols. Cleveland, 1904-1907.

Twinning, Thomas, *Travels in America one Hundred Years Ago.* New York, 1894.

Welby, Adlard, *A Visit to North America and the English Settlements in Illinois, with a Winter Residence at Philadelphia, solely to Ascertain the Actual Prospects of the Emigrant, Agriculturalist, Mechanic and Commercial Speculator.* London, 1821. In Thwaites, *Early Western Travels.*

> Welby has little to say about the Susquehanna Valley.

Weld, Isaac, Jr., *Travels through the States of North America and the Provinces of Upper and Lower Canada, 1795-97.* 2 vols. London, 1799.

Cuming, Fortescue, *Sketches of a Tour to the Western Country,* 1807-09, in Thwaites, *Early Western Travels,* Vol. IV.

> Contains a good account of the Susquehanna Valley.

E. Pamphlets and Reports.

Baltimore Commission, *Report of the Commissioners Appointed by the Mayor of the City of Baltimore to Explore and Survey the Route for a Canal and Still Water Navigation from the City of Baltimore to the Head of Tide Water, at Port Deposit.* Baltimore, 1825.

The Baltimore and Susquehanna Railroad.

> *Address to the Mayor and City Council of Baltimore on the trade of the Susquehanna & the Rail Road to that River.* Baltimore, 1830, 24 pp.

> *Annual Reports to the Stockholders,* 1828-54.

> *Laws and Ordinances relating to the Baltimore and Susquehanna Railroad Company.* Baltimore, 1831, 24 pp.; Baltimore, 1850, 238 pp.

> *Memorial of the President and Directors of the Baltimore and Susquehanna Rail Road Company,* signed January 13, 1835, 7 pp.

> *Memorial to the General Assembly of Maryland in behalf of the Baltimore and Susquehanna Rail Road,* n.d.n.p., 8 pp.

The Preamble and Resolutions offered by Mr. Logan as a Substitute for the Report and Resolutions of the Committee on Roads, Bridges and Inland Navigation in granting the Baltimore and Susquehanna Rail Road Company the privilege of extending their rail road into the State of Pennsylvania. Harrisburg, 1829.

The heart of the rivalry between Philadelphia and Baltimore over the chartering of the Baltimore and Susquehanna is found in this report.

Report of the City Director to the Mayor. Baltimore, 1831; Baltimore, 1847.

Baltimore had a director in the railroad company to care for its interests.

Report of the Directors on the part of the State. Baltimore, 1846.

Maryland likewise had a director on the board of directors of the railroad company.

Report of the Committee on Roads, Bridges and Inland Navigation on Granting the Baltimore and Susquehanna Rail Road Company the privilege of extending their rail road into the State of Pennsylvania, read in the Senate, January 17, 1829. Harrisburg, 1829.

This report was favorable to Philadelphia's interests and provoked the reply by Mr. Logan.

Report of the Committee on Internal Improvements Respecting the Baltimore and Susquehanna Rail Road Company. Annapolis, 1836. In the Maryland Historical Society.

Report on the Baltimore and Susquehanna Rail Road by General J. G. Swift, chief Engineer, Also the Annual Report of the President and Directors to the Stockholders. Baltimore, 1828. In the Maryland Historical Society.

Report and Proceedings in Relation to a Rail Road from Baltimore to the Susquehanna. Baltimore, 1828. B. Edes, printer.

An outspoken report for a railroad to the Susquehanna River which contains the importance of the river traffic to Baltimore and shows the ease of tapping the Pennsylvania State Works. This report led to years of struggle between two commercial centers.

Breck, Samuel, *Sketch of the Internal Improvements Already made by Pennsylvania; with Observations upon Her Physical and Fiscal Means for their Extension, Particularly as they have reference to the Future Growth and Prosperity of Philadelphia.* Philadelphia, 1818, 82 pp.

Breck attempted to wake the Pennsylvania metropolis from her lethargy; the pamphlet is of extreme importance for this study.

Camac, Turner, *Facts and Arguments respecting the Great Utility of an Extensive Plan of Inland Navigation in the United States,* by a Friend to National Industry. Philadelphia, 1805, 61 pp.

Carey, Mathew, *Brief View of the System of Internal Improvements of Pennsylvania containing a Glance at its Rise, Progress, Retardation, the Difficulties it Underwent, its Present State, and its Future Prospects.* Philadelphia, 1831. Printed by order of the Society for the Promotion of Internal Improvements.

Carey, Mathew, *A Connected View of the Whole Internal Navigation of the United States, Natural and Artificial, Present and Prospective,* by a "Citizen of Burlington." Philadelphia, 1825, 10 pp.

The Chesapeake and Delaware Canal.

Annual Reports to the Stockholders, 1804-60.

Bache, A. D., *Report of experiments on the navigation of the Chesapeake and Delaware canal by steam.* Philadelphia, 1834, 13 pp.

Carey, Mathew, *Letter on the Chesapeake and Delaware Canal,* May 9, 1825. Philadelphia.

"A Citizen of Philadelphia," *Views respecting the Chesapeake and Delaware Canal.* Philadelphia, 1824, 18 pp.
Shows Philadelphia's great interest in this project.

Memorial and Petition of the President and Directors of the Chesapeake and Delaware Canal Company to the Senate and House of Representatives, 1805; 1806; 1824.

A Collection of the Laws relative to the Chesapeake and Delaware Canal passed by the Legislatures of the States of Maryland, Delaware, and Pennsylvania. Published by order of the President and Directors of the Chesapeake and Delaware Canal Company. Philadelphia, 1823.

Exhibit of the shocking oppression and injustice suffered for sixteen months by John Randel . . . from Judge Wright. . . . Philadelphia, 1825.

Facts and Arguments respecting the Chesapeake and Delaware Canal and its Extension in the United States. Written by the President and Directors of the Canal; in Chesapeake and Delaware Canal Company Publications, ed. Gilpin. Philadelphia, 1809.

Gilpin, Joshua, *A Memoir of the Rise, Progress, and Present State of the Chesapeake and Delaware Canal, Accompanied with Original Documents and Maps,* 1821, 72 pp.

Reflections on the Proposition to communicate by a Navigable Canal the Waters of the Chesapeake with those of Delaware Bay, addressed to the Citizens of Maryland. To which is prefixed the Bill as published for consideration by the House of Delegates. Annapolis, 1797, 50 pp. In the Maryland Historical Society.

Early signs of rivalry appear in this important pamphlet.

Conewago Canal Company, *Account of the Conewago-canal, on the River Susquehanna. To Which is Prefixed, the Act for Incorporating the Company.* Philadelphia, 1798, 18 pp. Signed by William Smith, Henry Miller, Committee.

An official document which deals with the opening of the Conewago Falls.

Consideration on the Practicability and Utility of Immediately Constructing A Railway from Pottsville to Sunbury and Danville Through the Coal Region of Mahoney and Shamokin; with the Proceedings of a Meeting at Sunbury, December, 1830. Philadelphia, 1830, 37 pp.; Milton, 1830, 24 pp.

Correspondence with the War Department relative to a Grand National Sloop and Steam boat Navigation from the Atlantic, by the way of the Chesapeake Bay, Susquehanna River, Seneca or Cayuga Lake to Lake Ontario. Harrisburg, 1834.

The Cumberland Valley Railroad Company, *Annual Reports to the Stockholders,* 1835-58.

Description of the River Susquehanna with observations on the Present State of its Trade and Navigation, and their Practicability and probable Improvement. Illustrated with map and an appendix, 1796, Z. Poulson, Jr., printer.

A glowing account by an eighteenth century real estate agent.

Duane, William John, *Letters addressed to the People of Pennsylvania, respecting the Internal Improvements of the Commonwealth by Means of Roads and Canals.* Philadelphia, 1811, 125 pp.

Duane, William John, *Observations on the importance of Improving the Navigation of the River Schuylkill, for the Purpose of Connecting it with the Susquehanna,* Philadelphia, 1818

Facts and Arguments in favor of adopting Railways in preference to Canals in the State of Pennsylvania to which is added a few Remarks on the Subject of Internal Improvements. Philadelphia, 1825, 3rd edition.

Theme is that Pennsylvania must act or sink.

Charter, Supplements, and By-Laws of the Harrisburg, Portsmouth, Mt. Joy, and Lancaster Railroad Company. Harrisburg, 1853, 40 pp.

General Harper's Speech to the Citizens of Baltimore on the Expediency of Promoting a connection between the Ohio, at Pittsburg, and the waters of the Chesapeake at Baltimore, by a Canal through the District of Columbia with his Reply to some objections by Mr. Winchester, delivered at a meeting at the Exchange, December 20, 1823. Baltimore, 1824.

A very important pamphlet telling of Baltimore's decision to support a Susquehanna Canal project rather than the Chesapeake and Ohio Canal.

Historical Account of the Rise, Progress, and Present State of the Canal Navigation of Pennsylvania . . . with an Appendix and Explanatory Map. . . . Published by the Susquehanna and Schuylkill and Delaware and Schuylkill Navigation Companies, Philadelphia, 1795.

Letters on the Resources and Commerce of Philadelphia, from John R. Tyson to William Peter, Her Britannic Majesty's Consul for Pennsylvania, with Mr. Peter's Answer Prefixed. Philadelphia, 1851.

Lightner, George W., *Susquehanna Register of Arks, Rafts, etc., Arriving at Port Deposit, in the Year 1822.* Baltimore, 1823, in the Enoch Pratt Public Library, Baltimore.

This is a very detailed account of the Susquehanna River traffic recorded by a resident of Port Deposit.

Maryland, Citizen of, *A Short History of the Public Debt of Maryland and of the Causes which Produced it.* Baltimore, 1845, 95 pp. Contains numerous documents.

The Northern Central Railroad Company, *Annual Reports to the Stockholders,* 1855-60.

Pennsylvania, *A Compilation of the Canal and Railroad Laws of Pennsylvania, Prepared and Published Under the Authority of a Resolution of the House of Representatives, Passed the Sixteenth day of June, A.D. 1836.* Harrisburg, 1837.

Pennsylvania, *Compilation of the Laws of Pennsylvania, relating to Internal Improvements, together with the Canal and Railway Regulations, as Established by the Board of Canal Commissioners.* Harrisburg, 1840.

Pennsylvania Society for the Promotion of Internal Improvements, *The First Annual Report of the Acting Committee.* Philadelphia, 1826, 45 pp. Mathew Carey was in the chair.

Pennsylvania, *A Tabular View of the Financial Affairs of Pennsylvania from the Commencement of her Public Works to the Present Time in which are included the Cost, Revenue, and Expenditures of the Several Lines of Canals and Rail Roads, &c.* The Whole Prepared from Official Records by J. W. Hammond, late chief clerk of the Auditor General's Office. Philadelphia, 1844.

Remarks on the Advantages of the proposed Susquehanna and Lehigh Canal. Philadelphia, 1835, 24 pp.

Report from Reading Howells, Frederick Antes, and William Dean, Commissioners appointed to explore the Head-Waters of the rivers Delaware, Lehigh, and Schuylkill, and the north-east branch of Susquehanna. Philadelphia, 1791.

Report of the Committee on Roads and Inland Navigation, read in the House of Representatives, January 20, 1823, n.d.n.p., 8 pp. Mr. Lehman was chairman of the committee.

Report of the Maryland Commissioners on a proposed Canal from Baltimore to Conewago. F. Lucas, printer, 1825, 84 pp.

Report of the Susquehanna Commissioners on the subject of the Navigation of the River from Columbia to the head of Tide. Harrisburg, 1824, 8 pp.

Report on the proposed construction of a Rail Road from York to the Cumberland Valley Rail Road. Baltimore, 1847.

Report to the Legislature of Pennsylvania containing a description of the Swatara Mining District. Harrisburg, 1839. Henry K. Strong was chairman of the committee.

Strickland, William, *Reports on Canals, Roads and Other Subjects, Made to the Pennsylvania Society for the Promotion of Internal Improvements.* Philadelphia, 1826.

Susquehanna Railroad Company, *First Annual Report made January, 1854.* Includes the act of incorporation.

The Susquehanna and Tidewater Canal Company.

An Act for the Relief of the Bondholders of the Susquehanna Canal Company. Baltimore, 1861.

An Act of Incorporation of the Susquehanna Canal Company of Maryland together with subsequent Acts. Baltimore, 1835. Contains the laws authorizing the old canal of 1783.

Acts of Incorporation and the Supplements Thereto passed by the Legislatures of Pennsylvania and Maryland in reference to the Susquehanna and Tidewater Canal Companies. Baltimore, 1839.

Annual Reports of the President and Managers, 1839-1860, except 1840, 41, 42, 43, 45, and 46 which could not be located.

Baltimore City Council, *Report and Resolutions relative to Internal Improvements and the Susquehanna Canal Project, adopted January 5, 1827.* Baltimore, 1827, 29 pp.

Charter of the Susquehanna and Tidewater Canal Company. A printed copy in the Maryland Historical Society.

Documents Relative to the Susquehanna Canal Company, published by order of the Commissioners. Baltimore, 1835.

The Board of Managers of the Susquehanna Canal Company of Pennsylvania published these documents for the information of the stockholders and the public in general to inform them of the negotiations which they had had with the Maryland Canal Company for the purpose of extending the Pennsylvania Company's works through Maryland to the Chesapeake Bay.

Memorial to the State Legislature of Maryland for an Appropriation, in a collection of Pamphlets on Maryland Canals in the Princeton University Library.

Reasons why the Supplement to the Act of Incorporating the Susquehanna Canal Company should be passed, by a Committee of the Company. Harrisburg, 1836, 8 pp.

Susquehanna Canal Company to the Philadelphia and Reading Railroad Company-lease, in *Pamphlets* #2021 in the Pennsylvania State Library.

The Union Canal Company.

A Table of the Relative Distances on the Union Canal. Lebanon, n.d.

A Brief History, 1853.

A Supplement to the Act to Incorporate the Union Canal Company of Pennsylvania, and an extract from the "Act for the Improvement of the State"; together with the By-Laws, adopted by the Stockholders on the 22nd of May, 1821. Philadelphia, 1821, 18 pp.

An Act to Incorporate the Union Canal Company of Pennsylvania, with the By-Laws, Rules, Orders and Regulations, enacted at a meeting of the Stockholders on the 24th of July, 1811. Philadelphia, 1811, 24 pp.

Acts of the Legislature of Pennsylvania relating to the Union Canal Company of Pennsylvania. Philadelphia, 1825, 72 pp.

Additional Acts of the Legislature. 1826, 12 pp.

An Estimate of the Expense of Transporting Anthracite Coal on the Union Canal . . . n.p., 1840, 8 pp.

Annual Reports of the Managers of the Union Canal. 1812-60.

Mr. Aycrigg's Letter on the Supply of Water of the Union Canal, n.d.n.p., 7 pp.

Communication from the President of the Union Canal Company accompanied with a report of James D. Harris, principal Engineer relative to Enlarging the Union Canal. Read in the House of Representatives, February 9, 1839. Harrisburg, 1839.

Extracts from the Resolutions of the Stockholders of the Delaware and Schuylkill Canal. Philadelphia, 1800, 12 pp.

Letters on the Union Canal. Boston, 1826, 44 pp.
   These letters are from a former engineer of the Union Canal Company who believed in a wider canal than was built.

Memorial of a Convention of Citizens of the Commonwealth for aid to enlarge the Union Canal, read in the Senate, January 17, 1839. Harrisburg, 1839. A copy is found in *Pamphlets* #833 in the Pennsylvania State Library.

Observations on the Application for a Law to Incorporate the Union Canal Company, Respectfully Submitted to the Members of Both Houses of the Legislature of Pennsylvania, "On behalf of the Schuylkill and Susquehanna Navigation." 1808, 16 pp.

Paleske, Charles G., *Substance of an Address intended to be delivered on the 25th January, 1812, before the Special Committee of the House of Representatives. . . .* 7 pp.

Petition against the Incorporation of the Union Canal Company, n.d.n.p. In the Pennsylvania Historical Society, Philadelphia.

Report of the Committee of the Bondholders of the Union Canal Company of Pennsylvania. Philadelphia, 1860.

Report relative to the Enlargement of the Union Canal, n.d.n.p In the Historical Society of Pennsylvania, Philadelphia.

"The Union Canal Company," a paper read at a meeting of the Pennsylvania Society of Internal Improvements, January 10, 1826, 6 pp.

II. *Secondary Works.*

Adams, Henry, *Life of Albert Gallatin.* Philadelphia, 1880.

Adams, Henry, *History of the United States of America.* 9 vols. New York, 1891-1901.

Andrews, Israel D., *Report . . . On the Trade and Commerce of the British North American Colonies, and upon the Trade of the Great Lakes and Rivers.* Washington, 1853. (House Ex. Doc. No. 136, 32d Cong., 2d sess.)

Armroyd, George, *A Connected View of the Whole Internal Navigation of the United States, Natural and Artificial; Present and Prospective.* Philadelphia, 1826. 192 pages with maps.

Baker, George W., *Review of the Relative Commercial Progress of the Cities of New York and Philadelphia, tracing the Decline of the Latter, and showing the Necessity of Trans-Atlantic Steamship Communication to Reestablish Foreign Trade.* Philadelphia, 1859, 72 pp.
   This study was not of great importance for this volume, but, as its title shows, is an account of the rivalry between Philadelphia and New York.

Bartlett, Marguerite G., *Chief Phases of Pennsylvania Politics in the Jacksonian Period.* Allentown, Penna., 1919.
   This University of Pennsylvania thesis deals with internal improvements from political point of view.

Bates, S. P. and Richards, J. F., *History of Franklin County.* Chicago, 1887.

Bining, Arthur Cecil, *Pennsylvania Iron Manufacture in the Eighteenth Century.* Publications of the Pennsylvania Historical Commission. Vol. IV. Harrisburg, 1938.

Bishop, Avard Longley, *The State Works of Pennsylvania.* Yale Press, 1907. (In the *Connecticut Academy of Arts and Sciences,* XIII, 149-298.)
   A carefully written history of the canal and railroad system built and operated by the State of Pennsylvania, 1826-1859.

Bishop, James L., *History of American Manufactures from 1608 to 1860.* Philadelphia, 1868.
   An old-style history which contains detailed accounts of special industries.

Bogen, H. I., *Anthracite Railroads.* Philadelphia, 1929.
    This work does not include a study of the Northern Central Railway.

Bowen, Eli, *The Pictorial Sketch Book of Pennsylvania . . . Its Scenery, Internal Improvements, etc., Popularly Described.* Philadelphia, 1852.

Boyd, Julian P., ed., *The Susquehanna Company Papers.* 4 vols. Wilkes-Barre, Penna., 1933.
    The introduction to volume 4 contains an account of the sectional rivalry in Pennsylvania.

Burroughs, Thomas H., *State Book of Pennsylvania containing an account of the Geography, History, Government, Resources and Noted Citizens of the State with a Map of the State and of each County.* Philadelphia, 1845.
    This volume contains a map and description of the economic regions of the State.

Callender, Guy Stevens, "The Early Transportation and Banking Enterprises of the States in Relation to the Growth of Corporations." In *The Quarterly Journal of Economics,* XVII, 111-162, November, 1902.

Carter, C. F., *When Railroads were New.* New York, 1910.

Carter, W. C. and Grossbrenner, A. J., *History of York County.* 1834.

Clark, Victor L., *History of Manufacturing in the United States, 1607-1860.* Washington, 1929, new edition.
    The best study we have of manufacturing in America.

Clark, J. A., ed., *The Wyoming Valley, Upper Waters of the Susquehanna and Lackawanna Coal Region.* Scranton, 1875.

Conrad, H. D., *History of the State of Delaware,* 3 vols. Wilmington 1908.
    The economic material in this three volume history is extremely limited.

Coxe, Tench, *View of the United States of America in a Series of Papers, written at Various Times between the Years 1787 and 1794.* Philadelphia, 1794, 513 pp.

Craven, A. O., *Soil Exhaustion as a Factor in the Agricultural History of Virginia and Maryland, 1606-1860,* in the University of Illinois, *Studies in the Social Sciences,* vol. 13, the University of Illinois Press, 1926.
    This is an excellent study in the passing of the tobacco staple and the adoption of wheat in this region. This change had a wonderful effect on the rise of the city of Baltimore.

Davis, Joseph Stancliffe, *Essays in the Earlier History of American Corporations.* (Harvard Economic Studies, Vol. 16.) 2 vols. Harvard Press, 1917.

  The second volume dealing with "Eighteenth Century Business Corporations in the United States" had very good sections on inland navigations, corporations and turnpike corporations.

Day, Sherman, *Historical Collections of the State of Pennsylvania.* Philadelphia, 1843.

Defebaugh, J. E., *History of the Lumber Industry of America.* 2 vols. Chicago, 1907.

  This is not an altogether satisfactory study of this industry; it contains but little on rafting on the Susquehanna River during the early days of the lumberman.

Dunbar, Seymour, *A History of Travel in America.* 4 vols. Indianapolis, 1915.

  A readable running story of the whole subject. Illustrated with many interesting old prints.

Durrenberger, Joseph A., *Turnpikes; a Study of the Toll Road Improvement in the Middle Atlantic States and Maryland.* Valdosta, Ga., 1931.

  This study is a Columbia University thesis which is very well written and contains a great amount of spade work in original sources.

Egle, William H., *Illustrated History of the Commonwealth of Pennsylvania from Its Earliest Settlement to the Present Time.* Harrisburg, 1876; second edition, 1880.

Egle, William H., *Histories of the Counties of Dauphin and Lebanon.* Philadelphia, 1883.

  Contains a good section on the Union Canal.

Everts, Peck, & Richards, pub., *History of the Susquehanna and Juniata.* 2 vols. Philadelphia, 1886.

  Of little use in this study.

Faust, A. B., *The German Element in the United States.* Boston and New York, 1909.

  The part the German nationality played in the development of America.

Flick, A. C., ed., *History of the State of New York,* 8 vols. New York, 1933-1935.

  Volume five contains very good economic material.

Galpin, W. F., *Grain Supply of England during the Napoleonic Period*. (University of Michigan Publication. History and Political Science, Vol. 6.) New York, 1925.

Gallatin, A., *Report of the Secretary of the Treasury on the Subject of Public Roads and Canals; made in Pursuance of a Resolution of the Senate* . . . Washington, 1808.

Gibson, John, *History of York County*. Chicago, 1886.

Gordon, Thomas F., *A Gazetteer of the State of Pennsylvania*. Philadelphia, 1832.

Gould, Clarence P., *The Economic Causes of the Rise of Baltimore*, included in a volume of *Essays in Colonial History*. Yale Press, 1931.

Griffith, Thomas W., *Annals of Baltimore*. Baltimore, 1824.

Hall, Clayton C., ed., *Baltimore: Its History and its People*. 3 vols. New York, 1912.
    This work contains a good chapter on transportation systems by J. Wallace Bryan.

Hanna, Mary, "Trade of the Delaware District before the Revolution." In *The Smith College Studies*, II, No. 4, 239-345.
    This includes a study of the trade of this district to see its effect on legislation, and a study of legislative measures of the Empire to show their effect on the trade of the area.

Hanson, George A., *Old Kent: The Eastern Shore of Maryland*. Baltimore, 1876.
    Of no value for an economic study.

Harlow, Alvin F., *Old Towpaths, the Story of the American Canal Era*. New York, 1926.
    The plan of the book is very comprehensive but its quality is defective. No footnotes to information presented.

Higgins, Ruth L., *Expansion in New York*. Ohio State University Press, 1931.

Homans, J. S., *An Historical and Statistical Account of the Foreign Commerce of the United States*. New York, 1857.

Hulbert, Archer B., *The Paths of Inland Commerce*. New Haven, 1921. (Chronicles of America Series.)

Hulbert, Archer B., *Historic Highways of America*. 16 vols. Cleveland, 1902-05.

Johnston, George, *History of Cecil County, Maryland*. Elkton, 1881. A good county history for that time.

Johnson, E. R., *History of Domestic and Foreign Commerce in the United States.* Washington, D. C., 1915, for the Carnegie Institute. A cooperative work based on wide research. A standard commercial history.

Jones, U. J., *History of the Early Settlement of the Juniata Valley embracing an Account of the Early Pioneers, and the Trials and Privations Incident to the Settlement of the Valley. . . .* Philadelphia, 1856.

Jones, Chester Lloyd, *Economic History of the Anthracite-Tidewater Canals.* Philadelphia, 1908. (In the Publications of the University of Pennsylvania, Studies in Political Economy and Public Law, No. 22.)

This study deals with the important canals which led from New York and Philadelphia into the anthracite region. The canals taken up are well done but a number of important waterways were entirely omitted.

Klein, H. M. J., ed., *Lancaster County, Pennsylvania, a History.* 4 vols. New York, 1924.

A very comprehensive county history by a man who is an authority on the subject.

Klein, T. B., *The Canals of Pennsylvania, and the System of Internal Improvements of the Commonwealth.* 1900. (Report of the Pennsylvania Secretary of Internal Affairs.)

Kuhlman, Charles B., *The Development of the Flour Milling Industry in the United States.* Boston and New York, 1929.

One of the few adequate histories of a specific industry.

Lincoln, Charles H., *Revolutionary Movement in Pennsylvania, 1760-1776.* Philadelphia, 1901.

An excellent volume which shows the political, racial, religious, and economic sectionalism which led to a revolution within the colony of Pennsylvania.

Linn, John Blair, *Annals of Buffalo Valley, 1755-1855.* Harrisburg, 1877.

Luetscher, G. D., "Industries of Pennsylvania after the Adoption of the Federal Constitution, with Special Reference to Lancaster and York Counties," in *The American Ethnographical Survey, Conestoga Expedition, 1902.* New York, 1911.

McCarty, C., *Anti-Masonic Party: A Study of Political Anti-Masonry in the United States, 1827-40.* (American Historical Society, *Annual Report,* 1902, I, 365-574.)

The internal improvement question in Pennsylvania was the cause of the large membership that this following had in Pennsylvania. This study is of ground-breaking character.

McCauley, I. H., *Historical Sketch of Franklin County.* Chambersburg, Pa., 1878.

McClure, Alexander K., *Old Time Notes of Pennsylvania.* . . . 2 vols. Philadelphia, 1905.

McMaster, John Bates, *History of the People of the United States.* 8 vols. New York, 1883-1913.

McMaster, John Bates, *The Life and Times of Stephen Girard.* Philadelphia and London, 1918.

Taken mainly from Girard manuscripts, but has little material bearing on this study.

MacPherson, David, *Annals of Commerce, Manufactures, Fisheries, and Navigation.* 4 vols. London, 1815.

Main Line of the Pennsylvania State Improvements: its Building, Cost, Revenue, Expenditure, and Present and Prospective Value. No author. Printed by Collins, Philadelphia, 1850.

This is of little value compared to Bishop's work.

Mease, James, *The Picture of Philadelphia, giving an account of its origin, increases and improvements in Arts, Sciences, Manufacturing, Commerce, and Revenue.* . . . Philadelphia, 1811.

Meyer, Balthasar Henry, ed., *History of Transportation in the United States before 1860.* (By Caroline E. MacGill and a staff of collaborators.) Carnegie Institution, Washington, 1917.

Some data and tables are inaccurate and there are notorious errors in reference. Its fine bibliography, however, is of great importance to the scholar.

Mitchell, Samuel A., *Compendium of the Internal Improvements of the United States.* Philadelphia, 1935.

Maps of turnpikes, roads, and canals make this book valuable.

Oberholtzer, E. P., *Robert Morris: Patriot and Financier.* New York, 1903.

Only slight mention is found of Morris' activity in the canal companies which were projected in 1791.

Parkins, A. E., "The Development of Transportation in Pennsylvania," in *The Bulletin of Geographical Society of Philadelphia*, Vol. 14, 92-114, 148-168; Vol. 15, 1-18. Philadelphia, 1916, 1917.
This article contains many helpful suggestions.

Pearce, Stewart, *Annals of Luzerne County*. Philadelphia, 1866.

Pickell, John, *A New Chapter in the Early Life of Washington*. New York, 1856.

Pitkins, Timothy, *A Statistical View of the Commerce of the United States of America*. New York, 1817.

Plummer, Wilbur C., *The Road Policy of Pennsylvania*. Philadelphia, 1925.
An interesting study covering a tremendously long period (from Penn to 1924) done in one hundred and twenty pages and presented to the University of Pennsylvania as a Ph.D. thesis.

Poor, Henry V., *History of Railroads and Canals of the United States*. New York, 1860. A planned series, but only one volume was published. Contains many excellent and sound statistics.

Prescott, F. W., *Eastern Railroads*. An unpublished Ph.D. dissertation of the University of Wisconsin, 1925.
It deals chiefly with construction and construction problems of the eastern railroads built before 1860. Many valuable tables are included in this study.

Reizenstein, Milton, *The Economic History of the Baltimore and Ohio Railroad, 1827-1853*, in the Johns Hopkins University Studies in Historical and Political Science, Fifteenth Series, VII, VIII, 1897.

Ringwalt, John Luther, *Development of Transportation Systems in the United States*. Philadelphia, 1888.
This book is a reliable summary of the general subject for its time.

Ritter, Abraham, *Philadelphia and her Merchants as Constituted Fifty to Seventy Years ago. . . .* Philadelphia, 1860.
This work is of very limited value today.

Root, W. J., *Relations of Pennsylvania with the British Government, 1696-1765*. 1912.

Rupp, I. Daniel, *History of Lancaster County*. Lancaster, 1844.

Rupp, I. Daniel, *History of Northampton, Lehigh, Monroe, Carbon, and Schuylkill Counties*. Harrisburg, 1845.

Rupp, I. Daniel, *The History and Topography of Dauphin, Cumberland, Franklin, Bedford, Adams, and Perry Counties*. Lancaster, 1846.

Rutter, F. R., *South America Trade of Baltimore*, in the Johns Hopkins University Studies in Historical and Political Science, Fifteenth Series, IX, 1898.

Scharf, John Thomas, *History of Delaware, 1609-1888*. 2 vols. Philadelphia, 1888.
> Contains a good account of the Chesapeake and Delaware Canal.

Scharf, John Thomas, *The Chronicles of Baltimore*. Baltimore, 1874.
> This volume contains much good information but it is very difficult to use as it lacks an index.

Scharf, John Thomas, *History of Maryland from the Earliest Period to the Present Day*. 3 vols. Baltimore, 1879.

Scharf, John Thomas, and Wescott, T., *History of Philadelphia, 1609-1884*. 3 vols. Philadelphia, 1884.

Scott, *Geographical Dictionary*.

Semple, Ellen C., *American History and its Geographic Conditions*. Boston and New York, 1903.

Seybert, Adam, *Statistical Annals embracing views of the Population, Commerce, Navigation, Fisheries, Public Lands, Post Office Establishment, Revenues, Mint, Military and Naval Establishments, Expenditures, Public Debt, and Sinking Fund of the United States of America, 1789-1818*. Philadelphia, 1818.

Sharpless, I., *Two Centuries of Pennsylvania History*. 2 vols. Philadelphia, 1900.

Shenk, H. H., *A History of the Lebanon Valley in Pennsylvania*. 2 vols. Harrisburg, 1930.

Shepherd, W. R., *History of Proprietary Government in Pennsylvania*. 1896.

Simpson, Henry, *Eminent Philadelphians*. Philadelphia, 1859.

Sioussat, St. G. L., "Highway Legislation in Maryland and its Influence on the Economic Development of the State," in *The Maryland Geological Survey*, III, 1899.
> An excellent study.

Sipes, William B., *The Pennsylvania Railroad, its Origin, Construction, Conditions, and Connections*. Philadelphia, 1875.

Smith, W. Roy, "Sectionalism in Pennsylvania during the Revolution," in *The Political Science Quarterly*, XXIV, 208-35.
> A very good article with many references to original source material.

Sparks, Jared, "Baltimore," in *The North American Review,* XX, 1825.
This is a remarkably fine article written at an early date; the historian Sparks outlines in this study his reasons and beliefs why Baltimore prospered and grew so rapidly.

Sterns, Worthy P., "Foreign Trade of the United States from 1820-40," in *The Journal of Political Economy,* VIII, 34-57, December, 1899.

Tanner, H. S., *A Description of the Canals and Railroads of the United States; comprehending Notices of All the Works of Internal Improvements throughout the Several States.* New York, 1840.
Tanner gives a description, facts, etc., about each work in all states and considers the powerful influence of each on the pursuits and lives of the people.

Tanner, H. S., *Canals and Railroads of Pennsylvania and New Jersey.* Philadelphia, 1834.
A small, thirty-one-page volume containing the facts of the various projects within these two states.

Trego, Charles, *A Geography of Pennsylvania.* Philadelphia, 1844.

Turner, Morris K., *The Commercial Relations of the Susquehanna Valley During the Colonial Period.* A typed thesis of the University of Pennsylvania, 1916.
A lost opportunity for an important and colorful study.

Varle, Charles, *A Complete View of Baltimore with a Statistical Sketch.* Baltimore, 1833.

Warner, Beers, and Co., pub., *History of Cumberland and Adams Counties.* 1886.

Whitford, Noble E., *History of the Canal System of the State of New York.* 2 vols. Albany, 1906. (Supplement to the Annual Report of the State Engineer and Surveyors of the State of New York.)

Wilson, W. B., *History of the Pennsylvania Railroad Company, with Plans of Organization, Portraits of Officials, and Biographical Sketches.* 2 vols. Philadelphia, 1899.
A history to be used only with careful cross-checking.

Wood, Frederick J., *The Turnpikes of New England and the Evolution of the same through New England, Virginia, and Maryland.* Boston, 1919.

Young, John R., ed., *Memorial History of the City of Philadelphia, 1681-1895.* 2 vols. New York, 1895.

INDEX